ענינה של
תורת החסידות

ON THE
ESSENCE
OF CHASIDUS

ענינה של
תורת החסידות

O N   T H E
E S S E N C E
OF CHASIDUS

a chasidic discourse
by
The Lubavitcher Rebbe
Rabbi Menachem M. Schneerson
זצוקללה"ה נבג"מ זי"ע

KEHOT PUBLICATION SOCIETY
770 Eastern Parkway / Brooklyn, New York 11213

ON THE ESSENCE OF CHASIDUS

Published and Copyrighted © 2003
Second Printing 2005
by
KEHOT PUBLICATION SOCIETY
770 Eastern Parkway / Brooklyn, New York 11213
(718) 774-4000 / Fax (718) 774-2718

Orders:
291 Kingston Avenue / Brooklyn, New York 11213
(718) 778-0226 / Fax (718) 778-4148
www.kehotonline.com

ISBN 0-8266-0466-8

Manufactured in the United States of America

CONTENTS

ב"ה

PREFACE

On the Essence of Chasidus, a discourse by the Lubavitcher Rebbe, Rabbi Menachem M. Schneerson, of blessed memory, is a definitive, systematic exploration of the nature and idea of Chasidic philosophy. The discourse, originally delivered by the Rebbe on the 19th of Kislev 5726 (1965) and subsequently printed as *Inyana Shel Toras HaChasidus* in 5730 (1970), delves deeply into the essential nature of Chasidic thought, describing the unique role Chasidus plays within Torah, and its fundamental connection with the soul.

The discourse was first published in English by Kehot Publication Society on 11 Nissan 5738 (1978), in honor of the Rebbe's 76th birthday. The current edition contains revisions, clarifications and commentary, and presents both the Hebrew and English together for the first time.

An excerpt from a talk given by the Rebbe on the last day of Passover 5730 (1970), which touches upon matters that are relevant to the ideas discussed in the main text, appears as an appendix.

In addition to the translation of the discourse and the Rebbe's footnotes, additional footnotes were added to further clarify the text. Also, some of the Rebbe's footnotes have been elucidated and elaborated upon. The Hebrew text of the discourse has been re-typeset with Hebrew vowel marks to further enhance this volume's usability. The original Hebrew footnotes appear at the end of the text.[1]

The original translation was prepared by Rabbi Y. H. Greenberg and S. S. Handelman and editrd by Rabbis Zalman I. Posner and A. D. Sufrin. For preparing and editing the current edition, special thanks are due to Rabbis Ari Sollish, Avraham D. Vaisfiche and Yosef B. Friedman.

Kehot Publication Society

14 Iyar 5763
Pesach Sheini

---

1. A heretofore unpublished gloss from the Rebbe has been added to the Hebrew Notes.

THE LUBAVITCHER REBBE
RABBI MENACHEM MENDEL SCHNEERSON
זצוקללה״ה נבג״מ זי״ע

INTRODUCTION
AND
SUMMARY

INTRODUCTION AND SUMMARY

Chasidism, by now, is a familiar phenomenon, and a source of curiosity and fascination to many. Though its founders faced many difficult struggles, it has now become universally known and admired. Authors of all varieties of belief and practice have written countless volumes about its origins, history, and philosophy. Anthologies of stories and maxims told by and about Chasidim have been compiled and made available in English for many years.

Yet many of these works have been produced by outside admirers not always steeped in the knowledge of Chasidic philosophy, nor familiar with its more intricate and profound teachings. Hence many of these attempts made to define Chasidus, and to describe its precise relation to the rest of the Torah, have not been at all satisfactory. The need of the English reader for a definition of Chasidus from "within," from Chasidic leaders and thinkers themselves, has long been recognized.

On the Essence of Chasidus is a definitive explanation of the nature and idea of Chasidic philosophy. Indeed, one of the prime aims of Chabad Chasidus is to systematically define and elucidate "general Chasidus" in rational, intellectual terms, as will be explained at great length in the text.

Chasidus has been popularly conceived, especially by outside historians and biographers, as a teaching which primarily emphasizes joy, enthusiasm, emotion, etc.—albeit within the framework of the traditional Jewish Codes of Law, i.e., Talmud, *Shulchan Aruch*, etc. One who probes more deeply into works of Chasidic philosophy might be surprised, therefore, to find great emphasis placed on the actual, practical performance of *mitzvot*, on simple deed or action in itself. Though not explicitly referring to the seeming dilemma of whether Chasidus is expressed more in "affect" or in action, the Rebbe answers the question by presenting the concept of Chasidus as one of "essence," and analyzes the various modes in which "essence" comes to be revealed.

Hence, the focal point of the present discourse is the essence of Chasidus. It is a deep and searching inquiry into the central core of Chasidic philosophy and practice, and is not only an introduction to the subject, but also an integral part of classic Chasidic literature.

The Rebbe precisely defines the unique relationship Chasidus has with the other parts of Torah and the traditional forms of interpretation; with Kabbalah; with the various dimensions of the soul; with the concept of Moshiach; and with the Divine attributes (*sefirot*). He explains the role and function of Chasidus in the world, and the imperative reasons for its dissemination.

Furthermore, the Rebbe clarifies and illuminates the nature and essence of Chasidus by selecting one specific topic in Torah, analyzing it in light of the four traditional forms of interpretation, and then exploring the very same topic in the light of Chasidus. He thus proceeds to show how Chasidus vivifies and illuminates each of these four approaches to Torah. The topic, significantly, is the meaning of the first words a person utters when he awakens from his sleep in the morning—the prayer *Modeh Ani*, which is the fundamental starting point of a Jew's spiritual service for the entire day. Finally, the Rebbe demonstrates the manner in which all the ideas of Chasidus are reflected in, vitalize, and illumine even the technical and legalistic parts of Torah, using the example of the law of "acquisition through four cubits."

*   *   *

This discourse was delivered by the Rebbe on the Chasidic holiday of *Yud-Tes Kislev* 5726 (1965). It was originally published at the end of the first volume of *Sefer Ha'arachim* (the Chabad Encyclopedia) in 1970, and reprinted in a separate cover in 1971. A supplementary Appendix, excerpted from a talk given by the Rebbe on the last day of Passover 5730 (1970), was added to the 1971 edition. In it, the Rebbe explains why different parts of Torah come to be revealed at different times in Jewish history and, in particular, why Chasidus has been revealed only in these latter generations.[1]

---

1. Originally this Appendix was printed   at the end of a volume containing the

Since the subject matter of this Passover talk is relevant to the ideas discussed in *On the Essence of Chasidus*, it has also been translated into English and added as an appendix in the present edition.

Yud-Tes Kislev, the date on which the discourse was originally given, celebrates the day upon which the founder of Chabad Chasidus, Rabbi Schneur Zalman of Liadi, was released from a Russian prison. He had been arrested and falsely accused of subversive political activities and treason because of his leadership of the Chasidic movement. On the 19th day of *Kislev* 5559 (1798), he was completely exonerated and freed on express orders of the Czar. This date ever since has been celebrated by Jews the world over, and especially amongst Chabad Chasidim, for among other reasons, it marks the decisive turning point towards victory in the struggle to spread Chasidus. Hence, Rabbi Shalom DovBer of Lubavitch called it the "Rosh Hashanah" of Chasidus.[2]

Thus, the Rebbe's choice of *On the Essence of Chasidus* for his discourse on this special day is deeply connected to the meaning and inner significance of the holiday itself; for it was Rabbi Schneur Zalman who specifically brought the teachings of "general Chasidus" (as expounded by its founder, the Baal Shem Tov) into systematic, intellectual comprehension.

The Baal Shem Tov is well-known for his emphasis on and practice of the great principle of *Ahavat Yisrael* (the commandment to love a fellow Jew as oneself), even to the extent of self sacrifice, and for his affection for, encouragement, and teaching of the poor, unlettered, and oppressed masses of Jewry, who at that time were separated by a vast gulf from the scholarly elite by whom they were regarded as inferiors. The Baal Shem Tov emphasized the holiness of every Jew, stressing that everyone can serve G-d no matter what his or her background or knowledge. He also re-emphasized the importance of joy in Divine service and performance of *mitzvot*. Furthermore, he taught the deepest doctrines of the "esoteric" part of Torah in a manner that could be understood even by the simplest

---

maamarim of Rabbi Shalom DovBer of Lubavitch (the fifth-generation leader of Chabad) of the year 5666, for it also explains the distinctiveness of that work.

It was subsequently reprinted in *Likkutei Sichot* vol. 7, pp. 206-210.
2. This idea is explained in the text. See footnotes 59 and 61.

Jew, expressing these profound ideas through parables, stories, and aphorisms.

It was Rabbi Schneur Zalman, as has been said, who formulated the general Chasidus of the Baal Shem Tov into a systematic, comprehensible, intellectual philosophy. Among his numerous and lengthy Chasidic works, *Likkutei Amarim,* or *Tanya,* is the best known and most widely read, and has been translated into English and many other languages. This classic is a concise outline of his philosophy, written in a manner which enables people of all levels of understanding and knowledge to grasp and more deeply understand Chasidus.

Each of the six leaders of Chabad succeeding Rabbi Schneur Zalman have continued to expand and disseminate Chasidus—not only through their discourses and theoretical writings, but through their life-example, with their self-sacrificing work for the good of all Jews everywhere. They have intensely fought and resisted the efforts of oppressive governments to destroy Judaism, G-d forbid, placing themselves in great personal peril. The sixth Lubavitcher Rebbe, Rabbi Yosef Yitzchak Schneersohn, was imprisoned in 1927 and brutally treated by the Soviet government for his refusal to stop teaching Torah in Russia. After his arrival in the United States in 1940, he proceeded to establish Torah centers, determined to reawaken the flame of Torah and Judaism in America. Upon his passing in 1950, he was succeeded by his son-in-law, the Rebbe, Rabbi Menachem M. Schneerson, who continued and intensified this monumental task of spreading the light of Torah and Judaism throughout America and the entire world, to every Jew wherever he or she may be, and who has inspired countless Jews everywhere in love for G-d, Torah, and one's fellow man.

NOTE ON THE TRANSLATION AND HEBREW TEXT

In vowelizing the Hebrew words in this edition we have followed the grammatical rules of the Holy Tongue, which occasionally differ from the traditional or colloquial pronunciation.

In the original Hebrew text, 135 footnotes were added by the Rebbe—some citations of sources, and others quite lengthy and detailed explanations of ideas discussed in the text and their ramifications. These footnotes contain ideas of such profundity and importance that all have been completely translated. The reader is urged to make full use of them. In addition, the original Hebrew notes appear at the end of the text.

The translators have also added their own attempted clarifications, explanations of terms, concepts, names, etc. It should be understood that these commentaries and explanations are tentative and by no means an exhaustive or complete understanding of this text. They are meant to make the text clearer and more accessible to readers of all backgrounds. The text is a free translation, and the translators have attempted to make the language as clear and simple as possible. Nevertheless, the beginner may find some parts of the notes quite complex and perhaps difficult, but they are meant to be of aid to those who also already have some knowledge of Chasidus. Some of these notes develop independent topics and may be studied separately.

In addition, the translators have researched the Rebbe's references, and included summaries of the contents of those which they felt would be of invaluable aid to the reader, thus alleviating the reader of the task of looking up this information.

To facilitate distinguishing between the words of the Rebbe and those of the translators, minor variations in the text and notes have been made. All brackets are uniformly used to denote additions, remarks, and clarifications of the translators; parentheses are used for the words of the Rebbe. Footnotes added by the translators are enclosed in brackets. All chapter titles are the translators'.

TRANSLATION
AND
COMMENTARY

ON THE ESSENCE OF CHASIDUS

I.

THE CREATIVE CONTRIBUTIONS OF CHASIDUS

Many explanations have heretofore been given concerning the nature of Chasidus,[1] and the creative contribution which distinguishes it from those parts of the Torah which had been previously revealed.[2] And among them one finds the following:

1) In the times of the Baal Shem Tov the world was in a state of spiritual "unconsciousness," and through the revelations of the Baal Shem Tov and the teachings of Chasidus the world was aroused from this condition.[3]

2) "A Chasid is one who does more than what is required by the letter of the law."[4] (As our Sages of blessed memory have said: "The one who burns them [nail parings] is a Chasid, even though he might be harmed thereby."[5])

---

1. See also *On the Teachings of Chasidus* and *On the Learning of Chasidus* by R. Yosef Yitzchak Schneersohn [recently republished in *On The Study Of Chasidus*, Kehot.]

2. [See Appendix for an in-depth elaboration of this concept. It is one of the fundamental principles of Judaism that both the Written and the Oral Torahs in their entirety were given to Moshe at Sinai. The Written Torah, or *Tanach*, includes the Five Books of Moses, the Prophets, and the Writings. The Oral Torah comprises the *Mishnah*, Talmud, *Midrash*, commentaries, etc. The Talmud furthermore states, "Whatever any distinguished scholar will innovate in Torah study in the future was already given to Moshe at Sinai (*Megillah* 19b). That is to say, although all of Torah was given at Sinai, different parts were revealed at different times in Jewish his-

tory—for example, the Talmud in its appropriate time, the commentaries of Rashi in their appropriate time, etc. The fact that a particular idea or aspect of Torah was revealed at a specific time itself indicates that this was indeed the most fitting moment for its appearance, the time when it was most relevant. One of the earliest challenges to the Baal Shem Tov (the founder of Chasidism) and his new school of thought concerned the question of the contribution of Chasidus to the tapestry of Torah—how does it differ, and why was it not articulated in earlier generations.]

3. This explanation is found in an old Chasidic manuscript whose author is unknown.

[It has since been printed in *Sefer Hamaamarim 5663*, p. 142. When the Baal Shem Tov initiated his movement, the material situation of Eastern European

עִנְיָנָה שֶׁל תּוֹרַת הַחֲסִידוּת*

א.

בַּנּוֹגֵעַ לְעִנְיָנָה שֶׁל תּוֹרַת הַחֲסִידוּת* – וְהַחִידוּשׁ שֶׁבָּה עַל חֶלְקֵי הַתּוֹרָה שֶׁנִּתְגַּלּוּ לְפָנֶיהָ – נֶאֶמְרוּ בֵּיאוּרִים רַבִּים. וּמֵהֶם:

א) בִּזְמַנּוּ שֶׁל הַבַּעַל שֵׁם טוֹב הָיָה הָעוֹלָם**א בְּמַצָּב שֶׁל הִתְעַלְּפוּת, וְעַל יְדֵי גִילּוּי הַבַּעַל שֵׁם טוֹב וְתוֹרַת הַחֲסִידוּת, נִתְעוֹרֵר הָעוֹלָם מֵהִתְעַלְּפוּתוֹ.ד

ב) "חָסִיד הוּא שֶׁעוֹשֶׂה "לִפְנִים מִשּׁוּרַת הַדִּין"ג (וּכְמַאֲמַר רַבּוֹתֵינוּ זִכְרוֹנָם לִבְרָכָהד "שׂוֹרְפָן חָסִיד – אַף עַל גַּב שֶׁמַּזִּיק לוֹ").

Jewry—economic and political—was precarious, and the religious state was hardly better. The pogroms of 1648 and the false Messiahs were critical blows that the people barely survived. Their condition was virtually "comatose."]

See also *Kovetz Yud Shevat*, pp. 65-6. [*Likkutei Sichot* vol. 2 p. 516 ff. When a person faints, there is a tradition of whispering his name in his ear in order to revive him, because a person's Hebrew name has an essential connection to his general life-force. The soul of the Baal Shem Tov was the "general soul" of all the Jews, as indicated in his own name, "Yisrael," which he shared with all Jews. As Israel's "general soul," of which the particular soul of every individual Jew was a "component detail," the Baal Shem Tov's purpose and mission was to revive all Jews, even the lowliest, from their "unconsciousness," and to connect even the lowliest Jew with the Essence of G-d.]

4. *Padah b'Shalom 5675* (*B'Shaah Shehikdimu 5672*, p. 772-3); *Sefer Hamaamarim Melukat* vol. 6, p. 45.

[According to Torah law, one should desire, and is allowed, to pursue spiritual enlightenment for one's personal sake, and to strive for one's own spiritual interests. A Chasid, though, is one who reaches beyond that level and has no self-interest at all. An example is given (ibid.) of Moshe, who wanted to enter the Land of Israel not for his own attainment of spiritual revelations from on High, but rather so that the entire Jewish nation should have the ability to elicit G-dliness into the world.]

5. *Niddah* 17a and *Tosfot*, s.v. *sorfon chasid*. See also *Likkutei Dibburim* (Eng. Ed.) vol. 1, p. 149.

[The Talmud explains that one who cuts his nails should not throw the parings on the ground, lest a pregnant wom-

3) "The distinctive quality of Chasidus is that one's natural faculties are transformed into G-dly faculties."[4] As the Alter Rebbe [R. Schneur Zalman of Liadi], author of the *Tanya* and *Shulchan Aruch* said, "The entire idea of Chasidus is to change the nature of one's attributes."[6] This means to change not only one's natural characteristics themselves, but also the very "*nature* of one's character."[7]

4) The teachings of Chasidus created the possibility for every person, including even one who does not possess a lofty soul and who has not purified himself, to be able to grasp and comprehend G-dliness.[8] By explaining the ideas of the "esoteric"[9] part of Torah,

---

an step on them, causing her to miscarry. One who does throw away nail parings in this manner is a *rasha* (wicked); one who buries them, following the letter of the law, is a *tzaddik* (righteous); and one who burns them, thus taking extra precaution against them being uncovered, is a *Chasid* (pious).

Tosfot, quoting the *Aruch*, explains that the burning of any particle of one's body can cause harm to the one from whom the particle originated. Although one may be harmed, nevertheless one who burns his nail parings is a Chasid, for he goes beyond the requirement of the Law, and is prepared to suffer for it; the Law does not require a person to harm himself. See further *Ba'er Hetev* on *Shulchan Aruch, Orach Chaim* 260:2.]

6. *Likkutei Dibburim* ibid., p. 128. ["R. Menachem Mendel, the Tzemach Tzedek, once asked his grandfather Rabbi Schneur Zalman, the Alter Rebbe, at *yechidus*...: 'What is the ultimate point of Chasidus?' And the Alter Rebbe replied: 'The entire point of Chasidus is that one should transform the nature of his character traits (*middot*).'

"It should be noted that the question was, 'What is the ultimate point of Chasidus?' and not, 'What is Chasidus?' The Tzemach Tzedek knew what Chasidus is—a divine level of wisdom, the inner dimension of Torah. His question was, 'What is the ultimate *point* of Chasidus?'

And it was to this question that the Alter Rebbe answered that 'the entire point of Chasidus is that one should transform the nature of his *middot*.'

"...Now everyone understands with absolute clarity the difference between 'his natural *middot*' and 'the nature of his *middot*.' That much requires no explanation.

"Chasidus demands of everyone who studies its teachings that he should transform the nature of his *middot*. Chasidus is not only a schoolmaster who teaches one *how* to transform the nature of his *middot* [but a discipline that demands concrete action]."]

7. Ibid. See *Hatamim*, vol 3, p. 66 ff. [There are three basic souls in every Jew—the "G-dly soul," the "intellectual soul," and the "natural soul." Each of these three souls contains a full complement of both intellectual and emotional faculties in accordance with its nature. The natural soul is called the "animal soul," for all of its desires are directed towards materialistic and animalistic ends. The intellectual part of the animal soul engages in rationalizing actions according to its own understanding, and is concerned with self-preservation and self-justification. The emotional part of the animal soul is the "evil inclination" (*yetzer hara*). I.e., the emotional part of the animal soul is the inclination to do evil, while the intellectual part of the an-

ג) "מַעֲלַת הַחֲסִידוּת הוּא שֶׁהַכֹּחוֹת הַטִּבְעִים נַעֲשִׂים כֹּחוֹת

אֱלֹקִים"⁷. וּכְמַאֲמַר רַבֵּינוּ הַזָּקֵן בַּעַל הַתַּנְיָא וְהַשֻּׁלְחָן־עָרוּךְ

"כָּל עִנְיַן הַחֲסִידוּת הוּא לְשַׁנּוֹת טֶבַע מִדּוֹתָיו"⁸: לֹא רַק

לְשַׁנּוֹת מִדּוֹתָיו הַטִּבְעִים אֶלָּא גַם – "טֶבַע מִדּוֹתָיו"⁸.

ד) תּוֹרַת הַחֲסִידוּת חִידְּשָׁה אֲשֶׁר כָּל אֶחָד וְאֶחָד, גַם

מִי שֶׁאֵין לוֹ נְשָׁמָה גְבוֹהָה וְגַם לֹא זִכֵּךְ אֶת עַצְמוֹ, יוּכַל

לְהַשִּׂיג אֱלֹקוּת⁹. כִּי עַל יְדֵי זֶה שֶׁתּוֹרַת הַחֲסִידוּת בֵּיאֲרָה

---

imal soul is the means of justifying the act.

Until one has the appropriate instruments with which he can correct the inclinations of the animal soul, one must first *break* one's natural desires. True divine service, however, is not breaking, but fixing, mending (*tikkun*). And one begins this service of mending with the intellectual soul, the middle soul. The instrument is the study of Chasidus, which includes the contemplation of those ideas which are in consonance with one's level of understanding, and of material which also can be understood by, and is able to, arouse the heart.

Both the G-dly soul and the intellectual soul have emotional attributes, or "character traits": the intellectual soul is naturally drawn to that which is below it, and the G-dly soul is naturally drawn to that which is above it. To transform "the nature of one's *middot*" one is to transform the *middot* of both these souls. Thus, the intellectual soul should recognize that performance of a *mitzvah* should be because it is G-d's commandment, and not because it is rationally acceptable. Consequently, one transcends the confines of reason in pursuit of this. Conversely, the *middot* of the G-dly soul naturally desire to depart their physical holding, the body, and absorbed in their source, G-d. These *middot* can be "transformed" by directing them towards the service of G-d in this physical world,

within the confines of the body.]

8. *Torat Shalom*, p. 113. [Until the revelation of Chasidus, the esoteric elements of Torah (e.g. Kabbalah) were reserved for the spiritual elite, those with innately "lofty" souls, or those who had purified and refined themselves. Chasidus however, made the most abstruse concepts accessible to all by articulating them in intellectual, understandable, terms. Rabbi Shalom DovBer explains that this was consistent with what the Baal Shem Tov was told when he asked when Moshiach would come and was answered, "When your wellsprings will be dispersed outward (*chutzah*)"—i.e. when they will be dispersed even to unrefined and lowly people, so that even those who are *chutzah* should also understand G-dliness. And, Rabbi Shalom DovBer adds, *chutzah* ("outside, abroad") can even connote "rational understanding." That is, the articulation of Chasidus—which, as the text will soon note, transcends the realm of intellect—in rational terms, is already the first step in its extension to the "outside." See fn. 32.]

9. [There are four approaches or interpretations of Torah: *peshat* (plain meaning); *remez* (allusion); *drush* (homily); and *sod* (mystery)—the esoteric interpretation as found, for example, in Kabbalah. See below for detailed explanation and illustration of these four approaches.]

and making them accessible to the intellect through examples and analogies corresponding to the faculties and characteristics of the soul—as it is written, "From my flesh I perceive G-d"[10]—Chasidus enabled every one to comprehend even this part of Torah. Not only can one grasp it with the intelligence found in his G-dly soul, but also with the intelligence of his intellectual soul—and further, he can even comprehend it with the intelligence possessed by his animal soul.[11]

II

CHASIDUS AS THE "EXTENSION OF THE EIN SOF"

It is self-evident, for reasons which later will be explained, that Chasidus is one central point; it is a singular and indivisible core which is not a composite of various particular ideas. Now since all of the distinctive qualities mentioned in the preceding definitions (and also in numerous other explanations)[12] are different, one must conclude that these qualities do not define and capture the *essential* nature of the teachings of Chasidus. The fundamental nature of Chasidus is a quintessential point, which is completely abstracted and removed from any particular ideas; however, it is by virtue of this quin-

---

10. Job 19:26. [Chasidic literature explains this verse to mean that by examining the structure of one's own soul and its faculties, which are created in the image of G-d, one can comprehend Divinity itself.]

See *Likutei Dibburim* (Eng. Ed.) vol. 3, p. 5 ff. ["R. Shalom R. Hillel's once quoted an account which he had heard from his teacher, R. Hillel of Paritch, of the first lesson in Chasidus that he had ever heard… 'Before I became a Chabad Chasid,' recalled R. Hillel, 'I considered my body to be a loathsome thing, because all spiritual woes derive from it. But when I apprehended the spirit of the teaching that 'from my flesh I perceive G-d,' that the body is a magnifying glass through which one perceives G-dliness, my body acquired good standing in my eyes.'"]

See also *Torat Shalom*, p. 185, that "as

a result of this innovation of Chasidus—that the faculties of man can serve as an analogy to comprehend their parallels 'Above,' in G-d, as it were—these faculties thereby become G-dly." Thus, one can connect this fourth explanation of Chasidus with the third.

[The innovation of Chasidus over Kabbalah is that Chasidus makes Divinity comprehensible through the analogy of human faculties. Though Kabbalah in a sense does the same, it is not truly perfect comprehension. Chasidus, however, brings G-dliness to perfect human comprehension, for from one's own human faculties, he can understand supernal matters. (See below, fn. 71.) From one's own intellectual attributes, he can understand what the "intellect" of G-d is, and from his own emotional attributes, or *middot*, he can understand the *middot* of G-d. And through this understanding and,

אֶת הָעִנְיָנִים שֶׁל חֵלֶק הַ"סּוֹד" שֶׁבַּתּוֹרָה וְקֵירַבְתָּם אֶל
הַשֵּׂכֶל בְּדוּגְמָאוֹת וּמְשָׁלִים מִכֹּחוֹת וּתְכוּנוֹת הַנֶּפֶשׁ –
"מִבְּשָׂרִי אֶחֱזֶה אֱלוֹקַהּ"[11] – נִיתְּנָה הָאֶפְשָׁרוּת לְכָל אֶחָד
וְאֶחָד לְהַשִּׂיג גַּם חֵלֶק זֶה שֶׁבַּתּוֹרָה; וְלֹא רַק בְּהַשֵּׂכֶל
שֶׁבְּנַפְשׁוֹ הָאֱלֹקִית, אֶלָּא גַּם בְּהַשֵּׂכֶל שֶׁבְּנַפְשׁוֹ הַשִּׂכְלִית עַד
– בְּהַשֵּׂכֶל שֶׁבְּנַפְשׁוֹ הַבַּהֲמִית.

ב.

מוּבָן וּפָשׁוּט כִּדְלְקַמָּן, אֲשֶׁר תּוֹרַת הַחֲסִידוּת הִיא
נְקוּדָה אַחַת שֶׁאֵינָהּ מוּרְכֶּבֶת מִפְּרָטִים שׁוֹנִים. וּמִכֵּיוָן שֶׁכָּל
הַמַּעֲלוֹת שֶׁנֶּאֶמְרוּ בַּבֵּיאוּרִים הַנַּ"ל (וּבְעוֹד בֵּיאוּרִים[12]), מַעֲלוֹת
שׁוֹנוֹת הֵן, הֲרֵי מוּכְרָח – שֶׁמַּעֲלוֹת אֵלּוּ אֵינָן מַגְדִּירוֹת
וּמְמַצּוֹת אֶת **מַהוּתָהּ** שֶׁל תּוֹרַת הַחֲסִידוּת. מַהוּתָהּ שֶׁל
הַחֲסִידוּת הִיא נְקוּדָה עַצְמִית הַמּוּפְשֶׁטֶת מֵעִנְיָנִים פְּרָטִים,

---

consequently, purification, one's faculties thereby become G-dly—fitting vessels which can be absorbed into, and become a part of, G-dliness.

Thus the explanation of the fourth definition of Chasidus (that it enables even a simple person to understand Divinity through its analogies to the soul) is connected to the third definition (that Chasidus changes the nature of one's character). By understanding G-dliness, one's own faculties become *G-dly*.]

11. [See fn. 7. The intellectual soul bridges the gulf between the animal soul and the G-dly soul. Intellectual understanding is a vessel for G-dly understanding and thus can have an effect on the animal soul. See *Sefer Hamaamarim 5702*, p. 102.]

12. See *Sefer Hasichot Kayitz 5700*, p. 26

ff., and elsewhere. [R. Gershon Ber (a distinguished Chasid of Rabbi Menachem Mendel, the Tzemach Tzedek) was asked by a group of questioners, "What is Chasidus?" Though the questioners all agreed that Chasidus was a G-dly philosophy, they sought to know what advantage Chasidus had over Kabbalah and philosophy. R. Gershon Ber answered: Kabbalah describes the *sefirot*, the creative attributes and manifestations of G-d, while philosophy explains how G-d is beyond description and definition, how one cannot really understand Him at all—for if one would know G-d, he would "be G-d." Chasidus, however, maintains "Know Him and become like Him." Through the effort of actually understanding G-d, one becomes like Him. See also A.C. Glitzenstein, *Or Hachasidus* (Kehot, Kfar Chabad, 1965), for other explanations.]

tessential point that all the above-mentioned special qualities exist and are derived.[13]

This quintessential point of Chasidus (as discussed earlier in the *maamar*, which is based on the *maamar* of Rabbi Shalom DovBer of Lubavitch)[14] is the effusion of a "new light"[15] from the innermost level of *keter*,[16] and yet higher, an effusion from the innermost level of *atik*[17] itself, which is the level of the *Ein Sof*[18] [the Infinite] that is found in רדל״א—*radla*[19] [*reisha d'lo ityada*—"the head or beginning that is not known"].

---

13. Nevertheless, it is only through these specific different qualities that one can grasp the essential nature of Chasidus, as will be explained in Chapter XVIII.

14. Cited in footnote 4.

15. [NEW LIGHT. "Light" is used as a favorite metaphor in Kabbalah and Chasidus to represent and describe the various manifestations, emanations and forces of the Divinity. It is often used in contradistinction to what is called *Atzmut* (the "Essence" of G-d), the level beyond all definition, manifestation, etc. R. J. Immanuel Schochet in his *Mystical Concepts in Chassidism*, appended to the English-Hebrew Tanya (Kehot, 1998), uses Kabbalistic sources to explain the aptness of this metaphor as follows (pp. 884-885, see further there):

Of all physical phenomena, light is that which most closely approximates what is spiritual and freed from the limitations of matter. For example, it is not corporeal; it delights the soul; it enables one to see. It is also analogous to the nature of Divine emanations insofar as light is never separated from its source, spreads itself instantaneously, irradiates all physical objects, does not mix and mingle with any other substance, never *per se* changes, is essential to life in general, and is received and absorbed relative to the capacity of the recipient, etc.

Needless to say, however, the analogy is still only an approximation, and must not be taken in any literal sense. Terms and concepts related to the Divinity must be understood spiritually, without any temporal and spatial connotations whatsoever.]

16. *B'Shaah Shehikdimu 5672*, p. 768.

[KETER. Lit., "crown." In Kabbalah and Chasidic literature, *keter* refers to one of the most transcendent levels of G-dliness. It is the "crown," or level that transcends the ten so-called *sefirot*, creative divine attributes and manifestations of G-d. The *sefirot* are divided into two categories: *sechel* (intellect) and *middot* (emotions). The ten *sefirot* are the source of, and parallel to, the ten powers of the human soul. Just as man reveals himself through his attributes, or their "garments" (thought, speech, and deed), similarly G-d reveals Himself through His attributes, the *sefirot*.

There are four "worlds," or basic levels, each of which is a general category of Divine manifestation (see fn. 45), ranging from the highest level, where there is total unity with G-d, down to this lowest physical world which we inhabit, where the Infinite is all but concealed. (Each of these four worlds contains numerous subgradations also described as "worlds.") Now *keter* is the level which transcends all worlds, and which is the "crown" to the *sefirot*. It is identified with G-d's Supernal Will, which links G-d—the Infinite *Ein Sof*—with all His finite created worlds,

אֶלָּא – מִצַּד נְקוּדָתָהּ הָעַצְמִית, נִמְצָאוֹת וּמִסְתַּעֲפוֹת מִמֶּנָּה מַעֲלוֹת הַנַּ״ל.

הַנְּקוּדָה הָעַצְמִית שֶׁל הַחֲסִידוּת הִיא [כִּמְדוּבָּר לְעֵיל בְּהַמַּאֲמָר, שֶׁבִּיסוֹדוֹ הוּא מַאֲמָר שֶׁל כְּבוֹד קְדֻשַּׁת אַדְמוּ״ר (מהורש״ב) נִשְׁמָתוֹ עֵדֶן¹⁷] – הַמְשָׁכַת אוֹר חָדָשׁ מִבְּחִינַת פְּנִימִיּוּת הַכֶּתֶר¹⁷, וּלְמַעֲלָה יוֹתֵר – הַמְשָׁכַת בְּחִינַת פְּנִימִיּוּת עַתִּיק מַמָּשׁ, בְּחִינַת אֵין סוֹף שֶׁנִּמְצָא בְּרַדְלָ״א [בְּרֵישָׁא דְלָא אִתְיְדַע]¹⁹.

---

for an intermediary is necessary in order to link the infinite with the finite.

An analogy: The essence of the human soul itself is beyond all description. It is neither intellectual nor emotional. How then does the soul express itself and give rise to intellect and emotions if it entirely transcends these realms? It does so through the faculty of *ratzon* (will). *Ratzon* is a general power not limited to any particular part or function of the body, but is all-encompassing and unlimited. And though *ratzon* is still not the essence of the soul, but only an extension and reflection of it, it is the first state of movement from the pure soul to the faculties which express it; and thus it is an intermediary between the essence of the soul and its faculties.

Every "intermediary" must contain two parts; i.e., the factors it shares in common with the two levels between which it mediates. These may be described as: 1) The "head" of the lower level; 2) The lower part of the upper level. Likewise, in *ratzon* there are two parts: 1) *Ratzon*—an external aspect; 2) *Taanug* (delight), the internal aspect, which is the motivating force of all activity, including *ratzon.*

Hence, we can understand how *keter* (G-d's Will) is that which links the Four Worlds with the Infinite G-d. And, similarly, in *keter* there are also two levels of *ratzon*: the external, and the internal. The

external level of G-d's Will which transcends all worlds is called *arich anpin*; and the internal level is called *atik*, and corresponds to *taanug.*

When new light emanates from *keter*, all the *sefirot* are rejuvenated, as it were, and elevated. In our context, Chasidus is described as a "new light," a revelation of an aspect of G-d hitherto concealed; a deeper insight vouchsafed to man.

For further introduction and explanation of these concepts, see Schochet, *Mystical Concepts in Chassidism* (op. cit.) and Posner, *Translator's Explanatory Notes* to *On the Study of Chasidus* (Kehot, 1997).]

17. [ATIK. The innermost level of the Supernal Will, corresponding to "delight." See preceding note.]

18. [EIN SOF. Literally, "Infinite," "Endless." The most absolute, Infinite force of G-d, totally beyond description, knowledge, and comprehension, completely beyond any boundaries; the Essence of G-d Himself, the innermost aspect of the innermost level of *keter*. As explained above, *keter* (will) is the intermediary between the *Ein Sof* and the *sefirot.*]

19. *B'Shaah Shehikdimu 5672* p. 770; 773.

[RADLA. A Kabbalistic term indicating the deepest and innermost level of the Es-

It follows then, from this very idea (which was elaborated in the *maamar*), that all of the distinctive qualities of Chasidus which are explained in various places are but the ramifications of the quintessential point. For since Chasidus is the extension of the state of *Ein Sof*, it is self-understood that *Ein Sof* is the essence [of Chasidus], and all other particular aspects are only ramifications and derivatives of it.

III

TORAH: THE EPITOME OF PERFECTION

What has been stated above concerning Chasidus also applies *in general* to all parts of the Torah; for the Torah encompasses all manner of perfection and quality to be found in the world.

[Generally these virtues are divided—as illustrated in man, who is a "miniature world"[20]—into the attributes of intellect and those of the emotions (character traits).

Now in regards to the latter—to moral behavior and good character—the laws and ethical precepts of Torah (contained, for example, in the tractate *Avot* [Ethics of the Fathers][21] et al.) are the epitome of goodness and truth. All other systems of morality, however, which men by themselves have contrived, mix together good and evil, truth and falsehood.[22] And furthermore, the source of those portions of good that each one these systems contains is in Torah.

(There is a well-known story about the Rebbe, my sainted father-in-law [R. Yosef Yitzchak Schneersohn],[23] which illustrates this point. On one of his journeys, he encountered several men who were arguing and expressing differing opinions about the relationship of

---

sence of G-d which is entirely unknowable—not only because of its profundity, but because it is utterly beyond the realm of knowledge. Chasidus recognizes the bounds of intellect as innate. Intellect is a manifestation, a "power" of the soul or a *sefirah* of G-d, and is not Essence. Essence transcends intellect. Thus, *Ein Sof* transcends knowledge because knowledge itself originates on a lower plane than G-d's Essence.]

20. *Midrash Tanchuma, Pekudei* 3; *Tikkunei Zohar* 69, (p. 100a). See also *Avot d'R. Nattan*, ch. 31; *Kohelet Rabbah* 1:4; *Zohar* I:134b; Guide for the Perplexed I, ch. 72; *Likkutei Torah, Bamidbar* 5b.

21. See R. Ovadiah of Bartenura on Ethics of the Fathers, beg. [where he explains why this tractate begins with the statement that Moshe received the Torah from Sinai, and why it details its trans-

וְעִנְיָן זֶה עַצְמוֹ (שֶׁנֶּאֱמַר בְּהַמַּאֲמָר), מַכְרִיחַ אֲשֶׁר כָּל
הַמַּעֲלוֹת שֶׁחֲסִידוּת הַמְבוֹאָרוֹת בִּמְקוֹמוֹת שׁוֹנִים הֵן רַק
הִסְתַּעֲפוּת מִנְּקוּדָתָהּ הָעַצְמִית. כִּי מֵכֵּיוָן שֶׁהַחֲסִידוּת הִיא
הַמְשָׁכַת בְּחִינַת אֵין סוֹף, הֲרֵי מוּבָן וּפָשׁוּט אֲשֶׁר "אֵין סוֹף" הוּא
הָעַצְמִי, וְכָל שְׁאָר הָעִנְיָנִים אֵינָם אֶלָּא נִמְצָאִים וּמְסוּבָּבִים מִמֶּנּוּ.

ג.

הָאָמוּר לְעֵיל בַּנּוֹגֵעַ לְתוֹרַת הַחֲסִידוּת, הוּא **בִּכְלָלוּת** בְּכָל
חֶלְקֵי הַתּוֹרָה: הַתּוֹרָה כּוֹלֶלֶת כָּל הַמִּינֵי־שְׁלֵימוּת וּמַעֲלוֹת
הַנִּמְצָאוֹת בָּעוֹלָם

[הַנֶּחֱלָקוֹת בִּכְלָל – בְּעִנְיְנֵי הָעוֹלָם קָטָן הוּא הָאָדָם[כב] –
לְמַעֲלוֹת הַמּוֹחִין וּמַעֲלוֹת הַמִּדּוֹת:

בְּהַנְהָגוֹת מוּסָרִיּוֹת וּמִדּוֹת טוֹבוֹת – הֲרֵי הַמִּשְׁפָּטִים וְדַרְכֵי
הַמּוּסָר שֶׁבַּתּוֹרָה (דְּמַסֶּכֶת אָבוֹת[טו] וְכַדּוֹמֶה) הֵם תַּכְלִית הַטּוֹב
וְהָאֱמֶת. וְכָל שִׁיטוֹת הַמּוּסָר שֶׁבָּדוּ בְּנֵי אָדָם מִלִּבָּם, מְעוֹרְבוֹת
הֵן טוֹב וָרָע, אֱמֶת וָשֶׁקֶר*[טז]. וְחֶלְקֵי הַטּוֹב שֶׁיֶּשְׁנָם בְּכָל אַחַת
מֵהַשִּׁיטוֹת מְקוֹרָם הוּא בַּתּוֹרָה

(וְכַיָּדוּעַ הַסִּפּוּר מִכְּבוֹד קְדֻשַּׁת מוֹרִי וְחָמִי אַדְמוּ"ר[יז],
שֶׁבְּאַחַת מִנְּסִיעוֹתָיו, הִתְוַוכְּחוּ כַּמָּה אֲנָשִׁים וְהִבִּיעוּ דֵּיעוֹת

---

mission: While non-Jews contrived their own ethical systems, the ethics of the Jews are from Sinai, of *Divine origin*, and are the basis of all ethics.]

22. For G-d created the entire creation "*laasot*"—to be worked with, fixed, completed, and perfected. See *Bereishit Rabbah* 11:6, and Rashi's commentary there; *Zohar* I:47b ff.; *Or Hatorah* to Genesis 1:3 (p. 514 and p. 717). After Adam's sin

of eating from the Tree of Knowledge, good and evil, formerly totally separate, merged. Nothing is pure any longer; there is no good without evil and vice-versa. (*Torah Or, Toldot* 21b; *Torat Chaim, Toldot* 14b; and elsewhere. See *Likkutei Dibburim* (Eng. Ed.) vol. 1 p. 183-4.)

23. From a letter dated 4 *Tevet* 5698 [*Igrot Kodesh* vol. 4, p. 200 ff].

Torah to political systems, and debating with which system the Torah agreed. Each one of them brought forth as proof a source from Torah in support of his ideology. When they asked the Rebbe for his opinion on this question, he answered: "Since Torah is the absolute perfection of truth and goodness, it contains within itself all of the best ideas which one may find in all ideologies.")

[This pre-eminent perfection and superiority of Torah applies not only to moral and political systems.] The Torah is, furthermore, the most elevated and supreme wisdom in relation to all sciences and systems of knowledge—as it is written, "For it is your wisdom and understanding in the eyes of the nations."[24]]

Moreover, [not only does Torah encompass all perfection found within the world, but indeed] the entire vivifying and sustaining flow of life into the world (even into the Supernal Worlds)[25] depends upon (one minute detail of) Torah.[26]

Nevertheless, all of these profound attributes and superior virtues still do not constitute the essence of Torah. The essence of Torah is that it is "completely united with the infinite light of the *Ein Sof* which is enclothed within it in a perfect and total unity."[26] Therefore, since all of the worlds are as absolute nothingness in relation to the *Ein Sof,* so are they also in relation to the Torah; and hence, in this light, "It is no praise whatsoever to extol the Torah as the vivifying life force of all worlds, since they are reckoned as nothingness itself."[26] Rather, by virtue of its quintessential point, which is its union with the infinite light of the *Ein Sof,* the Torah automatically includes every kind of superior virtue and perfection found in the world; and by virtue of this same quintessential point, the Torah is also the world's vivifying flow of life, etc.

Now even though the quintessential point of *all* parts of Torah is that they are united with the light of the *Ein Sof,* in truth, the primary expression of this point is in Chasidus. (As was said of Chasidus in the *maamar* [quoted above], *it* (alone) is the effusion of the *Ein Sof* that is found in *radla.*)

---

24. Deuteronomy 4:6.

25. [In Kabbalah and Chasidus, the term "world" refers to the different

stages of spiritual and physical existence, and levels of concealment of G-d. All the worlds are elevated and sustained through the performance of

שׁוֹנוֹת אוֹדוֹת יַחַס הַתּוֹרָה לְהַשִּׁיטוֹת הַמְּדִינִיּוֹת וְעִם אֵיזוֹ מֵהֶן
הִיא מַסְכֶּמֶת, וְכָל אֶחָד מֵהֶם הֶרְאָה מָקוֹר בַּתּוֹרָה לְשִׁיטָתוֹ.
כְּשֶׁשָּׁאֲלוּ אֶת חַוַּת דַּעַת כְּבוֹד קְדֻשַּׁת מוֹרִי וְחָמִי אַדְמוּ"ר
בָּזֶה, עָנָה: הַתּוֹרָה, לִהְיוֹתָהּ תַּכְלִית הָאֱמֶת וְהַטּוֹב, יֶשְׁנָם בָּהּ
כָּל הָעִנְיָנִים הַטּוֹבִים שֶׁבְּכָל הַשִּׁיטוֹת).

בְּנוֹגֵעַ לְהַחָכְמוֹת – הַתּוֹרָה הִיא הַחָכְמָה הַיּוֹתֵר נַעֲלֵית,
כְּמוֹ שֶׁכָּתוּב" כִּי הִיא חָכְמַתְכֶם וּבִינַתְכֶם לְעֵינֵי הָעַמִּים]

וְלֹא זוֹ בִּלְבָד אֶלָּא שֶׁכָּל הַשְׁפָּעַת הַחַיּוּת בָּעוֹלָם (גַּם
בָּעוֹלָמוֹת הָעֶלְיוֹנִים) תְּלוּיָה בְּ(דִקְדּוּק קַל שֶׁל) תּוֹרָה".

אָמְנָם, לֹא זוֹהִי מַהוּתָהּ שֶׁל הַתּוֹרָה. מַהוּתָהּ שֶׁל תּוֹרָה
הוּא מַה שֶּׁהִיא "מְיוּחֶדֶת לְגַמְרֵי בְּאוֹר אֵין סוֹף בָּרוּךְ הוּא
הַמְלוּבָּשׁ בָּהּ בְּתַכְלִית הַיִּחוּד". וְלָכֵן, כֵּיוָן שֶׁכָּל הָעוֹלָמוֹת הֵם
כְּלֹא מַמָּשׁ לְגַבֵּי אֵין סוֹף בָּרוּךְ הוּא, כֵּן הֵם גַּם לְגַבֵּי הַתּוֹרָה,
וְלָזֹאת "אֵין לְשַׁבְּחָהּ כְּלָל בִּתְהִלַּת חַיּוּת כָּל הָעוֹלָמוֹת, מֵאַחַר
דְּלָא מַמָּשׁ חֲשִׁיבֵי"". אֶלָּא – מִצַּד נְקוּדָתָהּ הָעַצְמִית,
שֶׁמְּיוּחֶדֶת הִיא בְּאוֹר אֵין סוֹף בָּרוּךְ הוּא, כּוֹלֶלֶת הִיא בְּמֵילָא
גַּם אֶת כָּל הַמִּינֵי-מַעֲלוֹת וּשְׁלֵימוּת שֶׁבָּעוֹלָם, וְעַל יָדָהּ –
הַשְׁפָּעַת הַחַיּוּת וְכוּ'.

אָכֵן, אַף שֶׁפַּל חֶלְקֵי הַתּוֹרָה, נְקוּדָתָם הָעַצְמִית הִיא מַה
שֶּׁהֵם מְיוּחָדִים בְּאוֹר אֵין סוֹף בָּרוּךְ הוּא, בְּכָל זֶה, עִיקַר נְקוּדָה
זוֹ מִתְבַּטֵּא בְּתוֹרַת הַחֲסִידוּת (וְכָאָמוּר בְּהַמַּאֲמָר בְּנוֹגֵעַ
לְ"חֲסִידוּת", שֶׁהִיא (דַוְקָא) הַמְשָׁכַת אֵין סוֹף שֶׁנִּמְצָא בְּרִדְלָ"א),

---

mitzvot and the study of Torah; they depend on the appropriate observance of even its most minute detail, for the Torah is the wisdom of G-d. See be-

low, fn. 45.]

26. *Kuntres Acharon*, section 6; *Derech Mitzvotecha* 41 a-b.

This is primarily true of Chasidus because the state of *Ein Sof* which is found in all other parts of the Torah is clothed in a certain form, a form which defines and "expresses" the nature of that part. The form of that particular part of the Torah (whether it be *peshat*—the plain meaning; *remez*—the hinted, intimated meaning; *drush*—the homiletic, expounded meaning; or *sod*—the esoteric meaning) conceals the unformed abstractness[27] of the *Ein Sof* which is clothed therein. This form is a "concealing garment" that cannot be changed, so to speak.

Chasidus, however, is not bounded and defined by any form. And since those "forms" through which the ideas of Chasidus are revealed are, in the words of the Psalmist, "like a garment that You will change, and *they will be changed*"[28] (which is why Chasidus includes all the four levels of *Pardes* [*peshat, remez, drush, sod*] and gives life to them, as will later be explained),[29] the form does not truly conceal the unformed abstractness of the *Ein Sof* within.

IV

SOME RAMIFICATIONS OF THE CONCEPT OF MOSHIACH

We can further clarify the definition of the essential nature of Chasidus through explaining the inner meaning of the idea of Moshiach. For, "From the reward (of a commandment) we will know its essential nature"[30]; and since it is through (the dissemination[31] of the fountains of) Chasidus that "the Master comes,"[32] referring to King

---

27. [P'SHEETUS HA'EIN SOF. "Unformed abstractness"; lit., "Simplicity." In our context, "Simplicity" connotes not a "lack" or "deficiency," of course, but rather the most absolute level of *Ein Sof*, that which totally transcends description, boundary, form, or composition. That is, it is entirely abstracted from and beyond any form—even the forms and qualities of "perfection." It is utter *Essence*.]

28. Psalms 102:27. As it is known, there are two types of "garments." There are those that are impossible to exchange for others, such as garments of "skin and

flesh with which You have clothed me" (Job 10:11). [Then there are ordinary garments which one can change. In other words, *peshat, remez, drush* and *sod* are four *set* approaches through which the Torah can be comprehended. The "garment" of Chasidus, however, is not fixed in any form.]

29. Chapter VIII ff.

30. *Tanya*, ch. 39 (53a). [This is R. Schneur Zalman's interpretation on *Avot* 4:2, "The reward of a *mitzvah* is a *mitzvah*," that the reward of a *mitzvah* reflects the essential nature of that *mitzvah* itself.]

כִּי כָּל חֶלְקֵי הַתּוֹרָה, בְּחִינַת הָ"אֵין סוֹף" שֶׁבָּהֶם מִתְלַבֵּשׁ הוּא בְּאֵיזֶה צִיּוּר – צִיּוּר הַמַּגְדִּיר וּ"מְבַטֵּא" (גִיט אַרוֹיס) מַהוּתוֹ שֶׁל חֵלֶק זֶה, וְצִיּוּר זֶה שֶׁל חֵלֶק תּוֹרָה זֶה [פְּשַׁט, רֶמֶז, דְּרוּשׁ, סוֹד], מַעֲלִים הוּא עַל פְּשִׁיטוּת הָאֵין־סוֹף הַמְלוּבָּשׁ בּוֹ – הֶעְלֵם דִּלְבוּשׁ שֶׁכִּבְיָכוֹל אִי אֶפְשָׁר לְהַחֲלִיפוֹ.

וְאִילּוּ תּוֹרַת הַחֲסִידוּת, מִכֵּיוָן שֶׁאֵינָהּ מוּגְדֶּרֶת בְּאֵיזֶה צִיּוּר, וְהַ"צִיּוּרִים" שֶׁעִנְיָן שֶׁבַּחֲסִידוּת מִתְגַּלֶּה עַל יָדָם – כִּלְבוּשׁ[ט] תַּחֲלִיפֵם וְיַחֲלוֹפוּ (שֶׁלָּכֵן כּוֹלֶלֶת הִיא אֶת כָּל ד' הַחֲלָקִים פְּשַׁט־רֶמֶז־דְּרוּשׁ־סוֹד שֶׁבַּתּוֹרָה וּמְחַיֶּה אוֹתָם, כִּדְלְהַלָּן[י]), אֵין הַצִּיּוּר מַעֲלִים בְּהֶעְלֵם אֲמִיתִּי אֶת פְּשִׁיטוּת הָאֵין־סוֹף שֶׁבּוֹ.

ד.

בֵּיאוּר מַהוּתָהּ שֶׁל תּוֹרַת הַחֲסִידוּת יוּבְהַר עַל יְדֵי בֵּיאוּר תּוֹכְנוֹ הַפְּנִימִי שֶׁל מָשִׁיחַ. כִּי "מִשְׁכָּרָהּ (שֶׁל מִצְוָה) נֵדַע מַהוּתָהּ"[כא], וּמִכֵּיוָן אֲשֶׁר עַל יְדֵי [הֲפָצַת[כב] מַעְיְנוֹת] הַחֲסִידוּת

---

31. For the specifics of the expression "*dissemination*," or "*dispersal, spreading out*" of the fountains, see below, Chapter XXI.

32. When Moshiach was asked by the Baal Shem Tov when he would come, his response was, "When your fountains [of Chasidus] will be disseminated to the outside."

The Baal Shem Tov recorded this incident in his well-known letter describing his soul's ascension on High on Rosh Hashanah 5507. The letter is printed at the end of *Ben Porat Yosef*, and in a book of letters by the Baal Shem Tov and his stu-

dents (Lwow 1923, wherein the publisher notes that he copied this letter from the one written by R. Yechiel, the Baal Shem Tov's son-in-law, and signed by the Baal Shem Tov). It is also printed in *Ginzei Nistarot* (Jerusalem, 1924) part 1 ch. 65, and in part at the beginning of *Keter Shem Tov* and the Maggid of Mezritch's *Likkutei Amarim*.

Likkutei Dibburim vol. 2, chapters 16-18 explains the Baal Shem Tov's question and Moshiach's answer according to Chasidus. [To quote a segment (ch. 17 sect. 30-32):

The Baal Shem Tov asked Moshiach: "Master, when are you coming?" It would

Moshiach, thus, from the concept of Moshiach—the reward—we will know what is the essential nature of Chasidus.[33]

With the coming of Moshiach, many sublime events will be introduced. For example, Israel (and the *Shechinah*)[34] will be redeemed from Exile. Even greater: "All Israel will be great sages, they will know the things that are now concealed and will attain an understanding of their Creator... 'For the earth shall be full of the knowledge of G-d...'"[35] Even greater yet: there will be a change and great innovation in the works of Creation.[36]

---

seem that this was an unwarranted question. Consider the following explicit episode in *Sanhedrin* 98a:

R. Yehoshua ben Levi asked this question of Elijah the Prophet, and was told to ask Moshiach himself. Moshiach reply was, "Today." When Moshiach did not come, R. Yehoshua returned bitterly depressed to Elijah, who explained that this answer meant, "Today—if you will listen to My voice" (Psalms 95:7). That is, Moshiach could come only when Israel listened to the voice of G-d.

With such an explicit reply in the Talmud, why did the Baal Shem Tov again ask the question, "Master, when are you coming"?

The Baal Shem Tov is the Moshe Rabbeinu of the entire school of Chasidus, for he was chosen by G-d to be the one through whom the teachings of Chasidus at large were revealed. Similar to Moshe, the Baal Shem Tov was a "shepherd" of Israel who was concerned for even the least of his flock. Known for his great love for all Israel, the Baal Shem Tov could find virtue in every single Jew, and in every *mitzvah* he could perceive the true radiance within. He witnessed the great self-sacrifice of his fellow Jews, the pain which they were suffering in Exile, the splendor of all their *mitzvot*, and thus the way in which they were listening to G-d's voice. And so his soul ascended on High and visited the heavenly palace of Moshiach and asked him, "Master, when are you coming?"

In response, Moshiach told the Baal Shem Tov, "When your wellsprings will be disseminated abroad" (cf. Proverbs 5:16). Rashi comments: "You will ultimately acquire disciples and give forth instruction publicly, and your name will be renowned." Chasidus explains the term "wellspring": the space required by a wellspring is but sinewy and restricted, and its waters trickle forth by drops; a river, in contrast, covers considerable length and breadth and its abundant waters flow turbulently from its place of origin to the outside (*chutza*), to places which are not even fit for it. Likewise, Chasidus has to spread abroad and become so popular and widespread that everyone would be able to know the Baal Shem Tov's teachings and be familiar with this G-dly understanding.]

33. See *B'Shaah Shehikdimu 5672*, p. 771 ff., that the revelation of Chasidus is analogous to the future revelations of the era of Moshiach.

34. To quote *Megillah* 29a: "The Holy One blessed be He will return with them from Exile."

[SHECHINAH. The "Divine Presence," the immanent category of the Divine influence, brought down to earth by the study of the Torah and the practice of *mitzvot*. *Shechinah* is identified with *malchut* and the source of the souls, and also corresponds to the second letter *hay* of the Tetragrammaton, Y-H-V-H. One

"אָתֵי מַר"כג דָּא מַלְכָּא מְשִׁיחָא, הֲרֵי מֵעִנְיָנוֹ שֶׁל מָשִׁיחַ –
שֶׁכָּרָה, נֵדַע אֶת מַהוּתָהכד.

בְּבִיאַת הַמָּשִׁיחַ יִתְחַדְּשׁוּ כַּמָּה וְכַמָּה עִנְיָנִים נַעֲלִים. וּכְמוֹ:
גְּאוּלַת יִשְׂרָאֵל (וְהַשְּׁכִינָהכה) מֵהַגָּלוּת; לְמַעֲלָה מִזֶּה: "יִהְיוּ
יִשְׂרָאֵל חֲכָמִים גְּדוֹלִים וְיוֹדְעִים דְּבָרִים הַסְּתוּמִים וְיַשִּׂיגוּ
דַּעַת בּוֹרְאָם כו' מָלְאָה הָאָרֶץ דֵּעָה אֶת הוי' כו'"כו; לְמַעֲלָה
מִזֶּה: שִׁינּוּי וְחִידּוּשׁ בְּמַעֲשֵׂה בְּרֵאשִׁיתכז

---

who sins, on the other hand, breaks up the unity of the Divine Name, dragging down the *Shechinah* into "exile."]

35. *Rambam, Hilchot Melachim,* end. Even when the *Beit Hamikdash* stood, the entire world was not "full of the knowledge of G-d...," for that is set to take place only when Moshiach will come.

36. See *Rambam,* ibid., that in the era of Moshiach there will be no jealousy, etc., and there will be an abundance of all delights, etc. Although *Rambam* maintains (ibid., beg. chapter 12) that the prophecies concerning the era of Moshiach—such as "the wolf will lie down with the lamb"—are only to be taken allegorically and not literally, yet he included predictions that in the era of Moshiach there *will be* great change?
—According to the view (as also favored by Kabbalah and Chasidus) that the descriptions *are* to be taken literally, how much more so will there be great changes. See also *Raavad,* who disputes *Rambam's* allegorical interpretation (*Hilchot Teshuvah* 8:2); *Avodat Hakodesh,* part 2, ch. 41; and elsewhere.—
Perhaps the following explanation may be offered as a solution to this difficult issue: *Rambam* also maintains that there will be two distinct stages in the era of Moshiach after it has become certain that Moshiach has arrived. The *first stage*

of the Redemption is when "the earth will be filled with the knowledge of G-d..." (Isaiah 11:9); and it is this period—wherein there will be no great change in the nature of creation—which *Rambam* refers to in the entire chapter cited above. This corresponds to *Rambam's Hilchot Teshuvah* 9:2, that the era when "the earth will be filled with the knowledge..." refers to the period in which the world will operate according to its natural order.

Accordingly, one can answer the following question of *Lechem Mishneh* (*Hilchot Teshuvah* 8:7). How can *Rambam* follow the Talmudic opinion of Shmuel, that there will be no great change in Creation when Moshiach comes, and that all the prophecies are allegorical, if elsewhere he follows the opinion of the Sages, that there *will indeed* be a great change in Creation, and that the prophecies *are* to be taken literally?

[This question partly involves a discussion of whether one is allowed to carry a sword on Shabbat (*Shabbat* 63a). The Sages forbade it, for it constitutes the prohibited act of carrying on Shabbat. R. Eliezer, however, maintained that swords are defined as "ornaments," which one may carry on Shabbat. The Sages replied: Since Isaiah 2:4 prophesizes that "they shall beat their swords into plowshares...," a sword is not considered to be an ornament, but rather a lethal weapon which will be abolished in the era of Moshiach.

(Concerning the Talmudic saying that "the sole difference between the present and the days of Moshiach is delivery from servitude to foreign powers,"[37] this refers only to the *beginning* of the Era of Moshiach.[38] And particularly according to *Raya Mehemna*,[39] this statement was meant to pertain only to ignorant people, and not to those learned in Torah.)

Continuing to detail the innovations to accompany the coming of Moshiach: the aspect of Divinity which transcends nature will then be revealed. (Therefore, the Name of G-d will be *pronounced*[40] as it is written,[41] for throughout the entire world there will be a revelation of the Name of *Havaya*[42]—He was, He is, He will be,

---

Hence, it may not be carried on Shabbat.

Thus, the contrasting opinion—that one may carry a sword on Shabbat—will maintain that the Messianic prophecies are merely allegories, and thus, swords will exist in the era of Moshiach, since they are ornaments. The *Lechem Mishneh* therefore asks: How can *Rambam* rule in *Hilchot Shabbat* that one *cannot* carry a sword on Shabbat—meaning that he understands the prophecies in their literal sense—and at the same time follow the aforementioned opinion of Shmuel that the prophecies are allegories?]

One can answer: The statement in Talmud and *Rambam* concerning the era of Moshiach that, "there is no difference between the present age and the era of Moshiach besides the servitude to the nations," refers only to *beginning* of Redemption. However, in the second stage, *Rambam* also agrees that there will be a great change, and that the prophecies will be literal.

(This further clarifies and supports the answer of the *Kesef Mishneh* (*Hilchot Melachim*, beg. chapter 11) to *Raavad*, ibid.) [*Raavad* asks: *Rambam* maintains that Moshiach will not have to perform miracles to prove himself; but this is not so, for when Bar Kochba said that he was Moshiach, the Sages tested him to see if he could "judge according to his sense of scent" (Rashi, s.v. *Rava amar, Sanhedrin*

93b). That is, they tested him to see if he was so learned as to instantaneously know the answers. When he could not, they killed him. This proves that Moshiach *will* have to perform miracles and signs!

Kesef Mishnah answers: *Raavad's* account of Bar Kochba is correct if one follows the report given in *Sanhedrin* 93b. However, an alternate report in *Eichah Rabbah* relates that Bar Kochba was killed by non-Jews. *Rambam* is obviously following *Eichah Rabbah* because *Sanhedrin* 93b is not consistent with the opinion of Shmuel—that there will be no difference between the present and the era of Moshiach besides servitude to the nations. *Eichah Rabbah*, however, is consistent with Shmuel's opinion, which *Rambam* follows, which is why *Rambam* accepts *Eichah Rabbah* over *Sanhedrin*.] Thus, there is no contradiction, and *Rambam* is consistent with his own reasoning, that in the beginning of Redemption, Moshiach will not need to perform miracles and signs to prove himself, and he will not need to be able to "judge according to his sense of scent."

In the second stage, however, *Rambam* also agrees that there will be great *innovation* in the world, and the verse in Isaiah 2:4, "they will beat their swords into plowshares," is to be taken literally—not allegorically. And since swords will be abolished (at least) in the second

(וּמַה שֶּׁאָמְרוּ "אֵין בֵּין עוֹלָם הַזֶּה לִימוֹת הַמָּשִׁיחַ אֶלָּא
שֶׁעִבּוּד מַלְכִיּוֹת בִּלְבָד"כח הוּא רַק בִּתְחִלַּת הַזְּמַן שֶׁל יְמוֹת
הַמָּשִׁיחַכט. וּבִפְרָט עַל פִּי מַה שֶּׁכָּתוּב בָּרַעְיָא מְהֵימְנָאל, שֶׁמַּאֲמָר
זֶה נֶאֱמַר בַּנּוֹגֵעַ לְעַמֵּי הָאָרֶץ, מַה שֶּׁאֵין כֵּן בַּנּוֹגֵעַ לְתַלְמִידֵי
חֲכָמִים);

בְּחִינַת הָאֱלֹקוּת שֶׁלְּמַעְלָה מֵהַטֶּבַע יִהְיֶה אָז בְּגִילּוּי (שֶׁלָּכֵן
יִהְיוּ **קוֹרְאִין**לא אֶת הַשֵּׁם כִּכְתָבוֹלב, כִּי בְּכָל הָעוֹלָם כּוּלּוֹ יִהְיֶה

---

period of the Redemption, it is proof they are not ornaments [and thus cannot be carried on Shabbat, as discussed above].

37. *Berachot* 34b; *Rambam, Hilchot Teshuvah*, end of ch. 9; *Hilchot Melachim* 12:2.

38. See *Zohar* I:139a. See also above, footnote 36.

39. *Zohar* III:125a, explained in *Igeret Hakodesh*, epistle 26.

40. [KRI AND KTIV. Numerous words in Torah are not pronounced as they are written. These words are known by two terms, *kri* and *ktiv*. *Kri* refers to the manner in which the given word is read, while *ktiv* refers to manner how the word is spelled, or written in the Torah. The Name of G-d, the Tetragrammaton, is composed of four letters. It is written *yud, hey, vav, hey*. Its pronunciation in prayer, however, is *Ad-nay*. (The Tetragrammaton's colloquial pronunciation is *Havaya*.) The concept of *kri* and *ktiv* is pertinent only in our current era, before Moshiach's coming, for *kri*—the manner in which the word is "revealed" by speech—indicates the level of G-dliness presently revealed, while *ktiv*—that which is not pronounced—indicates the level of G-dliness that transcends nature, that

which is "hidden." When Moshiach comes, however, the aspect of G-dliness presently hidden within creation will be manifest and revealed. Consequently, we will pronounce the Tetragrammaton in the same manner as it is written, for G-dliness will be revealed and manifest within creation.] (See also *Igeret Hakodesh*, epistle 19 (128a); *Likkutei Torah, Vayikra* 6d; *Shir Hashirim* 31c.)

41. *Pesachim* 50a.

42. [HAVAYA. The Ineffable Divine Name, or Tetragrammaton, composed of the four letters Y-H-V-H, and pronounced in conversation as *Havaya*. (See footnote 40.) There are many Hebrew names for G-d in Scripture, each of which expresses a different aspect or attribute of the Divinity. *Havaya* refers to G-d the Infinite, transcending creation and nature, time and space, completely—the level of Divinity which brings everything into existence *ex nihilo*. The name *Elokim* represents the level of G-d which conceals the Infinite Light and life-force, for this Infinite force is too intense for finite creatures to endure. *Elokim* is the power of G-d that makes the world appear as though it exists naturally and independently. Therefore, *Elokim* has the numerical value of the word *hateva* (nature). In the era of Moshiach, however,

simultaneously[43]—the Name that is beyond time and space; and this
revelation will be similar to that which was manifest in the times of
the *Beit Hamikdash*.)[44]

These events, furthermore, will be innovations not only in this
world, but their spiritual corollaries will also be introduced into all
the worlds,[45] for the behavior of the supernal worlds proceeds according to the order of behavior of this world. (*Rosh Chodesh* and the
festivals, for example—into which is diffused an additional measure
of light—are established "above" in accordance with their establish-
ment "below.")[46] And because the coming of Moshiach will completely transform the general condition of this world and all its particular aspects, there will be likewise a corresponding change in the
supernal worlds.

Yet, in spite of all that has been explained above—and the great
magnitude, sublimity, and wondrousness of all these matters—in
truth, they are still only the ramifications of the essential point of
Moshiach.

---

the level of *Havaya* will be revealed and
perceived throughout nature.]

43. *Zohar* III:257b. *Shaar Hayichud
v'HaEmunah*, ch. 7 (82a).

44. [In the times of the *Beit Hamikdash*
they pronounced the Tetragrammaton as
it is written.]

However, the revelation of the era of
Moshiach will be even greater than the
revelation that existed during the time
that the *Beit Hamikdash* stood. For in the
era of Moshiach, the name *Havaya* will be
manifest throughout the entire world
(and not limited as it was when the *Beit
Hamikdash* stood. This can be compared
to *Likkutei Torah, Drushei Rosh Hashanah*
57c, discussing the superiority of the first
Beit Hamikdash over the second: when
the first *Beit Hamikdash* stood, the revelation of Divinity pervaded throughout the
borders of Israel). [When the second *Beit
Hamikdash* stood, Divine revelation was
limited to the *Beit Hamikdash*. When

Moshiach comes, however, this Infinite
Light will pervade the entire world.]

45. [THE FOUR WORLDS. Kabbalah and
Chasidus explain the phenomenon of the
creation of a finite physical universe by
an Infinite Creator with the concept of
tzimtzum, contraction and concealment.
G-d effected a series of concealments of
His presence and infinitude, resulting ultimately, in the creation of our physical
universe, through a virtually total concealment of G-d. The non-corporeal intermediate steps between the Creator
and this material world are called
"worlds," referring to the basic levels of
spiritual existence in the creative process.
The differentiation reflects their level of
concealment of the Divine light, the
higher worlds receiving this light in a
more revealed manner.

In general, there are four worlds: *Atzilut* (World of Emanation—a state of
proximity and relative unity with G-d);
Beriah (World of Creation); *Yetzirah*

גִּלּוּי בְּחִינַת שֵׁם הֲוָיָ׳ – הָיָה הֹוֶה וְיִהְיֶה כְּאֶחָד[דלג] – שֶׁלְּמַעְלָה מִזְּמַן וּמָקוֹם, בְּדוּגְמַת הַגִּילּוּי שֶׁהָיָה בְּבֵית הַמִּקְדָּשׁ[דלד]).

וְתוֹכֶן עִנְיָנִים אֵלּוּ יִתְחַדֵּשׁ לֹא רַק בָּעוֹלָם הַזֶּה אֶלָּא בְּכָל הָעוֹלָמוֹת. כִּי הַהַנְהָגָה בָּעוֹלָמוֹת הָעֶלְיוֹנִים הוּא כְּפִי סֵדֶר הַהַנְהָגָה בָּעוֹלָם הַזֶּה |וְעַל דֶּרֶךְ הַקְּבִיעוּת דְּרָאשֵׁי חֳדָשִׁים וּמוֹעֲדִים (שֶׁבָּהֶם נִמְשֶׁכֶת תּוֹסֶפֶת אוֹר) לְמַעְלָה, שֶׁהוּא כְּפִי אוֹפֶן קְבִיעוּתָם לְמַטָּה[דלה]]. וּמִכֵּיוָן שֶׁבְּבִיאַת הַמָּשִׁיחַ יִשְׁתַּנֶּה כְּלָלוּת הַמַּצָּב בָּעוֹלָם הַזֶּה וּפְרָטָיו, הֲרֵי שִׁינּוּי דוּגְמָתוֹ יִהְיֶה גַּם בָּעוֹלָמוֹת הָעֶלְיוֹנִים.

אָמְנָם, אַחֲרֵי כָל הַנַּ״ל, כָּל עִנְיָנִים אֵלֶּה – אַף שֶׁגָּדוֹל וְרַב הָעִילּוּי וְהַהַפְלָאָה שֶׁבָּהֶם – אֵינָם אֶלָּא הִסְתַּעֲפוּת מִנְּקוּדָתוֹ הָעִיקָרִית שֶׁל מָשִׁיחַ.

(World of Formation); *Asiyah* (World of Action or Making—the final stage in the creative process). The four worlds have been compared to the elements inherent to building a house. Four stages are necessary: 1) A general idea, as yet undefined; 2) A definite idea of the house in one's mind; 3) The architectural plan or design; 4) The actual building of the house (*Tanya*, Bi-lingual Edition, Kehot 1998, p. 343 fn. 3; p. 922).

"Higher" (or "Supernal") and "Lower" refer to stages closer or more distant from the Creator, with a greater or lesser awareness of Him (not, of course, implying physical distance). Lower Worlds appear to be independent entities apart from the Creator.

Through the performance of *mitzvot* and subordination of the physical world to the Divine purpose, all Worlds are elevated, and experience a clearer apprehension of G-d. See *Mystical Concepts in Chassidism*, ch. 2 (*Tzimtzum*) and ch. 4 (*Worlds*).]

46. See *Rosh Hashanah* 8b; Jerusalem Talmud, *Rosh Hashanah* 1:3; *Tanchuma* (Buber), *Bo* 13.

[Unlike Shabbat, which follows an inexorable cycle, the Hebrew months are determined by *Beit Din*, based on Biblical sanction. Since the lunar cycle is about 29 1/2 days, some months must be 29 days long and others 30. Based on testimony of witnesses who saw the new moon, the *Beit Din* declared that day *Rosh Chodesh* and counted the days for the next festival (*Pesach*, for example, on the fifteenth of *Nissan*). *Rosh Chodesh* was always on the thirtieth day or the thirty-first of the previous month. Now, reconciling the 354 days of 12 lunar months with the 365 days of the solar year created more complexity. The *Beit Din*, depending on when the witnesses arrived to testify, was empowered to add a thirteenth month periodically. Hence, *Rosh Chodesh* and the festivals were dependent on the actions of the human court.]

V

THE ESSENCE OF THE CONCEPT OF MOSHIACH

The essential idea of Moshiach is *Yechidah*. As it is known,[47] David possessed the level of *Nefesh*, Eliyahu of *Ruach*, Moshe of *Neshamah*, Adam of *Chaya*, and Moshiach will possess the level of *Yechidah*.[48]

The superior quality of *Yechidah* in relation to the other four levels of "*NaRaNaCh*" [the acronym for *Nefesh, Ruach, Neshamah, Chaya*] (within the context of these five levels which every individual soul possesses)[49] is that the four categories of *NaRaNaCh* are each particular individual levels, while the category of *Yechidah* is the *essence* of the soul which transcends particulars, as indicated by its name ("Sole, Only One"). It is important to clarify that although it is from the category of *Yechidah*—the essence of the soul—that the four levels of *NaRaNaCh* are drawn, this does not mean that the state of *Yechidah* may be classed as a source and "generalization" of these particular levels. For the very term *Yechidah* indicates that it is a simple, non-composite Oneness which excludes any relation whatsoever to details, even the relation of being their source (as is known from the difference between *Yachid*—"Sole, Only," and *Echad*—"One").[50] *Yechidah*, rather, is the quintessence of the soul, and from it also issue the four categories of *NaRaNaCh*.

Now, in the same way that the *Yechidah* of every individual soul is that soul's quintessential point, so also is the level of *Yechidah* the quintessence of the (life-force and) soul of the general *seder hishtalshelut*.[51] This latter category of the *Yechidah* of the entire world

---

47. *Sefer Hamaamarim 5699*, p. 207, in the name of *Ramaz*. See *Shaar* (and *Sefer) Hagilgulim*, beg., and elsewhere.

48. [NAMES OF THE SOUL. These five names are the five levels of the soul—see next footnote. In rough translation: *Nefesh* ("Vitality") is the lowest grade and life-force of the body, the natural soul and simple life of man. *Ruach* ("Spirit") the next grade, is the spiritual faculty vivifying man's emotional attributes. *Neshamah* ("Soul") is the Divine Force vivifying the intellect. *Chaya* ("Living") is

an even more refined G-dly level. *Yechidah* is the Divine spark itself enclothed in the most refined spark of the soul. *Yechidah* is the innermost point of the soul, "united" and one with G-d. It represents total *bittul*, self-nullification, nothingness. Since every one of Israel possesses each of the five, four obscure and one predominant, *Yechidah* in this sense is expressed in *mesirat nefesh*, literal self-sacrifice—martyrdom if need be.

David, Eliyahu, Moshe, Adam, and Moshiach each possess the general level of one of these five categories. Moshiach

ה.

עִנְיָנוֹ הָעִיקָרִי שֶׁל מָשִׁיחַ הוּא – יְחִידָה. כַּיָּדוּעַ⁴⁹, שֶׁדָּוִד זָכָה לִבְחִינַת נֶפֶשׁ, אֵלִיָּהוּ – לְרוּחַ, מֹשֶׁה – לִנְשָׁמָה, אָדָם הָרִאשׁוֹן – לְחַיָּה וּמָשִׁיחַ יִזְכֶּה לִיחִידָה.

מַעֲלַת הַיְחִידָה עַל ד' הַבְּחִינוֹת נֶפֶשׁ-רוּחַ-נְשָׁמָה-חַיָּה [בַּחֲמִשָּׁה הַמַּדְרֵיגוֹת שֶׁל כָּל נְשָׁמָה⁵⁰]: ד' הַבְּחִינוֹת נֶפֶשׁ-רוּחַ-נְשָׁמָה-חַיָּה הֵם מַדְרֵיגוֹת פְּרָטִיּוֹת, וּבְחִינַת יְחִידָה הִיא עֶצֶם הַנְּשָׁמָה שֶׁלְּמַעְלָה מִגֶּדֶר פְּרָטִים, כִּשְׁמָהּ. וְעִם הֱיוֹת אֲשֶׁר מִבְּחִינַת יְחִידָה – עֶצֶם הַנְּשָׁמָה – נִמְשְׁכוֹת ד' הַבְּחִינוֹת נֶפֶשׁ-רוּחַ-נְשָׁמָה-חַיָּה, אֵין זֶה שֶׁבְּחִינַת הַיְחִידָה הִיא בִּגְדֶר מָקוֹר וּ"כְלָל" לִפְרָטִים אֵלּוּ – כִּי לְשׁוֹן "יְחִידָה" מוֹרֶה עַל אַחְדוּת פְּשׁוּטָה הַמּוּשְׁלֶלֶת מֵאֵיזוֹ שֶׁהִיא שַׁיָּיכוּת לִפְרָטִים, גַּם מִגֶּדֶר מָקוֹר לִפְרָטִים (וְכַיָּדוּעַ הַהֶפְרֵשׁ בֵּין "יָחִיד" לְ"אֶחָד"⁵¹) – כִּי אִם שֶׁהִיא נְקוּדָה עַצְמִית שֶׁל הַנְּשָׁמָה, אֶלָּא שֶׁמִּמֶּנָּה נִמְצָאוֹת ד' הַבְּחִינוֹת נֶפֶשׁ-רוּחַ-נְשָׁמָה-חַיָּה.

וּכְמוֹ שֶׁבְּכָל נְשָׁמָה פְּרָטִית, בְּחִינַת הַיְחִידָה הִיא נְקוּדָה הָעַצְמִית שֶׁל הַנְּשָׁמָה, כֵּן הוּא בְּ(הַחַיּוּת וְ)הַנְּשָׁמָה שֶׁל כְּלָלוּת

---

possesses the general Yechidah of all souls.]

49. [As clarified in previous footnote.] See *Bereishit Rabbah* 14:9, *Devarim Rabbah* 2:37: "Five names are given to the soul—*Nefesh, Ruach, Neshamah, Chaya, Yechidah.*" In some editions of the *Midrash* there are changes in this order, and also in *piyutim* [liturgical hymns], etc. But in the writings of the Arizal (*Eitz Chaim, Shaar* 42, beg.; *Shaar Hagilgulim,* beg.) and in Chasidic literature this order is stated *specifically.* See also *Zohar* I:81a; 206a.

50. See *Imrei Binah, Shaar Hakriyat Shema,* ch. 8. See also *Likkutei Torah, Balak* 70a.

[The difference between *Yachid* (Sole, Only) and *Echad* (One) is the difference between G-d's Oneness as expressed within the multiplicity of creation (His Oneness, *Echad*), and His essential Oneness above multiplicity (His Soleness, *Yachid*), in relation to which nothing has any existence.]

51. [SEDER HISHTALSHELUT. Lit., "order of progression of worlds," or, "chain of

(which is the level of Moshiach) is the essential core of the life-force that completely transcends the limitations of form. And from this central, seminal point, all the particular qualities, which are the general *NaRaNaCh* of all Creation, are derived.

For the Essence of the life-force is altogether without limitations. It is unlimited not only in terms of immortality, i.e., it is not subject to temporal change—for every essence is unchanging—

[And herein is also one of the reasons why there will be eternal life in the Future Time.[52] At present, since only an extension of the life-force is elicited into the world, there is the presence of death, because within the category of "extension" [as opposed to "Essence"] there can be change—even unto cessation and destruction. In the future, however, the Essence of the life-force will pervade, and every essence is immutable.]

—but it is also unlimited in regards to quality and character; it is absolutely and completely perfect. Hence, when the category of *Yechidah* will be manifested in the worlds, and they will be imbued with the Essence of the life-force, they thereby will become consummately perfect and complete.

VI

CHASIDUS AS A NEW "LIFE-FORCE"

As has been said previously [in Chapter IV], from the reward for (the dissemination of) Chasidus we can know its essential nature. Now, all of the innovations which Chasidus introduced ([a] into Torah—which includes bringing the "esoteric" part to open revelation;[53] [b] into the service of man—behavior beyond that which is required by the letter of the law, and changing the nature of one's

---

worlds"; i.e., the transmission of life to the various levels of creation through a process of gradual and ordered descent and downward gradation, by means of numerous contractions of the Divine life-force. See footnote 45 for references.]

52. See *Sanhedrin* 92a. (See also *Midrash Hane'elam, Vayera* (*Zohar* I:114b): "The righteous do not return to dust...but endure forever." The opinions of *Rambam* and *Ramban* as to when the essential part of the reward will be manifest and the decisions concerning this are discussed in *Likkutei Torah, Tzav* 15c; *Drushim L'Shabbat Shuva* 65d; and *Derech Mitzvotecha* 14b.

[Concerning the nature of eternal life, *Rambam* is of the opinion that after the

הַהִשְׁתַּלְשְׁלוּת, שֶׁבְּחִינַת הַיְּחִידָה שֶׁבָּהּ (בְּחִינָתוֹ שֶׁל מָשִׁיחַ) הִיא – עֶצֶם נְקֻדַּת הַחַיּוּת שֶׁלְּמַעְלָה מִגֶּדֶר צִיּוּר. וּמִנְּקוּדָה זוֹ, מִסְתַּעֲפוֹת כָּל מַעֲלוֹת הַפְּרָטִיּוֹת, נֶפֶשׁ־רוּחַ־נְשָׁמָה־חַיָּה דִּכְלָלוּת,

כִּי עֶצֶם הַחַיּוּת הוּא בִּלְתִּי מוּגְבָּל. וְהַבְּלִי־גְבוּל שֶׁלּוֹ אֵינוֹ רַק בְּעִנְיַן הַנִּצְחִיּוּת, שֶׁאֵינֶנּוּ נִתְפָּס בְּשִׁנּוּיֵי הַזְּמַן כִּי כָּל עֶצֶם בִּלְתִּי מִשְׁתַּנֶּה

[שֶׁגַּם זֶה מֵהַטְּעָמִים שֶׁלֶּעָתִיד לָבֹא יִהְיוּ חַיִּים נִצְחִיִּים‎[ט‏‎]: עַכְשָׁיו, שֶׁנִּמְשָׁךְ בָּעוֹלָם רַק בְּחִינַת הִתְפַּשְּׁטוּת הַחַיּוּת, יֶשְׁנוֹ עִנְיַן הַמִּיתָה. כִּי בִּבְחִינַת הַהִתְפַּשְּׁטוּת שַׁיָּךְ עִנְיַן הַשִּׁנּוּי וְעַד – הֶפְסֵק וְכִלָּיוֹן. מַה שֶּׁאֵין כֵּן לֶעָתִיד שֶׁיּוּמְשַׁךְ עֶצֶם הַחַיּוּת, הֲרֵי כָּל עַצְמִי בִּלְתִּי מִשְׁתַּנֶּה]

אֶלָּא גַּם בְּעִנְיַן הָאֵיכוּת וְהַמַּעֲלָה, שֶׁשָּׁלֵם הוּא בְּתַכְלִית הַשְּׁלֵימוּת. וְלָכֵן, כְּשֶׁתּוּמְשַׁךְ בָּעוֹלָמוֹת בְּחִינַת הַיְּחִידָה וְיִהְיוּ בְּחִינַת עַצְמִי, יִהְיוּ בְּמֵילָא בְּתַכְלִית הַמַּעֲלָה וְהַשְּׁלֵימוּת.

ו.

כָּאָמוּר לְעֵיל, מִשְּׂכָרָהּ שֶׁל [הֲפָצַת הַ]חֲסִידוּת – בִּיאַת הַמָּשִׁיחַ, נֵדַע אֶת מַהוּתָהּ: כָּל הַחִידוּשִׁים שֶׁחֲסִידוּת חִידְשָׁה [בַּתּוֹרָה (כּוֹלֵל הֲבָאַת חֵלֶק הַ"סוֹד" שֶׁבָּהּ לִידֵי גִּילּוּי‎[מ‏‎]); בַּעֲבוֹדַת הָאָדָם (הַהַנְהָגָה דִּלְפָנִים מִשּׁוּרַת הַדִּין וְשִׁנּוּי טֶבַע הַמִּדּוֹת‎[מא‏‎]);

---

first stage, which is the Resurrection of the Dead, the final and ultimate stage will be the existence of the soul without the body (termed and/or known as the World to Come). *Ramban* disagrees, and is of the opinion that the Resurrection of the Dead is the ultimate stage, wherein the body and soul exist together. *Chasidus* agrees with *Ramban*.]

53. It is only in relation to *seder hishtalshelut* that this limitation exists, i.e., that *peshat, remez,* and *drush* are revealed and the esoteric part, *sod,* is concealed. In relation to the *essence* and *inner being* of Torah, however, the level of *Yechidah,* there is no division between the esoteric part and the other portions; even the esoteric part can be revealed.

character;[54] [c] into the world in general—the arousal of the world from its spiritual "unconsciousness"[55]) were not separate innovations originating *individually* and *independently*. Chasidus, rather, is a new life-force, an "essential energy"[56] of the state of *Yechidah*.[57] Consequently, when this new flow of life was brought into the world (general Chasidus through the Baal Shem Tov, the Maggid of Mezritch[58] et al.; and afterwards, the teachings of Chabad Chasidus[59] through the "new soul"[60] of Rabbi Schneur Zalman of Liadi, whose liberation we commemorate and celebrate

---

54. In terms of the four levels of *Nefesh, Ruach, Neshamah,* and *Chaya,* a person retains his individual entity, and it is "he" who serves his Creator. Since his self is undiminished, therefore: 1) His intention in his service of G-d is for the sake of the desirable consequences of serving G-d. (In general, this is the idea of behavior according to the standards of the law, as explained in the aforementioned *Padah B'Shalom,* p. 772-3.) For even on the sublime level of *Chaya* one has some objective, some self-interest (*Sefer Hamaamarim 5670* p. 151; *Kuntres Ha'avodah* ch. 5); 2) The nature of his *middot* is not changed, but rather he exploits and makes use of those *middot* which he already naturally possesses to love G-d, etc.

On the level of *Yechidah,* however, one attains complete nullification of one's own "existence," and therefore: 1) One has no "self-interest" in his service of G-d whatsoever—corresponding to behavior beyond what is required by the law; 2) The very nature of one's *middot* are also changed (from *gevurah* to *chesed,* or *chesed* to *gevurah,* etc.).

55. For this "unconsciousness" is only in relation to the manifest levels of the soul, but does not extend to its essence, *Yechidah*; and therefore it is possible to arouse it.

56. [The adjective "essential" in "essential energy"—used here as well as oth-

er places in the text in translation of *chayut atzmi*—does not mean "important," but refers to Essence.]

57. See *Sefer Hamaamarim 5699* ibid., that the innermost part of the Torah that Moshiach will teach is by virtue of his level of *Yechidah*. It is noteworthy that Achiyah the Shilonite—who was the teacher of the Baal Shem Tov, the founder of Chasidus (the inner part of the Torah, and a foretaste of the Inner Torah to be revealed in the future)—is called "Master of *Chaya-Yechidah*" (*Sefer Hasichot 5700,* p. 159). Similarly, the leaders and heads of Israel in every generation—the masters who revealed Chasidus—are of the category of the general *Yechidah* of all Israel (R. DovBer, *Shaar Hateshuvah, Padah B'Shalom,* ch. 12).

[Achiyah the Shilonite is a Biblical figure mentioned in I Kings 11:29 ff. In *Rambam's* introduction to his *Mishneh Torah,* he mentions that Achiyah was one of those who left Egypt (cf. *Bava Batra* 121b). The Jerusalem Talmud (*Eruvin* 5:1) states that "he was one of those who left Egypt, a teacher of Eliyahu."]

58. The Baal Shem Tov's successor was Rabbi DovBer, the "Maggid of Mezritch" (d. 19 *Kislev* 1772). He is credited with being the organizer of the Chasidic movement during the twelve years of his leadership in succession to the Baal Shem Tov. He was the teacher of Rabbi Schneur Zalman of Liadi, founder of the

בִּכְלָלוּת הָעוֹלָם (הִתְעוֹרְרוּת מֵהִתְעַלְפוּת‎מּב)], אֵינָם חִידּוּשִׁים
שֶׁכָּל אֶחָד וְאֶחָד מִתְחַדֵּשׁ הוּא **בִּפְנֵי עַצְמוֹ,** כִּי אִם, שֶׁחֲסִידוּת
הִיא חַיּוּת חָדָשׁ, חַיּוּת עַצְמִי דִּבְחִינַת יְחִידָה‎מּג. וְכַאֲשֶׁר חַיּוּת
חָדָשׁ זֶה שֶׁל הַחֲסִידוּת נִמְשָׁךְ בָּעוֹלָם [תּוֹרַת חֲסִידוּת הַכְּלָלִית
עַל יְדֵי כְּבוֹד קְדֻשַּׁת הַבַּעַל שֵׁם טוֹב, הָרַב הַמַּגִּיד וְכוּ' וְאַחַר כַּךְ
– תּוֹרַת חֲסִידוּת חַבַּ"ד‎דּ‎מּד עַל יְדֵי הַ"נְּשָׁמָה חֲדָשָׁה"‎מּה – כְּבוֹד
קְדֻשַּׁת אַדְמוֹ"ר הַזָּקֵן בַּעַל הַשִּׂמְחָה וְהַגְּאוּלָה‎מּו], הִתְחִילוּ כָּל

Chabad movement. Like his predecessor, he left no written works, but his disciples compiled his teachings in two books, *Maggid Devaro l'Yaakov* and *Likkutei Amarim*.

59. Within Chasidus itself, Chabad Chasidus was the part that brought general Chasidus into the realm of understanding and comprehension by *ChaBaD*, the three intellectual attributes—*chochmah* (wisdom), *binah* (understanding), and *daat* (knowledge). Thereby, Chabad Chasidus revealed the essence of the inner part of Torah. (*Padah B'Shalom 5685*, quoting R. Shalom DovBer, *Yud-Tes Kislev 5679*. See also *Likkutei Sichot* vol. 4, p. 1138.)

[The Baal Shem Tov and the Maggid of Mezritch revealed the inner part of Torah, but their revelations were in a form higher than rational understanding and beyond intellectual comprehension. The doctrines were trans-rational, appealing to faith, and called for a largely emotional response. Intellect was not the obvious instrument for dealing with their Chasidic teachings.

R. Schneur Zalman, the founder of Chabad Chasidus, articulated these doctrines in a form which intellect *could* comprehend. Thus he revealed the essence of the teachings of the inner part of Torah. That is, he was able to take that which totally transcended reason and logic, and bring it into the realm of intellect.

One can accomplish such a feat only by penetrating to the essence of the inner part of Torah. For although essence is that which is not limited to any particular form—be they rational, or emotional—nevertheless, essence is expressed through all of these forms. See below, Chapter VII, and footnote 64. Hence the revelations of the Baal Shem Tov and the Maggid were the preparation for the revelation of the essence of the Inner Torah, which was accomplished by R. Schneur Zalman.

Sefer Hamamarim 5688, p. 201 ff. (also in *Sefer Hasichot 5688*, p. 18 ff.) analogizes the contributions of the founders of Chasidus, the Baal Shem Tov and the Maggid, to the contributions of the Patriarchs before the Torah was given at Sinai. The Patriarchs fulfilled all the commandments of the Torah even before they were given (see *Kiddushin* 82a). Yet, as *Shir Hashirim Rabbah* 1:3 states, this was but the "fragrance"—not the substance—of Torah. The revelation at Sinai, however, was the essence of Torah. Just as the deeds and teachings of the Patriarchs were a preparation for the giving of the Torah at Sinai through Moshe, similarly the Baal Shem Tov and the Maggid prepared the way for the revelation of the essence of Chasidus through R. Schneur Zalman.]

60. *Sefer Hasichot 5705*, p. 127 ff.
[The Arizal explains (*Sefer Hagilgulim*

today),[61] all aspects of the world then began to live with a new vitality—an "essential life-force." And *thereby*, [from the all-pervasive flow of this essential life-force,] all of those innovations were engendered.

VII

OIL: A METAPHOR FOR CHASIDUS

For the same reason [that it is the Essence of the life-force], Chasidus is compared[62] to oil, which represents the "secret of secrets."[63]

Oil symbolizes the distilled essence of everything. Hence it necessarily possesses the following two characteristics: on the one hand, it is in itself distinct and separate from everything (for were it to be bound to any one *particular* thing, it could not then be the essential aspect of *every* thing); yet at the same time, because it is "essence," it must also pervade and be found within everything,[64] for the essence, by definition, exists and is found everywhere.

This concept, like all matters pertaining to the Inner Torah,[65] is

---

ch. 7) that there are two kinds of souls: 1) Those included in Adam's soul; 2) Those not included in Adam's soul. This second category of souls is superior to all others; thus, they are termed "new souls."] See *Likkutei Torah, Shir Hashirim* 50a.

61. [This talk was delivered on *Yud-Tes Kislev*, the nineteenth day of the Hebrew month of *Kislev*, the anniversary of liberation of R. Schneur Zalman from Russian prison, after having been arrested for his teaching of Chasidus and falsely accused of treason.] The festival of *Yud-Tes Kislev* marks the turning point at which Chasidus was presented in intellectual terms (*Torat Shalom*, p. 114; see *Likkutei Dibburim* vol. 1, p. 22a ff.). Thus, as explained in footnote 59, the essence of the inner Torah was expressed. Significantly, *Yud-Tes Kislev* is termed *Rosh Hashanah of Chasidus*. "Rosh Hashanah" (the "head" of the year) is inclusive of the entire year, as a head is comprehensive of the entire body, and on Rosh Hashanah there is elicited "depth and innerness... from the core and Essence of the blessed *Or Ein Sof*." (Letter

by R. Sholom DovBer, *Yud-Tes Kislev 5662, Igrot Kodesh*, vol. 1 p. 259; *Kuntres Umaayan*, intro., p. 17).

[Concerning *Yud-Tes Kislev*, see *The Arrest and Liberation of Rabbi Schneur Zalman of Liadi*, (Kehot, 1999), and *Rabbi Schneur Zalman of Liadi, A Biography* (Kehot, 2002).]

62. This analogy of Chasidus to oil is even more appropriate after Rabbi Schneur Zalman's liberation, as expressed in Rabbi Shalom DovBer's well-known aphorism of this event: "Just as the olive gives forth its oil when it is squeezed and pounded, similarly, it was only through the accusations that took place in Petersburg that the essence was revealed..." (*Torat Shalom*, p. 26).

[A striking difference can be noted in the style of R. Schneur Zalman's teachings before his arrest and after his release, named among Chasidim, "before Petersburg" and "after Petersburg." His earlier teachings were brief, pithy, difficult to absorb. His later works were expansive, rich in elaboration, no less deep

עִנְיְנֵי הָעוֹלָם לִחְיוֹת בְּחַיּוּת חָדָשׁ – חַיּוּת עַצְמִי, **וּבְמֵילָא** נִתְחַדְּשׁוּ בָּהֶם כַּמָּה וְכַמָּה עִנְיָנִים.

ז.

גַּם מִטַּעַם זֶה, נִמְשְׁלָה תּוֹרַת הַחֲסִידוּת[סג] – לְשֶׁמֶן, רָזִין דְּרָזִין[סד]:

שֶׁמֶן הוּא נְקוּדַּת הַתַּמְצִית (״עֶסֶענץ״) שֶׁל כָּל דָּבָר. וּמִזֶּה מוּכְרָח, שֶׁמִּצַּד עַצְמוֹ מוּבְדָּל הוּא מִכָּל דָּבָר (כִּי בְּאִם הָיְתָה לוֹ שַׁיָּיכוּת לְדָבָר **פְּרָטִי**, לֹא הָיָה יָכוֹל לִהְיוֹת נְקוּדַּת הַתַּמְצִית שֶׁל **כָּל** דָּבָר), אֶלָּא שֶׁהוּא בְּחִינַת ״עַצְמִי״, וְלִהְיוֹתוֹ עַצְמִי, נִמְצָא הוּא בְּכָל דָּבָר[סה], כִּי הָעַצְמִי נִמְצָא בַּכֹּל.

וְדָבָר זֶה, כְּכָל הָעִנְיָנִים שֶׁבִּפְנִימִיּוּת הַתּוֹרָה, מִתְבַּטֵּא גַּם

---

but more accessible because of the more generous exposition. The fact that the hardships and ominous arrest marked the turning point is not fortuitous, for "oil" only comes forth after "pounding." Chasidic tradition interprets the arrest as symbolic of the test of the validity of Chasidus and its "right" to prevail. The release demonstrated that the "wellsprings may spread abroad" without hindrance.]

63. *Imrei Binah, Shaar Hakriyat Shema*, ch. 54 ff., explaining the difference between "wine" (secret) and "oil" (secret of secrets). As long as wine is withheld and concealed inside the grape, it gains strength and quality. Conversely, oil does not gain any additional power at all by being contained and withheld in the olive. Thus wine is the category of the hidden—and has the numerical value of the word *sod*, "secret." (Hence it derives strength from being withheld and concealed.) Oil however, transcends the sense of "concealment and revelation" (and therefore the constraints of conceal-

ment do not give it any additional strength). Thus, Chasidus, compared to oil, also transcends "concealment and revelation" (and therefore has the power to reveal the hidden, as explained above in footnote 53).

64. See *Torah Or* 39a; 110d; *Likkutei Torah, Naso* 27d; *Imrei Binah*, ibid., ch. 56 (54b).

[The "essence" is apart from all particular aspects, manifestations, or qualities derived from it, and yet is the foundation and central point of everything. "Essence refers to the absolute, fundamental, nonderivative state of any being, the state which transcends revelation. It is noncomposite. Manifestation does not involve the Essence of being, the Essence being the Source of the manifestation..." (See the *Explanatory Notes* mentioned in footnote 16.)]

65. [INNER TORAH—REVEALED TORAH. "Inner Torah" (*Pnimiyut Hatorah*; *Nistar*) is a term used to describe the esoteric aspects of Torah, dealt with for example

also expressed in the Revealed Torah, even in an actual *halachah* [a practical law]: on the one hand, oil does not mix with any liquids,[66] and conversely, it penetrates into all matter.[67]

And thus, Chasidus is likened to oil, for it also possesses these two properties. By virtue of its nature as Essence, it does not mix with any other thing—it is the essential core of the life-force, higher than any radiation and reflection.[68] And on the other hand, Chasidus diffuses into and permeates every single thing, as explained above.

VIII

THE FOUR LEVELS OF TORAH INTERPRETATION (PARDES)

The life and vitality which the teachings of Chasidus infuse into all aspects of the world (the "miniature world" of man, and the "real," literal world) issue from the vitality that Chasidus infuses into all the elements of Torah, and are generated from that life-force—for all the elements of Creation are drawn from[69] and are derived through the Torah.

In the Torah itself there are four levels of interpretation: *peshat, remez, drush* and *sod*,[70] and the teachings of Chasidus imbue each one with life and vitality.

That is, in addition to the explanations which Chasidus gives to various subjects within *all* four parts of Torah (which negates the common misconception that Chasidus arose in order to explain only the "esoteric" part of Torah)[71]

---

in Kabbalah, etc. The "Revealed Torah" (*Torah haniglit; Nigleh*) refers to the exoteric parts, e.g., the Talmud, its commentaries, and the Codes of Law. The Inner Torah is also called the "soul" of the Torah, and the Revealed Torah its "body." Just as the soul and body are correspondent to each other, there is a correspondence of the Inner Torah to the Revealed Torah.]

66. *Tevul Yom*, 2:5; *Rambam, Hilchot Tumat Ochlin*, 8:10. (Even according to R. Yochanan ben Nuri that "the two of them (wine and oil) join," the meaning

is not that oil *mixes* with wine, rather that the oil touches and adheres to wine. See *Imrei Binah*, ibid., beg. ch. 56). See also *Shemot Rabbah* 36:1.

[The discussion in the Mishnah concerns the ritual purity of wine on top of which oil is floating, if someone who is ritually impure touches the oil. One opinion in the Mishnah is that only the oil is contaminated because the two do not mix. R. Yochanan ben Nuri, however, maintains that the wine is also contaminated because they are attached. It is evident though, that even according to R. Yochanan the contamination is not because the oil *mixes*

בְּנִגְלֶה דְתוֹרָה, עַד בַּהֲלָכָה לְמַעֲשֶׂה: מִצַּד אֶחָד, הַשֶּׁמֶן אֵינוֹ מִתְעָרֵב בִּשְׁאָר מַשְׁקִין, וּלְאִידָךְ גִּיסָא, מְפַעְפֵּעַ הוּא בְּכָל דָּבָר‎.

וְלָכֵן נִמְשְׁלָה תּוֹרַת הַחֲסִידוּת לְשֶׁמֶן, כִּי גַּם בָּהּ – שְׁתֵּי תְכוּנוֹת אֵלּוּ: מִצַּד עִנְיָנָהּ הָעַצְמִי – אֵינָהּ מִתְעָרֶבֶת בְּשׁוּם דָּבָר – עֶצֶם נְקוּדַת הַחַיּוּת שֶׁלְּמַעְלָה מֵהִתְפַּשְּׁטוּת, וּלְאִידָךְ גִּיסָא – מִתְפַּשֶּׁטֶת הִיא וּמְפַעְפַּעַת בְּכָל דָּבָר וְדָבָר, כַּנַּ"ל.

ח.

הַחַיּוּת שֶׁתּוֹרַת הַחֲסִידוּת מַכְנִיסָה בְּכָל עִנְיְנֵי הָעוֹלָם (קָטָן זֶה הָאָדָם, וְהָעוֹלָם – כִּפְשׁוּטוֹ), נִמְשֶׁכֶת מֵהַחַיּוּת שֶׁחֲסִידוּת מַכְנִיסָה בְּכָל עִנְיְנֵי הַתּוֹרָה וּבָאָה עַל יְדֵי חַיּוּת זוֹ. כִּי כָּל עִנְיְנֵי הַבְּרִיאָה נִמְשָׁכִים מֵהַתּוֹרָה‎ וּבָאִים עַל יָדָהּ.

בַּתּוֹרָה – ד' חֲלָקִים: פְּשָׁט, רֶמֶז, דְּרוּשׁ, סוֹד. וְתוֹרַת הַחֲסִידוּת מַכְנִיסָה חַיּוּת בְּכָל אֶחָד מֵהֶם. אֲשֶׁר

– נוֹסָף עַל זֶה שֶׁבְּתוֹרַת הַחֲסִידוּת בָּאוּ בֵּיאוּרִים לְעִנְיָנִים שׁוֹנִים **שֶׁבְּכָל** ד' חֶלְקֵי הַתּוֹרָה (שֶׁגַּם זֶה, שׁוֹלֵל אֶת הַסְּבָרָא שֶׁהַחֲסִידוּת בָּאָה בִּכְדֵי לְבָאֵר אֶת חֵלֶק הַ"סּוֹד" שֶׁבַּתּוֹרָה בִּלְבָד‎) –

---

with the wine, but only because the oil *touches* and adheres to the wine.]

67. See *Chullin* 87a. *Shulchan Aruch, Yoreh De'ah* 105:5.

68. [Note the distinction between radiation or reflection of the life-force, and its Essence. The radiation of the life-force is merely a dimmed manifestation, or reflection of its source, whereas the source is the Essence of the Divine Light itself. Radiation is not G-d's Essence but only an emanation from Him, comparable to the light (radiation) shining from the

sun. The Essence of His life-force, however, is that which encompasses and transcends creation, and permeates it in a hidden manner. Chasidus comes from this Essence of the life-force.]

69. *Zohar* II:161a. See also *Bereishit Rabbah*, beg.

70. [See footnote 9, and below.]

71. See *Torat Shalom*, p. 172: "The world considers Chasidus to be an explanation of Kabbalah. That is a mistake..."

The statement concludes, "Kabbalah is

—the learning of Chasidus also infuses life into every subject (in all the parts of *Pardes* [the acronym for *peshat, remez, drush, sod*]) which we learn in Torah. And the subject then "lives" in an entirely different manner, with an Essential life-force. This vitality strikingly illuminates and profoundly deepens one's understanding of the idea.

An analogy to this concept of additional illumination and vitality in the Revealed part of Torah,[72] and in a practical law, is as follows:

"The *entire* service of Yom Kippur is only acceptable when done by him" (the High Priest).[73] In the same manner that the holiness of Yom Kippur is effective for the special services of Yom Kippur, it also affects the daily and extra (Shabbat) sacrifices that are in them-

---

an explanation of Chasidus." To explain: Chasidus is the comprehension of Divinity. (*Yechidah* is in the feminine form—it receives from *Yachid* [G-d, the Sole One]. See *Eitz Chaim, Shaar* 42, beg. ch. 1: "The small spark [of G-d]...clothes itself in the small spark [of man]...and is called '*Yechidah.*'") Chasidus achieves this comprehension of G-d by using analogies, parallels, and explanations. Kabbalah, though, explains "the location" [of G-d] in terms of "the Body of the King," and the *sefirot*, etc.

It should also be noted that the revelation of *keter* (analogous to darkness) is in *chochmah*. [As discussed in Chapter II, Chasidus is the effusion of new radiance from the innermost level of *keter*, the crown or highest of the *sefirot*. Kabbalah corresponds to *chochmah*, the following *sefirah*. Each spiritual level in the order of descent of creation is revealed in the subsequent level:] The top point of the letter *yud* [of *Havaya*, representing *keter*] is revealed in the yud; similarly *Yechidah* is revealed in *Chaya*; *ratzon* is revealed in *chochmah*, etc. But the intensity and essence of *keter* is expressed only through physical action.

[There are two major ideas discussed here: 1) The manner in which Kabbalah is an explanation of Chasidus, and not vice versa; 2) The fact that Kabbalah is

only an explanation, a reduced reflection, and does not capture the essence of Chasidus.

In the first part, the Rebbe distinguishes between the nature and methods of comprehending G-d in Chasidus and Kabbalah. Kabbalah is a descriptive "anatomy," so to speak, of the "Body of the King"; i.e., the various manifestations of Divinity. It is interested in "indexing," "cataloging," and "locating" these Divine revelations, assigning them "places" and names. Hence Kabbalah is concerned with the technical identities and relations between the *sefirot*, the worlds, *seder hishtalshelut*, etc. Chasidus, however, is concerned with the direct perception of Divinity underlying all these terms, forms, and "locations." It will thus employ all manner of explanation, example, parallels—including Kabbalah—in order to reveal the Essence of Divinity expressed in all levels. That is, Kabbalah is the technical explanation of these forms and terms in themselves, while Chasidus only uses, and is interested in, these forms as a means for perceiving Divinity. As discussed earlier in Chapter III, Chasidus is not limited to any "forms."

An analogy: A physician uses biology, chemistry, anatomy, etc., only to gain comprehension of the body's essential life-force, in order that he may be able to

לִימּוּד הַחֲסִידוּת מַכְנִיס חַיּוּת בְּכָל עִנְיָן וְעִנְיָן (בְּכָל חֶלְקֵי הַפְּשַׁט־רֶמֶז־דְּרוּשׁ־סוֹד שֶׁבּוֹ) שֶׁלּוֹמְדִים בַּתּוֹרָה, שֶׁ"חַי" הוּא בְּאוֹפֶן אַחֵר לְגַמְרֵי, בְּחַיּוּת עַצְמִי. וְחַיּוּת זֶה, מוֹסִיף גַּם בְּהִירוּת וְעוֹמֶק יוֹתֵר בַּהֲבָנַת הָעִנְיָן.

דּוּגְמָא לָזֶה בַּנִּגְלֶה דְּתוֹרָה, וּבַהֲלָכָה:

"כָּל עֲבוֹדוֹת יוֹם הַכִּפּוּרִים אֵינָן כְּשֵׁירוֹת אֶלָּא בּוֹ" (בְּכֹהֵן גָּדוֹל)עֹד: כְּמוֹ שֶׁקְּדוּשַׁת יוֹם כִּפּוּר מוֹעִילָה לַעֲבוֹדָה הַמְּיוּחֶדֶת דְּיוֹם כִּפּוּר, כָּךְ הִיא פּוֹעֶלֶת גַּם בְּהַתְּמִידִין וּמוּסָפִין (דְּשַׁבָּת)

---

heal. He is not interested in anatomy in and for its own sake, but only insofar as it helps him further understand the nature of the body's existence. Similarly, Kabbalah is an "anatomy," so to speak, while Chasidus is concerned with the essential comprehension of G-d's being and existence.

The Rebbe then proceeds to analyze the nature of Kabbalah as a "revelation" of Chasidus. Another analogy: the anatomy textbook helps the physician understand the body; nevertheless, the text is only a schematized, secondary reflection of the body and not, of course, the essence of the body's life-force itself. Furthermore, the full force and essence of the physician's understanding of the human body is demonstrated not in his particular knowledge of anatomy, but in the practical effects of his healing. Similarly, Kabbalah, while it is a "revelation" and "explanation" of Chasidus, is merely an explanation, and not the essence of Chasidus itself. The essence of Chasidus is captured only in action, in practical deed.

Chasidus is likened above to the state of Yechidah, to keter, to the top point of the yud, to ratzon—all of which refer to transcendent, concealed levels of G-d. Yechidah is the quintessence of the soul that transcends all form; keter transcends the ten sefirot and is analogous to "darkness,"

a hidden level; the top point of the yud is an unformed seminal point; ratzon is a general force (see note 16 above). Now all these levels—although essentially beyond comprehension—are reflected in a reduced, dim way in their next lower manifestations. That is, in the sefirot, a reduced reflection of keter is "revealed" in chochmah; the top point of the yud is manifested in the yud, etc. Yet, these lower manifestations do not capture the essence of these higher transcendent levels. As explained in Chapter VII and note 64, "Essence" is a fundamental, non-derivative state which at once transcends all revelation, and yet permeates all. Hence in Chasidic terminology, the concept of "revelation" has a dual sense: it is a "manifestation" of the "essence," but at the same time is merely a manifestation, a secondary reflection or glimmer of the "essence." Kabbalah, therefore, is an explanation, but only a dimmed manifestation of Chasidus. The true inner force and essence of Chasidus is expressed in action. See further in Chapters XVII and XVIII.]

72. [See footnote 65.]

73. Yoma 32b. See also Tzofnat Paneach (by the Rogatchover Gaon) on the Torah, beg. Korach.

selves connected to all the regular days of the year; they, too, become sanctified through the sanctity of Yom Kippur.[74]

The same is true of Chasidus, the "*Shabbat Shabbaton*" of Torah:[75] it likewise affects and influences all the parts of Torah. For the four parts of *Pardes* are the four levels of the *Nefesh, Ruach, Neshamah* and *Chaya* of Torah, and Chasidus is the Torah's *Yechidah*; and the manifestation and revelation of the *Yechidah* elevates all the other four levels of *NaRaNaCh*, as explained above.

IX

THE SIGNIFICANCE OF THE PRAYER MODEH ANI

Needless to say, the subjects discussed in Torah are boundless and inexhaustible. We will attempt to explain only one topic in Torah as it is interpreted according to *peshat,* according to *remez,* according to *drush,* and according to *sod*—and then consider it in light of the vitality, illumination and depth that Chasidus brings to each of these four approaches. From the analysis of this one topic, we will learn that all of the conclusions also hold true for the rest of Torah.

The topic we will choose as an example is *Modeh Ani Lefanecha...*[76] [the morning prayer, "I offer thanks[77] to You, living

---

74. [This explains why even these "common" sacrifices had to be performed by the High Priest on Yom Kippur.]

Similarly in relation to the prayers of Yom Kippur ("prayers correspond to the sacrifices"—*Berachot* 26b): The cause for the addition of the *Ne'ilah* prayer (in which is the primary revelation of the fifth level, *Yechidah*) also affects the other four prayers of Yom Kippur (although they are also recited during the rest of the year). These other four correspond to *Nefesh, Ruach, Neshamah,* and *Chaya* respectively. The affect of *Yechidah* is indicated in the expression (*Likkutei Torah, Pinchas* 81b), "the day on which one is obligated to pray five prayers" (see *Likkutei Sichot* vol. 4, p. 1154).

[When the *Beit Hamikdash* stood, the essence of the Jewish people was bound with the Essence of G-d by the High Priest entering the Holy of Holies on Yom Kippur. Today, this union is achieved by the five prayers which we recite on Yom Kippur, for prayer takes the place of the sacrifices. Yom Kippur is the only day of the year when one is obligated to offer five separate prayers: *Maariv, Shacharit, Musaf, Minchah,* and *Ne'ilah.* These five prayers correspond to the five levels of the soul, *Nefesh, Ruach, Neshamah, Chaya,* and *Yechidah.* The fifth prayer, *Ne'ilah,* or "closing prayer," is said only on Yom Kippur. By reciting it, one reveals the *Yechidah* of the soul, which is the state of complete union with G-d. Hence the meaning of *Ne'ilah* or "closing": all the doors are closed, excluding everything but the union of Israel with the Essence of G-d.

Although *Yechidah* is associated specifically with *Ne'ilah,* it nonetheless per-

הַמִּשְׁתַּיְּכִים מִצַּד עַצְמָם לְכָל יְמֵי הַשָּׁנָה, שֶׁגַּם הֵם, מִתְקַדְּשִׁים בִּקְדוּשָׁתוֹ שֶׁל יוֹם הַכִּפּוּרִיםעה.

וְכֵן הוּא גַם בַּנּוֹגֵעַ לְתוֹרַת הַחֲסִידוּת – בְּחִינַת "שַׁבַּת שַׁבָּתוֹן" שֶׁבַּתּוֹרָהעו – שֶׁפּוֹעֶלֶת הִיא בְּכָל חֶלְקֵי הַתּוֹרָה. כִּי ד' הַחֲלָקִים פְּשַׁט־רֶמֶז־דְּרוּשׁ־סוֹד שֶׁבַּתּוֹרָה הֵם ד' הַבְּחִינוֹת נֶפֶשׁ־רוּחַ־נְשָׁמָה־חַיָּה שֶׁבַּתּוֹרָה, וְתוֹרַת הַחֲסִידוּת הִיא בְּחִינַת יְחִידָה שֶׁבַּתּוֹרָה, וּמִצַּד גִּלּוּי הַיְחִידָה, מִתְעַלִּים גַּם הַנֶּפֶשׁ־רוּחַ־נְשָׁמָה־חַיָּה, כַּנַּ"ל.

ט.

הָעִנְיָנִים שֶׁבַּתּוֹרָה הֲרֵי הֵם בְּרִיבּוּי לְאֵין קֵץ. וּנְבָאֵר – בְּדֶרֶךְ אֶפְשָׁר, עַל כָּל פָּנִים – עִנְיָן אֶחָד בַּתּוֹרָה כְּמוֹ שֶׁהוּא עַל פִּי פְּשַׁט, עַל פִּי רֶמֶז, עַל פִּי דְרוּשׁ וְעַל פִּי סוֹד, וְאֶת הַחַיּוּת וְהַבְּהִירוּת וְהָעוֹמֶק שֶׁתּוֹרַת הַחֲסִידוּת מַכְנִיסָה בְּכָל ד' הַחֲלָקִים שֶׁבּוֹ. וּמִמֶּנּוּ נִלְמַד שֶׁכֵּן הוּא בְּכָל הָעִנְיָנִים שֶׁבַּתּוֹרָה.

הָעִנְיָן שֶׁנִּבְחַר אוֹתוֹ בְּתוֹר דּוּגְמָא הוּא – "מוֹדֶה אֲנִי

meates the entire day of Yom Kippur, as indicated in the expression "the day on which one is obligated to pray five prayers." That is, throughout the entire day, at the time of each prayer, this fifth category, *Yechidah*, illuminates and permeates.]

75. See *Likkutei Torah, Drushei Yom Kippur* 70d, that "*Shabbat Shabbaton*" [i.e., a *Shabbat* over regular *Shabbatot*, as Yom Kippur is called], is [a revelation of] *Or Ein Sof* that is vested in *radla*. And this is the level of Chasidus, as explained above in Chapter II.

76. The source of the text of *Modeh Ani* is *Seder Hayom*. It is quoted in *Ateret Z'kenim*, beg. of *Shulchan Aruch Orach Chaim, Shulchan Aruch Harav* 1:5 (and

in the second version 1:6); *Siddur Admur Hazaken*, beg.

77. [*Modeh* may be translated as "acknowledging" and "giving thanks," and also as "confessing," "admitting," or "conceding." It is an expression of confronting a "fact" greater than the person. Contrasting our usage of the term *Modeh*, as Chasidus explains it, is not "denial," but "comprehension." One is able to comprehend only that which is not greater than himself; he can master it and contain it intellectually. *Modeh Ani*, then, is certainly a declaration of gratitude, but of a specific kind: it is a pre-rational or supra-rational declaration, not the reasoned product of sharp thinking. It is instinctive and spontaneous, emanating from the soul.]

and eternal King, for having restored my soul within me with mercy; Your faithfulness is great"]. The reasons for this choice are the following:

1) Since it is incumbent upon every person to accustom himself to say *Modeh Ani* immediately upon awakening from his sleep, "and thereby to remember G-d who stands over him, and arise with zeal,"[78] this statement is the foundation and beginning of a person's service (namely, the fulfillment of *all* the teachings of Torah), and of his life, for the rest of the entire day.

2) The idea behind this saying is that one should "contemplate immediately upon awakening before Whom he lies—before the King of the King of Kings, the Holy One Blessed be He, as it is written,[79] 'Behold, the heavens and the earth I fill...'"[80]—"Of this should one be aware during *all* his dealings and affairs."[81] "This is a great principle in Torah, and a distinguishing quality of the righteous who walk always before G-d, as it is written, 'I place G-d *constantly* before me.'"[82] That is to say, the whole day should be conducted in this same manner.

3) All of the preceding—the service of man to his Maker—first comes[83] through man's *awakening from his sleep*, his slumber in the vanities of the world, to use the well-known expression of Maimonides.[84]

(And in light of all the foregoing, we can also understand the proverb which Rabbi Shalom DovBer said in his youth: that we must spread out the "dot" (i.e., the period which is after the word "mercy") in *Modeh Ani* over into the entire day—because the service of *Modeh Ani* is required at every moment of the whole day.)

---

78. *Shulchan Aruch Harav*, second version, ibid. In the *Siddur* it reads, "remember G-d *hanitzav*..." [instead of the word *omed*, used in *Shulchan Aruch*. Although both *omed* and *nitzav* are identically translated as "standing," the term "*nitzav*" denotes a stronger presence than "*omed*." See *Or Hatorah, Devarim*, p. 1202.]

79. Jeremiah 23:24.

80. *Siddur Admur Hazaken*, loc. cit.

81. *Shulchan Aruch Harav*, first version, 1:2. See also *Darkei Moshe* on the *Tur*, ibid. (from *Guide for the Perplexed* III, ch. 52).

82. *Shulchan Aruch Harav*, second version, 1:5. Note numerous changes from the first version. This, however, is not the place for further examination.

לְפָנֶיךָ כו'‎"נז. כִּי

א) מִכֵּיוָן שֶׁעַל הָאָדָם לְהַרְגִּיל עַצְמוֹ לוֹמַר "מוֹדֶה אֲנִי" מִיָּד כְּשֶׁנֵּיעוֹר מִשְּׁנָתוֹ, "וְעַל יְדֵי זֶה יִזְכֹּר אֶת ה' הָעוֹמֵד עָלָיו וְיָקוּם בִּזְרִיזוּת"נח, הֲרֵי אֲמִירָה זוֹ, יְסוֹד וְרֵאשִׁית הִיא לַעֲבוֹדַת הָאָדָם (קִיּוּם **כָּל** הַהוֹרָאוֹת שֶׁבַּתּוֹרָה) וּלְחַיָּיו – בְּמֶשֶׁךְ כָּל הַיּוֹם.

ב) תּוֹכֶן אֲמִירָה זוֹ שֶׁהוּא "לְהִתְבּוֹנֵן מִיָּד לִפְנֵי מִי הוּא שׁוֹכֵב לִפְנֵי מֶלֶךְ מַלְכֵי הַמְּלָכִים הַקָּדוֹשׁ בָּרוּךְ הוּא כְּמוֹ שֶׁכָּתוּבנט הֲלֹא אֶת הַשָּׁמַיִם וְאֶת הָאָרֶץ אֲנִי מָלֵא כו'"ס – כֵּן יַחֲשׁוֹב **בְּכָל** עֲסָקָיו וְעִנְיָנָיו"סא, "וְזֶה כְּלָל גָּדוֹל בַּתּוֹרָה וּבְמַעֲלוֹת הַצַּדִּיקִים הַהוֹלְכִים לִפְנֵי הָאֱלֹקִים כְּמוֹ שֶׁכָּתוּב שִׁוִּיתִי ה' לְנֶגְדִּי **תָמִיד**"סב. זֹאת אוֹמֶרֶת אֲשֶׁר עַל דֶּרֶךְ זֶה צָרִיךְ לִהְיוֹת כָּל הַיּוֹם כֻּלּוֹ.

ג) כָּל הַנַּ"ל – עֲבוֹדַת הָאָדָם לְקוֹנוֹ – הֲרֵי זֶה עַל יְדֵי הַקְדָּמַתסג **נֵיעוֹר מִשֵּׁינָתוֹ** בְּהַבְלֵי הָעוֹלָם – כִּלְשׁוֹן הָרַמְבַּ"ם הַיָּדוּעַסד.

(וּבָזֶה יוּבַן פִּתְגָּמוֹ שֶׁל כְּבוֹד קְדֻשַּׁת אַדְמוֹ"ר (מְהוֹרַשַׁ"ב) נִשְׁמָתוֹ עֵדֶן שֶׁאָמַר בִּימֵי יַלְדוּתוֹ, אֲשֶׁר הַ"נְּקוּדָה" (שֶׁאַחֲרֵי תֵּיבַת בַּחֶמְלָה) שֶׁבְּ"מוֹדֶה אֲנִי" צְרִיכִים לְפוֹשְׁטָהּ (פֿאַנאַנדֶערשְׁפְּרֵייטֶן) עַל כָּל הַיּוֹם כֻּלּוֹ – כִּי בְּכָל רֶגַע וָרֶגַע שֶׁבְּמֶשֶׁךְ כָּל הַיּוֹם צְרִיכָה לִהְיוֹת הָעֲבוֹדָה דְמוֹדֶה אֲנִי).

---

83. Perhaps one can say that the obligation of Torah study, which is *constant* and *ceaseless* (and is a manner of study that brings to practice—i.e., Divine service throughout the *entire* day), always contains *an element* of "waking from one's sleep." For, as stated in *Likkutei Torah*, *Shelach* 44a, one is able to attain Torah knowledge only because previously, when one was in his mother's womb, he was taught the entire Torah, until being tapped by an angel above the mouth [making him forget] (*Niddah* 30b). Through Torah study, one *regains* what he had known before, but had forgotten (and left him). [Thus, Torah study is analogous to "waking from one's sleep."]

84. *Hilchot Teshuvah* 3:4.

X

MODEH ANI INTERPRETED ON FOUR LEVELS

To begin, then, our analysis: the subject of *Modeh Ani* according to *peshat* [the plain meaning of Torah] is giving thanks to G-d for "having restored my soul within me." Though we make the blessing of *Elokai Neshamah*[85] for the restoration of the soul, it is still also necessary to say *Modeh Ani*, because the obligation to give thanks for the return of the soul applies *immediately* upon awakening from one's sleep.

For just as the blessing for the enjoyment of food [*Birchat Hanehenin*][86] is obligatory immediately when pleasure is derived (and even before[87] one benefits[88]), likewise, the blessing of thanksgiving for the restoration of the soul (which is the greatest benefit of all, and includes all specific worldly pleasures and benefits) is obligatory immediately upon awakening from one's sleep.[89]

And inasmuch as the blessing of *Elokai Neshamah* contains mention of G-d's Name, and so cannot be said (in our times[90]) before the morning washing of the hands,[91] one must therefore give thanks for the restoration of the soul immediately upon awakening at least through saying *Modeh Ani*. (Nevertheless, it is still necessary to say the blessing of *Elokai Neshamah* later, for not only does the blessing *Elokai Neshamah* contain certain details not found in *Modeh Ani*, but also in *Modeh Ani* there is no mention of G-d's name, and any

---

85. [The blessing *Elokai Neshamah* follows the blessing for washing the hands, and the blessing of thanksgiving for physical health, *Asher Yatzar*. See *Siddur Tehillat Hashem*, Morning Blessings.]

86. [There are two catergories of blessings: 1) *Birchot Hanehenin* are blessings of gratitude for enjoying G-d's Creation, include *Hamotzi* before bread, and similar blessings. 2) *Birchot Hoda'ah* are blessings of praise and acknowledgment, recognizing G-d in all His works. Although it is *Birchot Hanehenin* that are recited before partaking of the food, the Rebbe ap-

plies the principle to *Birchot Hoda'ah* as well.]

87. In our case, however, it is obviously not possible to make a blessing for the restoration of the soul before (it is restored, the parallel of) deriving benefit; it is nevertheless obligatory to make the blessing immediately upon awakening. This would correspond to (and even surpass) the concept of the blessing recited on purification by immersion in a *mikvah*. Although the blessing cannot be recited before immersion, since "the person is not yet fit [to recite it]," one does not

י.

עִנְיָנוֹ שֶׁל "מוֹדֶה אֲנִי כו'" עַל פִּי חֵלֶק הַפְּשַׁט שֶׁבַּתּוֹרָה
הוּא – הוֹדָאָה לַה' עַל "שֶׁהֶחֱזַרְתָּ בִּי נִשְׁמָתִי". וְאַף שֶׁמְּבָרְכִים
עַל הַחֲזָרַת הַנְּשָׁמָה בְּבִרְכַּת אֱלֹקַי נְשָׁמָה, מִכָּל מָקוֹם צָרִיךְ
לוֹמַר גַּם "מוֹדֶה אֲנִי כו'", כִּי הַחִיּוּב לְהוֹדוֹת עַל הַחֲזָרַת
הַנְּשָׁמָה הוּא מִיָּד כְּשֶׁנִּיעוֹר מִשֵּׁינָתוֹ

– כִּי כְּמוֹ שֶׁהַחִיּוּב דְּבִרְכַּת הַנֶּהֱנִין הוּא מִיָּד כְּשֶׁנֶּהֱנֶה
(וְעוֹד טֶרֶם⁹⁰ שֶׁנֶּהֱנֶה⁹¹), כֵּן גַּם הַחִיּוּב דְּבִרְכַּת הַהוֹדָאָה עַל
הַחֲזָרַת הַנְּשָׁמָה [שֶׁהִיא הֲנָאָה הַיּוֹתֵר גְּדוֹלָה, וְכוֹלֶלֶת אֶת כָּל
הַהֲנָאוֹת הַפְּרָטִיּוֹת שֶׁבָּעוֹלָם] הוּא מִיָּד כְּשֶׁנִּיעוֹר מִשֵּׁינָתוֹ⁹² –

וּבִהְיוֹת שֶׁבְּבִרְכַּת אֱלֹקַי נְשָׁמָה, לִהְיוֹתָהּ בְּהַזְכָּרַת הַשֵּׁם, אִי
אֶפְשָׁר לְאוֹמְרָהּ (עַכְשָׁיו) קוֹדֶם נְטִילַת יָדַיִם⁹³, צָרִיךְ לְהוֹדוֹת
עַל הַחֲזָרַת הַנְּשָׁמָה מִיָּד כְּשֶׁנִּיעוֹר מִשֵּׁינָתוֹ בַּאֲמִירַת מוֹדֶה
אֲנִי עַל כָּל פָּנִים. (אֶלָּא שֶׁמִּכָּל מָקוֹם צָרִיךְ לְבָרֵךְ אַחַר כָּךְ גַּם
בִּרְכַּת "אֱלֹקַי נְשָׁמָה", כִּי (נוֹסָף לָזֶה שֶׁבְּבִרְכַּת אֱלֹקַי נְשָׁמָה
יֶשְׁנָם כַּמָּה פְּרָטִים שֶׁאֵינָם בְּ"מוֹדֶה אֲנִי", עוֹד זֹאת) בְּ"מוֹדֶה

---

postpone the blessing to a later time. Rather, the blessing is said immediately upon emerging from the water (*Pesachim* 7b; see also *Shulchan Aruch Harav* 6:5: "One should recite the blessing as close to the action as possible..."). [Hence, the blessing of acknowledgment for the restoration of the soul in the morning certainly should not be delayed.]

88. For one is not allowed to enjoy anything of Creation without reciting the appropriate blessing (*Berachot* 35a).

89. *Berachot* 60b; *Shulchan Aruch Harav*,

1:7.

90. [See below.]

91. *Rosh* on *Berachot*, ibid.; *Shulchan Aruch Harav* 46:3.

[*Modeh Ani* only contains the words "Everlasting King" in its reference to G-d, but does not mention any of His Names directly, for one is not permitted to pronounce any of G-d's names until after the morning ritual washing of the hands. Washing the hands restores purity and cleanliness to the mind and body. *Shulchan Aruch Harav* first version, 4:1,4.]

blessing which does not contain the Name and attribute of G-d's kingdom is not truly a *beracha*.)[92]

All the above will help us understand why in Talmudic times, *Modeh Ani*, in fact, was not said, and only the blessing of *Elokai Neshamah* was recited—for in *Modeh Ani* there is nothing new or additional to the blessing *Elokai Neshamah* (on the contrary, as explained before). Saying *Modeh Ani* is required in our times only in order that the thanks may be given immediately upon awakening from one's sleep. In the Talmudic era, they said *Elokai Neshamah* immediately upon awakening from their sleep,[93] and had, therefore, no need to say *Modeh Ani*.

Proceeding to the level of *remez* [the allusion, or intimated meaning], the idea of *Modeh Ani* is that the restoration of the soul every morning *alludes* to the Resurrection of the Dead. For sleep is called "one-sixtieth of death";[94] and hence, the restoration of the soul upon awakening is of an order of Resurrection. That is the meaning of "for having restored my soul within me... great is Your faithfulness": from this "restoring my soul within me," we know that "great is Your faithfulness" to the Resurrection of the Dead.[95]

Continuing the analysis further, according to *drush* [the homiletic, expounded meaning], the interpretation of *Modeh Ani* is that through the restoration of the soul every morning—"They are new every morning"—G-d returns to a person the soul which was entrusted to Him, and does not withhold it for the "debts" which the person owes Him. This act shows the great faithfulness of the Holy One blessed be He—"Great is Your faithfulness." From this we *expound* and learn that a person should also be faithful and trusting in the same manner, and not withhold an article entrusted to him by another because of the debts owed to him.[96]

---

92. *Berachot* 40b, *Shulchan Aruch Harav* 214:1.

[A "blessing" in Jewish law is defined by its mention of G-d's name and His Kingdom, as in the formula: "Blessed are You, L-rd our G-d, King of the universe..." The text of *Modeh Ani* does not contain these elements.]

93. Being "holy," they were able recite this blessing amid cleanliness immediately upon awakening from their sleep. (*Rabbenu Yonah, Berachot* 60b, s.v. *Ki Shama*).

94. *Berachot* 57b, *Zohar* I:169b; III:119a.

אֲנִי״ אֵין בָּהּ הַזְכָּרַת הַשֵּׁם, וְכָל בְּרָכָה שֶׁאֵין בָּהּ שֵׁם וּמַלְכוּת
– אֵינָהּ[צ] בְּרָכָה).

וְעַל פִּי זֶה מוּבָן זֶה שֶׁבִּזְמַן הַשַׁ״ס לֹא אָמְרוּ מוֹדֶה אֲנִי וְהָיוּ
מְבָרְכִים רַק ״אֱלֹקַי נְשָׁמָה״, כִּי בְּ״מוֹדֶה אֲנִי״ אֵין הוֹסָפָה
וְחִידוּשׁ עַל בִּרְכַּת אֱלֹקַי נְשָׁמָה (וְאַדְרַבָּה כַּנַּ״ל). דְּמַה שֶׁהִצְטָרְכוּ
לוֹמַר עַכְשָׁיו גַּם מוֹדֶה אֲנִי, הַיְינוּ רַק בִּכְדֵי שֶׁהַהוֹדָאָה תִּהְיֶה
מִיָּד כְּשֶׁנֵּיעוֹר מִשְׁנָתוֹ, וּבִימֵיהֶם שֶׁהָיוּ מְבָרְכִים אֱלֹקַי נְשָׁמָה
מִיָּד כְּשֶׁנֵּיעֲרוּ מִשְּׁנָתָם[ע] – לֹא הוּצְרְכוּ לוֹמַר מוֹדֶה אֲנִי.

עִנְיָנוּ שֶׁל מוֹדֶה אֲנִי כו' עַל פִּי חֵלֶק הָרֶמֶז שֶׁבַּתּוֹרָה: הַחֲזָרַת
הַנְּשָׁמָה בְּכָל בּוֹקֶר **רוֹמֶזֶת** לִתְחִיַּית הַמֵּתִים. כִּי שֵׁינָה הִיא אֶחָד
מִשִּׁשִּׁים בְּמִיתָה[א], וּבְמֵילָא, הַחֲזָרַת הַנְּשָׁמָה הִיא מֵעֵין תְּחִיַּת
הַמֵּתִים. וְזֶהוּ ״שֶׁהֶחֱזַרְתָּ בִּי נִשְׁמָתִי כו' רַבָּה אֱמוּנָתֶךָ״: מִזֶּה
שֶׁ״הֶחֱזַרְתָּ בִּי נִשְׁמָתִי״, אָנוּ יוֹדְעִים שֶׁ״רַבָּה אֱמוּנָתֶךָ״ לִתְחִיַּת
הַמֵּתִים[ע].

עִנְיָנוּ שֶׁל מוֹדֶה אֲנִי כו' עַל פִּי חֵלֶק הַדְּרוּשׁ שֶׁבַּתּוֹרָה:
הַחֲזָרַת הַנְּשָׁמָה בְּכָל בּוֹקֶר – ״חֲדָשִׁים לַבְּקָרִים״ – ״מַה שֶׁהַקָּדוֹשׁ
בָּרוּךְ הוּא מַחֲזִיר לָהָאָדָם אֶת נִשְׁמָתוֹ שֶׁהִפְקִידָהּ אֶצְלוֹ וְאֵינוֹ
מְעַכְּבָהּ בְּעַד הַחוֹב שֶׁהָאָדָם חַיָּיב לוֹ, מַרְאֶה עַל גּוֹדֶל אֱמוּנָתוֹ
שֶׁל הַקָּדוֹשׁ בָּרוּךְ הוּא – ״רַבָּה אֱמוּנָתֶךָ״. וּמִזֶּה אָנוּ **דּוֹרְשִׁים**
וּלְמֵדִים, שֶׁגַּם הָאָדָם צָרִיךְ לִהְיוֹת אִישׁ אֱמוּנִים בְּאוֹפֶן כָּזֶה,
וְאָסוּר לוֹ לְעַכֵּב אֶת פִּקְדוֹנוֹ שֶׁל חֲבֵירוֹ בִּשְׁבִיל הַחוֹבוֹת
שֶׁהַמַּפְקִיד חַיָּיב לוֹ[ע].

---

95. See *Eichah Rabbah* on Lamentations 3:23, "They are new every morning, great is Your faithfulness." *See references there.*

96. *Zohar* III ibid. *Nitzutzei Zohar* (on *Zohar* ibid.; and 198b) refers to the following sources: *Sifri, Hazinu* 32:4; *Zohar Chadash, Bereishit* 18b and *Rut* 88d; *Mordechai, Bava Metzia* sect. 406 (likewise in *Kol Bo*, 116) from Responsa and Rabbinical Edicts of *Rabbenu Tam.* Ibid., 408 from Jerusalem Talmud; *Radvaz* 1:483; *Baal Haturim, Teitzei* 24:14;

And according to the "esoteric" part of Torah [*sod*], *Modeh Ani* is explained in the following manner: the words "living and eternal King" refer to the Divine attribute of *malchut*[97] [sovereignty, kingship] as it is united with the attribute of *yesod*[98] [foundation]. (For the word *melech*—King—indicates G-d's attribute of *malchut*, and "living and eternal" His attribute of *yesod*.[99]) "Living and eternal King who has restored my soul within me" means, then, that the restoration of the soul comes from the level of *malchut* as it unites with the level of *yesod*.

XI

A CHASIDIC INSIGHT INTO MODEH ANI

The preceding exposition, which is based on the four levels of *Pardes* —the *Nefesh, Ruach, Neshamah,* and *Chaya* of Torah—elaborates upon various particular ideas in the thanksgiving of *Modeh Ani* (in contrast to the "great general principle"). Chasidus—the *Yechidah* of Torah—comes forth to articulate the general, comprehensive explanation, by elucidating the quintessential point of *Modeh Ani,* which comes from the level of the *Yechidah* within a person.

According to Chasidus, the explanation of *Modeh Ani* is as follows: We begin the order of the day with *Modeh Ani,* which we say before washing the hands, and even with hands which are ritually unclean, because all the impurities of the world cannot contaminate the *Modeh Ani* of a Jew.[100] It is possible that a person may be lacking

---

Rema, Choshen Mishpat 72:17; *Shach* sect 5 on *Choshen Mishpat* 292 from Responsa of *Mahara Sasoon; Ketzot Hachoshen* on *Choshen Mishpat,* 4; *Pitchei Teshuva* sect. 2 on *Choshen Mishpat,* ibid., from *Birkei Yosef* in the name of Rabbi Menachem Azaria of Fano.

97. [MALCHUT. Lit., Royalty or Kingship; the tenth and last of the ten *sefirot. Malchut* is referred to in the *Tikkunei Zohar* (intro. 17a) as the "Mouth of G-d," the Word or speech of G-d by which the world comes into actual being. (Mouth and speech are used for communication with "others" outside of the self.) The world and the creatures (the "others") make it possible to speak of a Divine Kingdom, since "there cannot be a King without a nation"—G-d cannot be a ruler without the element of "others."

Eitz Chaim (6:5, 8:5, et passim) speaks of *malchut* as "a dim speculum because it has no (light) of its own." The *Zohar* (I:249b, 251b) therefore compares *malchut* to "the moon that has no light of its own save that which is given to it from the sun." Paradoxically, although *malchut* is a passive sphere that only contains that which the other *sefirot* pour into it, it is specifically through *malchut* that the orig-

עִנְיָנוֹ שֶׁל מוֹדֶה אֲנִי כו' עַל פִּי חֵלֶק הַסּוֹד שֶׁבַּתּוֹרָה:
"מֶלֶךְ חַי וְקַיָּים" הוּא בְּחִינַת הַמַּלְכוּת כְּמוֹ שֶׁהִיא מְיוּחֶדֶת עִם
בְּחִינַת הַיְסוֹד [כִּי "מֶלֶךְ" מוֹרֶה לִסְפִירַת הַמַּלְכוּת, וְ"חַי
וְקַיָּים" – לִסְפִירַת הַיְסוֹד[98]], וְזֶהוּ "מֶלֶךְ חַי וְקַיָּים שֶׁהֶחֱזַרְתָּ בִּי
נִשְׁמָתִי", שֶׁהַחֲזָרַת הַנְּשָׁמָה בָּאָה מִבְּחִינַת הַמַּלְכוּת כְּמוֹ שֶׁהִיא
מְיוּחֶדֶת עִם בְּחִינַת הַיְסוֹד.

יא.

הַבֵּיאוּר הַנַּ"ל שֶׁעַל פִּי ד' חֶלְקֵי הַפְּשַׁט־רֶמֶז־דְּרוּשׁ־סוֹד –
נֶפֶשׁ־רוּחַ־נְשָׁמָה־חַיָּה – שֶׁבַּתּוֹרָה, מְבָאֵר עִנְיָנִים פְּרָטִיִּים
(בְּעֶרֶךְ הַ"כְּלָל גָּדוֹל" שֶׁבָּזֶה) בְּהַהוֹדָאָה דְמוֹדֶה אֲנִי. וּבָאָה
תוֹרַת הַחֲסִידוּת – יְחִידָה שֶׁבַּתּוֹרָה, וּמְבָאֶרֶת בֵּיאוּר כְּלָלִי,
מְבָאֶרֶת אֶת הַנְּקוּדָה הָעַצְמִית אֲשֶׁר בְּמוֹדֶה אֲנִי הַבָּאָה
מִבְּחִינַת הַיְחִידָה שֶׁבָּאָדָם.

הַבֵּיאוּר עַל פִּי תוֹרַת הַחֲסִידוּת עַל מוֹדֶה אֲנִי כו' הוּא:
הַתְחָלָתוֹ שֶׁל סֵדֶר הַיּוֹם הוּא בְּמוֹדֶה אֲנִי, שֶׁאוֹמְרִים אוֹתוֹ
קוֹדֶם נְטִילַת יָדַיִם, אֲפִילוּ בְּיָדַיִם טְמֵאוֹת, לְפִי שֶׁכָּל הַטּוּמְאוֹת
שֶׁבָּעוֹלָם אֵינָן מְטַמְּאוֹת אֶת הַ"מוֹדֶה אֲנִי" שֶׁל יְהוּדִי[99]. אֶפְשָׁר

---

inal creative plan is actualized. But *malchut* can only actualize the potential of the earlier *sefirot*. See *Mystical Concepts in Chassidism*, ch. 3 (*Sefirot*).]

98. YESOD. Lit., "Foundation"; the ninth of the ten *sefirot*. *Yesod* is the Divine Attribute which is the blending channel of all the preceding *sefirot*. *Yesod* is the all-inclusive principle which joins heaven and earth and makes it possible for all the emanations of the *sefirot* to issue forth—it is the "foundation" of creation.

In the words of Rabbi Schneur Zalman (*Igeret Hakodesh*, epistle 15): "The aspect of *yesod* is, by way of example, the

bond by which the father binds his intellect to the intellect of the son when teaching him with love and willingness, for he wishes his son to understand. Without this bond, even if the son would hear the very same words from the mouth of his father, he would not understand them as well..." I.e., *yesod* is the bond uniting Emanator and recipient. See also *Mystical Concepts in Chassidism*, ibid.]

99. *Siddur HaArizal* (*Kol Yaakov*), beg.

100. See footnote 103.

in one respect or another—but his *Modeh Ani* always remains perfect.[101]

And this perfection and purity are due solely to the *Yechidah*: The four categories of *NaRaNaCh* allow for imperfections and even impurities; but in the *Yechidah* of the soul, which is constantly united with the Essence of G-d, there is no connection to or possibility whatsoever for defects and impurities, G-d forbid. It always remains perfect and whole.

(This is the "inner" reason why *Modeh Ani* has no mention of any of the "seven names of G-d which one is not allowed to erase or destroy"—for *Modeh Ani* comes from the level of *Yechidah*, which is the essence of the soul, and the thanksgiving expressed by the essence of the soul is directed to the Essence of G-d "which is not[102] contained in any name.")[103]

Therefore, this explanation is given only in Chasidus, for since the four parts of *Pardes* comprise only the *NaRaNaCh* (of Torah), they do not *explain* and *elaborate*[104] upon the idea of *Yechidah*. We

---

101. *Hayom Yom*, p. 19.

102. *Likkutei Torah*, *Pinchas* 80b. See also *Zohar* III:257b.

103. *In simple terms, the fact that Modeh Ani contains no mention of G-d's name and therefore may be recited even before the morning washing of the hands (see sources in fn. 76) indicates that Modeh Ani is of a lower realm than that of G-d's names. But on an inner level, the reason why there are none of the Divine names in Modeh Ani (and also why we recite it before the washing of the hands) is that Modeh Ani transcends the level of G-d's names.* (Note also *Torah Or* 100b and

If, as according Chasidus, Modeh Ani has a trascendant quality [of Yechidah] not shared by Elokai Neshamah (though on the "revealed" plane—as noted in Chapter X, Elokai Neshamah contains all of Modeh Ani and more), why was it not recited in the days of the Talmud? A possible solution: The arousal and expression of Yechidah is

121b, explaining why none of G-d's name's are mentioned in the Book of Esther.)

This idea [that *Modeh Ani* transcends G-d's names] does not contradict the fact that "there is no holiness in *Modeh Ani*, for *Modeh Ani* is comparable to the word "*Anochi (Hashem Elokecha)*" ["I am the L-rd your G-d," Exodus 20:2]. Though *Anochi* ["I"] refers to the Essence that transcends all names (as explained in the

specifically when even one who is in a state of ritual impurity acknowledges the Eternal King (as will be explained later in Chapter XVIII ff.). This idea is similar to the fact (Sefer Hamaamarim 5709, p. 107) that the capacity for self-sacrifice (engendered by Yechidah) is more evident during Exile, especially towards its end, than when the Beit Hamikdash stood. The same is true of Chasidus, the level of Yechidah: it was only revealed in the later generations, when the world was in a state of "unconsciousness," as explained at the beginning of this talk.

שֶׁיִּהְיֶה חָסֵר בְּעִנְיָן זֶה אוֹ בְּעִנְיָן אַחֵר – אֲבָל הַ"מוֹדֶה אֲנִי"
שֶׁלּוֹ נִשְׁאָר תָּמִיד בִּשְׁלֵימוּתⁱ.

וְעִנְיָן זֶה הוּא מִצַּד הַיְּחִידָה דַּוְקָא: כִּי ד' הַבְּחִינוֹת
נֶפֶשׁ-רוּחַ-נְשָׁמָה-חַיָּה שַׁיָּיךְ עִנְיַן הַפְּגָם אוֹ גַּם טוּמְאָה כוּ', אֲבָל
מִצַּד הַיְּחִידָה שֶׁבַּנְּשָׁמָה שֶׁמְּיוּחֶדֶת תָּמִיד בְּעַצְמוּתוֹ יִתְבָּרֵךְ, אֵין
שַׁיָּיךְ כָּל פְּגָם וְטוּמְאָה חַס וְשָׁלוֹם וְנִשְׁאָר תָּמִיד בִּשְׁלֵמוּתוֹ.

(וְזֶהוּ טַעַם הַפְּנִימִי עַל מַה שֶׁבְּ"מוֹדֶה אֲנִי" לֹא נִזְכָּר שׁוּם
שֵׁם מִז' הַשֵּׁמוֹת שֶׁאֵינָם נִמְחָקִים, כִּי מִכֵּיוָן שֶׁהַ"מוֹדֶה אֲנִי" בָּא
מִצַּד בְּחִינַת הַיְּחִידָה – עֶצֶם הַנְּשָׁמָה, הֲרֵי הַהוֹדָאָה שֶׁל עֶצֶם
הַנְּשָׁמָה הִיא לְעַצְמוּתוֹ יִתְבָּרֵךְ "דְּלָא" אִתְפַּס בְּשֵׁם"ⁿ).

וְלָכֵן נֶאֱמַר בֵּיאוּר זֶה בַּחֲסִידוּת דַּוְקָא, כִּי ד' הַחֲלָקִים
פְּשַׁט-רֶמֶז-דְּרוּשׁ-סוֹד, מִכֵּיוָן שֶׁעִנְיָנָם הוּא – נֶפֶשׁ-רוּחַ-נְשָׁמָה-
חַיָּה (שֶׁבַּתּוֹרָה), אֵינָם מְבָאֲרִיםⁿ עִנְיַן הַ"יְּחִידָה" וְעַד שֶׁמָּצִינוּ

---

sources cited in the previous footnote), nevertheless (and for this very reason) the name *Anochi* does not possess any holiness (because the *word Anochi* is not a *vessel* for the Essence; it only alludes to it and represents it).

[The "Seven Names of G-d" are "vessels" for what they represent—e.g., Kindness, Eternity, etc.—and as such are "holy" and must be treated with reverence (they cannot be erased, for example). *Anochi*, however, is not a "name" or a "vessel" for His Essence, but *refers* to Essence, and hence does not "contain" holiness.]

104. Although *Yechidah* is, in fact, *mentioned* in the *Midrash*, as noted above in footnote 49. Also in *Zohar* II:158b, and addendum to the *Zohar* (from *Sefer Habahir*) vol. 1 (267a), etc. (One should further note that the category of *Yechidah* written of in *Zohar* II ibid. is the level of "with all your *soul*," and not the more sublime level of "with all your *might*"—

implying that the *Zohar* is not referring to the true level of *Yechidah*.)

[That is, the *Zohar* does mention, although it does not elaborate upon, the idea of *Yechidah*, in its interpretation of the Shema: "You shall love the L-rd your G-d with all your heart, with all your soul, and with all your might..." Here the *Zohar* associates *Yechidah* with the second level of love, "with all your soul," and not with the highest form of love, "with all your might." The latter is the highest level and corresponds to the true *Yechidah*; for "with all your might" represents an unlimited, boundless love that leads one to self-sacrifice, and can result only from *Yechidah*. Thus the *Yechidah* of which the *Zohar* speaks is not the same as that which Chasidus expounds upon. (*Yechidah*, however, is sometimes applied to a lower level, the level of *Chaya*, to represent what is beyond the natural order in relation to, and in context of, the lower faculties. See *Likkutei Sichot*, vol. 19, p. 151 fn. 33.)]

find, moreover, (in the Zohar,[105] though it is the "esoteric" aspect [*sod*] of Torah,) that in the enumeration and detailing of the levels of the soul—"*Nefesh, Ruach, Neshamah, Neshamah of Neshamah*"— the category of *Yechidah* is not even listed. It is included, instead, in the category or "*Neshamah of Neshamah*," which is the level of *Chaya*.

In Chasidus, however, which is the *Yechidah* of Torah, the subject of *Yechidah* is expounded upon at great length.[106]

And since the *Yechidah* is the category of the essence of the soul from which the other four levels of *NaRaNaCh* are drawn, the explanation of Chasidus (which elucidates the quintessential point of *Modeh Ani* that comes from the level of *Yechidah*) thus also invigorates and sharply illuminates the four interpretations of *Pardes* discussed above (which themselves elaborate on the specifics of *Modeh Ani*), as will now be explained.

XII

AWAKENING FROM SLEEP: THE RESTORATION OF A JEWISH SOUL

The vitality that Chasidus introduces into the level of *peshat* in *Modeh Ani* (the idea that the thanksgiving is expressed for "restoring my soul within me") lies in the emphasis on the word *nishmati*—"my soul." That is to say, all the gratitude is for the restoration of a Jewish soul. If a different soul were to be restored to the person (that of a non-Jew, or a bondsman)[107]—even though that other soul would also revive him from the state of (one-sixtieth of) death to life—he would not give thanks. For through the illumination of the *Yechidah*, he feels deeply within him that "life" is Jewish life only. (This is the life of *man, Adam*—"you are called *Adam*,"[108] wherein "the spirit of man is that which rises upwards."[109]) The life of the flesh *by itself* (the life of an animal—the nation that is compared to a donkey,[110] or labeled "donkey"[111]—wherein "the spirit of the animal descends

---

105. *Zohar* I:79b; 81a. (Also quoted in *Or Hachaim, Emor* 22:12.) The term *Neshamah of Neshamah* ["soul of the soul"] (and similar expressions) is also mentioned in *Zohar* III:152a; *Zohar Chadash, Rut* 78c.

106. In contrast, [the subject of *Yechidah*

is not explained and elaborated in depth] in *Eitz Chaim*, etc. See also note in *Eitz Chaim, Shaar* 42 (*Drushei Abiya*) beg. ch. 1 and notes and explanations there.

107. See *Shulchan Aruch Harav* 46:4.

108. *Yevamot* 61a. [The Talmud quotes

יְתֵרָה מִזּוֹ (כַּזֹּהַרᵖ – אַף שֶׁהוּא חֵלֶק הַ"סּוֹד" שֶׁבַּתּוֹרָה), אֲשֶׁר מוֹנֶה וּמְפָרֵט אֶת הַמַּדְרֵגוֹת שֶׁבַּנְּשָׁמָה "נֶפֶשׁ, רוּחַ, נְשָׁמָה וּנְשָׁמָה לַנְּשָׁמָה" – וּבְחִינַת הַיְּחִידָה אֵינָהּ נִמְנֵית, כִּי נִכְלֶלֶת הִיא בְּהַ"נְּשָׁמָה לַנְּשָׁמָה" – בְּחִינַת חַיָּה,

אֲבָל בַּחֲסִידוּת – יְחִידָה שֶׁבַּתּוֹרָה – מְבוֹאָר, וּבַאֲרוּכָהᵖᵃ עִנְיָנָהּ שֶׁל הַיְּחִידָה.

וּמִכֵּיוָן שֶׁהַיְּחִידָה הִיא בְּחִינַת עֶצֶם הַנְּשָׁמָה שֶׁמִּמֶּנָּה נִמְשָׁכוֹת ד' הַבְּחִינוֹת נֶפֶשׁ-רוּחַ-נְשָׁמָה-חַיָּה, הֲרֵי הַבֵּאוּר שֶׁבַּחֲסִידוּת (הַמְבָאֵר אֶת הַנְּקוּדָה הָעַצְמִית דְּ"מוֹדֶה אֲנִי" הַבָּאָה מִבְּחִינַת הַיְּחִידָה) מְחַיֶּה וּמַבְהִיר גַּם אֶת ד' בֵּיאוּרִים הַנַּ"ל שֶׁבְּפַשֵׁט-רֶמֶז-דְּרוּשׁ-סוֹד הַתּוֹרָה (הַמְבָאֲרִים אֶת הַפְּרָטִים דְּ"מוֹדֶה אֲנִי", כְּדִלְהַלָּן.

יב.

הַחַיּוּת שֶׁחֲסִידוּת מַכְנִיסָהּ בְּחֵלֶק הַ"פְּשָׁט" שֶׁבְּמוֹדֶה אֲנִי (שֶׁהַהוֹדָאָה הִיא עַל "שֶׁהֶחֱזַרְתָּ בִּי נִשְׁמָתִי") הוּא – הַהַדְגָּשָׁה בְּפֵירוּשׁ "נִשְׁמָתִי" נְשָׁמָה שֶׁלִּי. זֹאת אוֹמֶרֶת שֶׁכָּל הַהוֹדָאָה הִיא עַל הַחֲזָרַת נִשְׁמַת יְהוּדִי. וְאִילוּ הָיוּ מַחֲזִירִים לוֹ נְשָׁמָה אֲבָל אַחֶרֶת (דְּנָכְרִי וְעֶבֶדᵖᵍ) – אַף שֶׁגַּם אָז הָיָה יוֹצֵא מִכְּלַל (אֶחָד מִשִּׁשִּׁים בְּ)מִיתָה לְחַיִּים – לֹא הָיָה מוֹדֶה. כִּי מִצַּד הֶאָרַת הַיְּחִידָה, נִרְגָּשׁ אֶצְלוֹ שֶׁ"חַיִּים" הֵם – חַיִּים יְהוּדִיִּים דַּוְקָא [חַיּוּת שֶׁל **אָדָם** (אַתֶּם קְרוּיִים אָדָםᵖᵍ) אֲשֶׁר "רוּחַᵖᵈ בְּנֵי הָאָדָם הָעוֹלָה הִיא לְמַעְלָה"], וְחַיִּים בְּשָׂרַיִים **בִּפְנֵי עַצְמָם** [חַיּוּת שֶׁל בְּהֵמָה (עִם הַדּוֹמֶה לַחֲמוֹרᵖᵉ) אוֹ – נִקְרָא חֲמוֹרᵖᶠ) אֲשֶׁר "רוּחַᵖᵈ

Ezekiel 34:31, "You are my sheep, the sheep of my pasture, you are Man," to explain: "You are called 'man,' but idol-worshippers are not."]

109. Ecclesiastes 3:21.

110. In reference to a slave, see *Yevamot* 62a.

111. In reference to a non-Jew, see Ezekiel 23:20. See also *Shabbat* 150a, *Yevamot* 98a (and *Ketubot* 3b *Tosfot* s.v. *Lidrosh*) and elsewhere.

downwards") in *his estimation* is not life at all, and *he* has no reason to give thanks for it.

Though the physical life is assuredly also a very important state of existence[112]—especially if it is human life[113]—yet "all Israel are sons of Kings,[114] and the concept of "life" for a prince is his bond with his father, the King. If a prince were to be offered life, but one in which he would be torn from his father, the King, and brought to a stable to live as an animal, he would not only not enjoy such an existence, but on the contrary, he would be thoroughly disgusted by and despise his life.

(As is known in the famous story of Reb Yekusiel Liepler, when the Alter Rebbe wanted to give him a blessing for long life, Reb Yekusiel said: "But not with peasant years (not the life of peasants) who have eyes and do not see, ears and do not hear, who do not see the Divine and do not hear the Divine."[115] At first glance, though, this response is most surprising. When someone is offered a gift, and especially a great gift, it is not appropriate for him to say that he will not accept it unless the gift is made even larger. And inasmuch as long life itself is a great thing (especially in light of what was mentioned earlier—that the pleasure and benefit of life includes in itself all other pleasures and benefits in the world), how then could Reb Yekusiel stipulate conditions for the blessing?

The explanation, however, is that Reb Yekusiel's stipulation was not that the measure of the blessing be *increased*, but rather that his longevity should be a true existence of *living* days. For it

---

112. Genesis 1:29-30 and commentary of the Sages there.

[The verse states: "And G-d said: Behold I have given you every herb yielding seed which is upon the face of all the earth, and every tree in which is the fruit of a tree yielding seed; to you it shall be for food. And to every beast of the earth, and to every fowl of the heaven and to everything that crawls upon the earth, wherein there is a living soul, I have given every green herb for food. And it was so." Rashi comments, from *Sanhedrin* 59b,

that "He made equal the animals and the beasts as regards food, and He did not permit Adam and his wife to kill a creature and to eat its flesh..." Hence the sanctity of physical life in any form.]

113. Genesis 9:5-6 and commentary of the Sages there.

[The verse states: "And surely your blood of your lives will I demand; at the hands of every beast will I demand it; and at the hand of man, even at the hand of every man's brother will I demand the life

הַבְּהֵמָה הַיּוֹרֶדֶת הִיא לְמַטָּה"] – **בְּעֶרְכּוֹ** אֵינָם חַיִּים, **וְהוּא** –
אֵין לוֹ לְהוֹדוֹת עַל זֶה.

וְאַף שֶׁגַּם חַיִּים בְּשָׂרִיִּים הֵם מְצִיאוּת חֲשׁוּבָה בְּיוֹתֵר[פז]
וּבִפְרָט – שֶׁל מִין הַמְּדַבֵּר[פח], הֲרֵי כָּל יִשְׂרָאֵל בְּנֵי מְלָכִים הֵם[פט],
וְהַמּוּשַׂג שֶׁל "חַיִּים" אֵצֶל בֶּן מֶלֶךְ הוּא – הִתְקַשְּׁרוּתוֹ עִם
אָבִיו הַמֶּלֶךְ. וּבְאִם יִתְּנוּ לוֹ חַיִּים אֲבָל יְנַתְּקוּ אוֹתוֹ מֵאָבִיו
הַמֶּלֶךְ וְיַכְנִיסוּהוּ לְרֶפֶת לִחְיוֹת חַיֵּי בְּהֵמָה – הֲרֵי לֹא לְבַד
שֶׁלֹּא יִתְעַנֵּג בְּחַיּוּת זֶה, אֶלָּא אַדְּרַבָּה יִמְאַס וְיָקוּץ בְּחַיָּיו וכו'.

[וְכִידוּעַ הַסִּפּוּר מֵהֶחָסִיד רַבִּי יְקוּתִיאֵל לְיֶעפְּלֶער,
שֶׁכְּשֶׁרָצָה אַדְמוּ"ר הַזָּקֵן לְבָרְכוֹ בַּאֲרִיכוּת יָמִים, אָמַר: "אַבֶּער
נִיט מִיט פּוֹיֶעְרשֶׁע יָארֶן (לֹא חַיֵּי אִכָּר), וָואס עֵינַיִם לָהֶם וְלֹא
יִרְאוּ אָזְנַיִם לָהֶם וְלֹא יִשְׁמָעוּ, מֶען זֶעהט נִיט קֵיין
גֶעטְלִיכְקַייט אוּן מֶען הֶערט נִיט קֵיין גֶעטְלִיכְקַייט" (שֶׁאֵין
רוֹאִים וְשׁוֹמְעִים אֱלֹקוּת)[צ]. וְלִכְאוֹרָה תָּמוּהַּ: כְּשֶׁנּוֹתְנִים מַתָּנָה
לְאָדָם וּבִפְרָט מַתָּנָה גְּדוֹלָה, הֲרֵי אֵין מָקוֹם שֶׁיֹּאמַר שֶׁאֵינֶנּוּ
רוֹצֶה בָּהּ רַק בִּתְנַאי שֶׁהַמַּתָּנָה תִּהְיֶה גְּדוֹלָה עוֹד יוֹתֵר, וּמִכֵּיוָן
אֲשֶׁר גַּם אֲרִיכוּת יָמִים מִצַּד עַצְמָהּ הוּא דָּבָר גָּדוֹל בְּיוֹתֵר
(וּבִפְרָט שֶׁכַּנַּ"ל הֲנָאַת הַחַיּוּת כּוֹלֶלֶת אֶת כָּל הַהֲנָאוֹת
שֶׁבָּעוֹלָם), אֵיךְ הִתְנָה הָרַב יְקוּתִיאֵל תְּנָאִים בְּהַבְּרָכָה?

אַךְ הַבֵּיאוּר בָּזֶה, שֶׁתְּנָאוֹ שֶׁל הָרַב יְקוּתִיאֵל הָיָה לֹא
שֶׁיּוֹסִיפוּ לוֹ בְּהַבְּרָכָה, כִּי אִם שֶׁהָאֲרִיכוּת יָמִים תִּהְיֶה מְצִיאוּת
שֶׁל יְמֵי-חַיִּים. כִּי הָיָה מוּנָח (אַפְגֶעלֵייגְט) אֶצְלוֹ בִּפְשִׁיטוּת שֶׁכָּל

---

of man. He who sheds the blood of man,
by man shall his blood be shed; for in the
image of G-d made He man."

Rashi comments from *Bava Kama*
91b, that one is not allowed to take his or
her own life, or injure oneself.]

114. *Shabbat* 67a. Moreover, it is explained in the "*Inner Torah*"(*Zohar* II:26b;
Tikkunei Zohar, intro., beg.) that they are
actually *kings* (in their *inner* aspect).

115. *Hayom Yom* p. 102.

was absolutely basic and self-evident to him that all true existence and life consists in perceiving, seeing, and hearing G-dliness. Hence he made the condition, "But not with peasant years," because to him days and years without seeing and hearing the Divine could not be considered existence at all; on the contrary, he *despised* such days and years.)

Such a feeling comes only from the manifestation of the *Yechidah*. The four categories of *NaRaNaCh* are cast in a particular form (intellectual attributes, emotional attributes, etc.), and are, therefore, entities of a sort, and the Divinity in them is as an additional aspect, not of their essence. Consequently, these four levels also have a measure of accommodation and potentiality (albeit very subtle) for life without perceiving, seeing, and hearing G-dliness. In contrast, the level of *Yechidah*—which by definition is union with the Essence of G-d—gives utterly no allowance for, nor significance to, anything else but G-d.

XIII

RESURRECTION AS A DAILY PHENOMENON

It can be seen from this exposition of the simple meaning of *Modeh Ani* that Chasidus does not *add* another *interpretation* to the one already given in the *peshat* of *Modeh Ani* (for according to Chasidus also, the plain meaning is the thanksgiving for "restoring my soul within me"). Rather, Chasidus sharply clarifies and illumines this very meaning by emphasizing *what is* the soul (and vitality) of a Jew, and *for what* he gives thanks. The same holds true for the interpretations of *remez, drush,* and *sod* of *Modeh Ani*; Chasidus strikingly clarifies and illumines these same interpretations [as can be demonstrated through the following analysis]:

On the level of *remez*, the allusion to the Resurrection of the Dead in the restoration of the soul every morning (without the elucidation of Chasidus) is, it would appear, very remote. For (not only is sleep merely "one-sixtieth" of death and not actually death itself, but) the entire act of renewal in restoring the soul after sleep is restricted to the *reconnection* of the soul with the body; whereas the renewal at the time of the Resurrection of the Dead will affect both body and soul *proper*. Prior to the Resurrection, the *luz* bone will be

מְצִיאוּת הַחַיּוּת הוּא רְאִיַּת וּשְׁמִיעַת אֱלֹקוּת. וְלָכֵן הִתְנָה "אָבֶּער נִיט מִיט פּוֹיעֶרְשֶׁע יָאְרֶן", כִּי יָמִים וְשָׁנִים שֶׁאֵין רוֹאִים וְשׁוֹמְעִים אֱלֹקוּת לֹא הָיוּ נֶחְשָׁבִים אֶצְלוֹ לִמְצִיאוּת כְּלָל, וְאַדְרַבָּה – **מָאס** בְּיָמִים וְשָׁנִים כָּאֵלּוּ].

וְהַרְגֵּשׁ זֶה בָּא מִצַּד גִּלּוּי הַיְּחִידָה דַּוְקָא: מִצַּד ד' הַבְּחִינוֹת נֶפֶשׁ-רוּחַ-נְשָׁמָה-חַיָּה, מִכֵּיוָן שֶׁמְּצוּיָּירִים הֵם בְּאֵיזֶה צִיּוּר (מוֹחִין, מִדּוֹת כו'), הֲרֵי יֵשׁ בָּהֶם עִנְיָן לְעַצְמָם, וְעִנְיָן הָאֱלֹקוּת שֶׁבָּהֶם הוּא כְּמוֹ עוֹד דָּבָר, וּבְמֵילָא יֵשׁ בָּהֶם אֵיזֶה יַחַס וּנְתִינַת מָקוֹם (בְּדַקּוּת דְּדַקּוּת עַל כָּל פָּנִים) לְחַיִּים בְּלִי שֶׁשּׁוֹמֵעַ וְרוֹאֶה אֱלֹקוּת. מַה שֶּׁאֵין כֵּן בְּחִינַת הַיְּחִידָה, שֶׁכָּל עִנְיָנָהּ הוּא מַה שֶׁהִיא מְיֻחֶדֶת בְּעַצְמוּתוֹ יִתְבָּרֵךְ – אֵין בָּהּ שׁוּם נְתִינַת מָקוֹם לְשׁוּם עִנְיָן זוּלָתוֹ יִתְבָּרֵךְ.

יג.

כְּמוֹ שֶׁבַּחֵלֶק הַפְּשָׁט זֶה שֶׁבְּמוֹדֶה אֲנִי, אֵין הַחֲסִידוּת **מוֹסִיפָה** עוֹד **פֵּירוּשׁ** – נוֹסָף עַל הַפֵּירוּשׁ הַפָּשׁוּט (שֶׁהֲרֵי גַּם עַל פִּי חֲסִידוּת הַפֵּירוּשׁ דְּמוֹדֶה אֲנִי כִּפְשׁוּטוֹ – הוּא הוֹדָאָה עַל שֶׁהֶחֱזַרְתָּ בִּי נִשְׁמָתִי), אֶלָּא שֶׁמַּבְהִירָה וּמְאִירָה פֵּירוּשׁ זֶה עַצְמוֹ עַל יְדֵי הַדְגָּשָׁתָהּ **מַהִי** נִשְׁמָתוֹ (חַיּוּתוֹ) שֶׁל יְהוּדִי וְעַל **מָה** הִיא הוֹדָאָתוֹ, כֵּן הוּא בְּחֵלֶק הָרֶמֶז, הַדְּרוּשׁ וְהַסּוֹד שֶׁבְּמוֹדֶה אֲנִי, שֶׁהַחֲסִידוּת מְאִירָה וּמַבְהִירָה אֶת הַפֵּירוּשִׁים אֵלֶּה עַצְמָם.

הָרֶמֶז שֶׁבְּהַחֲזָרַת הַנְּשָׁמָה בַּבּוֹקֶר לִתְחִיַּת הַמֵּתִים (בְּלִי הַבֵּיאוּר שֶׁל חֲסִידוּת), הוּא רֶמֶז רָחוֹק בְּיוֹתֵר לִכְאוֹרָה, כִּי (נוֹסָף לָזֶה שֶׁהַשֵּׁינָה הִיא רַק אֶחָד מִשִּׁשִּׁים בְּמִיתָה וְלֹא מִיתָה מַמָּשׁ, הֲרֵי) כָּל הַחִידּוּשׁ שֶׁבְּהַחֲזָרַת הַנְּשָׁמָה לְאַחַר הַשֵּׁינָה הוּא רַק **בְּקִישּׁוּר** הַנְּשָׁמָה בַּגּוּף. וְאִילּוּ הַחִידּוּשׁ בִּתְחִיַּת הַמֵּתִים יִהְיֶה גַּם בְּהַגּוּף וְהַנְּשָׁמָה **עַצְמָם**: קוֹדֶם הַתְּחִיָּה יִשָׁאֵר מֵהַגּוּף רַק עֶצֶם לוּז בִּלְבָד*, וּמִזֶּה מוּבָן שֶׁגַּם בַּנְּשָׁמָה (שֶׁהַנְּשָׁמָה וְהַגּוּף

the only remnant left of the entire body,[116] and from this fact it follows that the soul also will undergo a fundamental change (since the soul and body are—in general—related and correspondent to each other). At the time of the Resurrection, a complete body will be constructed from this bone,[116] and in similar fashion, the soul will also pass through several stages until it, too, will be "built" and enter the body. And hence, the allusion to the Resurrection of the Dead in the morning restoration of the soul is but a faint representation.

Chasidus, however, proceeds to clarify and explain that even in the daily restoration of the soul, the renewal is not only a reconnection of the soul to the body, but is also, in fact, a regeneration of the body and soul *themselves* (which is why it is said that every morning a person becomes a *new* being).[117] This is because at every instant the entire creation is being brought into existence anew, literally, just as in the first six days of the original creation of the world.[118] (However, the Resurrection of the Dead is still indicated specifically in the morning restoration of the soul, because the precise expression and revelation of the continuous creation of the world *ex nihilo* [*yesh me'ayin*] is clearest in every morning.)[119]

One truly recognizes and feels this [constant creation *ex nihilo*] only through the revelation of the *Yechidah*. Since the four levels of *NaRaNaCh* are themselves inherently bounded by their respective

---

116. *Bereishit Rabbah* 28:3; *Zohar* II:28b. The *luz* bone [a bone located at the back of the neck] is *completely* different from the rest of the body. (See these references and their commentaries).

117. *Yalkut Shimoni, Tehillim,* 702; *Shulchan Aruch Harav* 6:1. See also *Eicha Rabbah* referred to in footnote 95.

118. See *Shaar Hayichud v'HaEmunah,* beg.
[Rabbi Schneur Zalman explains the concept of constant creation *ex nihilo* through the Baal Shem Tov's interpretation of Psalms 119:89, "Forever, O G-d, Your word stands firm in the heavens." "Your word," the Baal Shem Tov explains, means the original ten utter-

ances of G-d by which the world was created in the six days of creation. Furthermore, Rabbi Schneur Zalman explains, these words "stand firmly forever within the firmament of heaven and are forever clothed within all the heavens to give life to them... for if the letters were to depart [even] for an instant, G-d forbid, and return to their source, all the heavens would become naught and absolute nothingness, and it would be as though they had never existed at all... And so it is with all created things, in the upper and lower worlds."
In chapter 2, Rabbi Schneur Zalman points out the error of those who conceive of creation through the false analogy of "comparing the work of G-d, the Creator of heaven and earth, to the work of

הֵם – בִּכְלָל – בְּעֵרֶךְ וְשַׁיָּיכוּת זֶה לָזֶה) יִהְיֶה שִׁינּוּי עִיקָּרִי, וּבִזְמַן הַתְּחִיָּה, יִיבָּנֶה מֵעַצְם זֶה גּוּף שָׁלֵם¹¹⁸, וְעַל דֶּרֶךְ זֶה גַּם הַנְּשָׁמָה תַּעֲבוֹר דֶּרֶךְ כַּמָּה עִנְיָנִים עַד שֶׁ"תִּבָּנֶה" וְתִכָּנֵס בְּגוּפוֹ. וּבְמֵילָא הָרֶמֶז שֶׁבְּהַחֲזָרַת הַנְּשָׁמָה לִתְחִיַּת הַמֵּתִים – הוּא רַק סִימָן בְּעָלְמָא.

וּבָאָה תּוֹרַת הַחֲסִידוּת וּמְבָאֶרֶת, שֶׁגַּם בְּהַחֲזָרַת הַנְּשָׁמָה הַחִידּוּשׁ הוּא לֹא רַק בְּקִישּׁוּר הַנְּשָׁמָה בְּהַגּוּף, אֶלָּא גַּם בְּהַגּוּף וְהַנְּשָׁמָה **עַצְמָם** (שֶׁלָּכֵן אָמְרוּ שֶׁבְּכָל בּוֹקֶר נַעֲשֶׂה הָאָדָם בְּרִיָּה **חֲדָשָׁה**¹¹⁹). כִּי בְּכָל רֶגַע וָרֶגַע מִתְהַוֵּית כָּל הַבְּרִיאָה מֵחָדָשׁ מַמָּשׁ כְּמוֹ בְּמַעֲשֵׂה בְרֵאשִׁית¹¹²ⁱ. (אֶלָּא שֶׁמִּכָּל מָקוֹם נִרְמֶזֶת תְּחִיַּת הַמֵּתִים בְּהַחֲזָרַת הַנְּשָׁמָה שֶׁבַּבּוֹקֶר דַּוְקָא, כִּי בִּיטּוּי וְהִתְגַּלּוּת הַחִידּוּשׁ שֶׁל הַבְּרִיאָה שֶׁמִּתְהַוֵּית תָּמִיד מֵאַיִן לְיֵשׁ – הוּא בְּכָל בּוֹקֶר דַּוְקָא¹¹²ⁱ).

וַאֲמִיתִּית הָרֶגֶשׁ זֶה הוּא מִצַּד גִּילּוּי הַיְּחִידָה דַּוְקָא: ד' הַבְּחִינוֹת נֶפֶשׁ־רוּחַ־נְשָׁמָה־חַיָּה, מֵכֵּיוָן שֶׁהֵם עַצְמָם נִמְצָאִים בָּ"עוֹלָם" [נֶפֶשׁ – בַּעֲשִׂיָּה, רוּחַ – בִּיצִירָה, נְשָׁמָה – בִּבְרִיאָה וְחַיָּה – בַּאֲצִילוּת¹¹²²], הֲרֵי מַה שֶׁנִּרְגָּשׁ אֶצְלָם **בִּפְשִׁיטוּת** הוּא –

---

man and his schemes. For, when a gold-smith has made a vessel, that vessel is no longer dependent upon the smith, and even when his hands are removed from it and he goes away, the vessel remains in exactly the same image and form as when it left the hands of the smith. In the same way, these fools conceive the creation of heaven and earth. But their eyes are covered [and they fail] to see the great difference between the work of man and his schemes—which consists in making one thing out of another which already exists, merely changing the form and appearance from an ingot of silver to a vessel—and the making of heaven and earth, which is creation *ex nihilo*... With the withdrawal of the power of the Creator from the thing created, G-d forbid, it would revert to naught and complete non-existence. Rather, the activating force of the Creator must continuously be in the thing created to give it life and existence."]

119. See *Likkutei Torah, Achrei* 26a: "He renews [His works]...from absolute nothingness. No example or illustration at all of creation from nothingness may be found below in this physical world. One may only perceive this in minute form when the light of each new day breaks forth from the darkness of the night...which is thus somewhat like creation *ex nihilo*."

"worlds" (*Nefesh* in *Asiyah*; *Ruach* in *Yetzirah*; *Neshamah* in *Beriah*; and *Chaya* in *Atzilut*),[120] their *spontaneous* apprehension is the indisputable existence of their worlds. The feeling that there is no independent existence to the worlds whatsoever, and that their entire being is constantly created anew from utter nothingness is, on these four planes, a novel concept. Solely on the level of *Yechidah*,[121] which transcends all the worlds, is there an innate comprehension that all the worlds are absolute nothingness and that their entire existence is a completely new creation, which is continuously renewed at every moment.

XIV

OBSERVANCE OF THE MITZVOT FOR THEIR OWN SAKE

The manner in which Chasidus vitalizes and illuminates the level of *drush* of *Modeh Ani* [homiletic interpretation] may be seen through the following discussion:

The prohibition against withholding an article with which one has been entrusted [*pikadon*] on account of the debts of the depositor [*mafkid*] (without the elucidation of Chasidus), is also, it would appear, not comprehensible. For since the depositor owes money to the one to whom he entrusted the article, and since this guardian [*shomer*] has no other means of collecting his debt, then when the opportunity arises for the guardian to obtain what is rightfully his, why should he not seize it? What differentiates this case from that of an object which has been stolen from the guardian? If a stolen object cannot be recovered from the thief through the courts, the victim is allowed to tell another person to buy the object from the thief in order to regain it.[122]

---

120. *Shaar Hagilgulim*, beg., and elsewhere. [See footnote 45.]

121. To say that solely in *Yechidah* is there an innate feeling that all the worlds are as nothing does not contradict what is mentioned elsewhere (see *B'Sukkot Teishvu* (ch. 27); *Mi Yiten 5706* [*Sefer Hamaamarim 5706* pp. 29, 114], that (also) in *Atzilut*, Divinity is absolutely primary and intrinsic (*Elokut b'pshitut*),

and the worlds considered novel creations (*olamot b'hitchadshut*)—for in their *particular* aspects, the existence of the worlds begins from *Beriah*, but on the general level, even *Atzilut* is called the *World of Atzilut*. See also *Vayehi He'anan v'Hachoshech 5675* [in *B'Shaah Shehikdimu 5672* vol. 2, p. 934], where this distinction (between Divinity as absolutely and intrinsically felt, and Divinity as an acquired perception) is applied

מְצִיאוּת הָעוֹלָמוֹת. וְהַהֶרְגֵּשׁ שֶׁאֵין שׁוּם מְצִיאוּת לָעוֹלָמוֹת
וְכָל מְצִיאוּתָם מִתְחַדֶּשֶׁת תָּמִיד מֵאַיִן וְאֶפֶס הַמּוּחְלָט, הוּא
בְּדֶרֶךְ הִתְחַדְּשׁוּת אֶצְלָם. וְרַק בְּחִינַת הַיְּחִידָה⁵¹ שֶׁלְּמַעְלָה
מֵעוֹלָמוֹת, נִרְגָּשׁ אֶצְלָהּ בִּפְשִׁיטוּת שֶׁכָּל הָעוֹלָמוֹת הֵם אַיִן
וְאֶפֶס הַמּוּחְלָט וְכָל מְצִיאוּתָם הוּא חִידוּשׁ גָּמוּר שֶׁמִּתְחַדֵּשׁ
תָּמִיד בְּכָל רֶגַע וָרֶגַע.

יד.

הַחַיּוּת וְהַהַבְהָרָה שֶׁחֲסִידוּת מַכְנִיסָה בְּחֵלֶק הַדְּרוּשׁ
שֶׁבְּ"מוֹדֶה אֲנִי" הוּא:

הָאִיסוּר לְעַכֵּב פִּקָּדוֹן בְּעַד הַחוֹבוֹת שֶׁל הַמַּפְקִיד (בְּלִי
הַבֵּיאוּר שֶׁל חֲסִידוּת), אֵין לוֹ הֲבָנָה לִכְאוֹרָה: מִכֵּיוָן
שֶׁהַמַּפְקִיד חַיָּיב לוֹ מָמוֹן, וְאֵין לוֹ דֶּרֶךְ לְהִפָּרַע מִמֶּנּוּ, הֲרֵי
כְּשֶׁבָּאָה לְיָדוֹ הַהִזְדַּמְנוּת לְקַבֵּל אֶת הַמַּגִּיעַ לוֹ – לָמָּה לֹא יַצִּיל
אוֹתָהּ? וּמַאי שְׁנָא מֵחֵפֶץ הַגָּזוּל מִמֶּנּוּ, שֶׁבָּאם אֵינוֹ יָכוֹל
לְהוֹצִיאוֹ מֵהַגַּזְלָן עַל יְדֵי בֵית דִּין, מוּתָּר לוֹ לוֹמַר לְאַחֵר
שֶׁיִּקְנֶה אֶת הַחֵפֶץ מֵהַגַּזְלָן בִּכְדֵי לְהַצִּיל עַל יָדוֹ אֶת הַגְּזֵילָה⁵²?

וּבָאָה תּוֹרַת הַחֲסִידוּת וּמְבָאֶרֶת, שֶׁכָּל הַמִּצְוֹת, גַּם הַמִּצְוֹת

---

to the following situations: before the *tzimtzum* and after it; to Adam in the Garden of Eden; and also to great *tzaddikim*, etc. And thus it will be in the *Future Time*. [In the Era of Moshiach, the entire world will be on this sublime level where Divinity is innately and absolutely felt.] Hence, there are numerous levels in the application of this concept.

[That is, the category of feeling Divinity innately and fundamentally (*Elokut b'pshitut*) is applied to many levels relative to what is under particular consideration. There are numerous uses of the terms.

Thus it is no contradiction that in certain contexts, *Atzilut* is also said to be on this level and not just *Yechidah* alone. *Yechidah*, however, is the highest degree of this level of *Elokut b'pshitut*.]

122. In terms of one's responsibility to the buyer there is, however, (*a different* prohibition:) the prohibition against putting a stumbling block before the blind (*S'meh* on *Choshen Mishpat* 146:39). But regarding retrieving one's object in this manner, there is no prohibition involved.

Chasidus explains that the fundamental principle of all the commandments, even those which have a discernible logic and intelligible reason, is the Supernal Will which transcends reason[123] (for the Divine Will, even when it is embodied in reason, retains its own nature and abstractness).[124] Therefore, even the rational commandments which are called *mishpatim* ["judgments" or "ordinances"] must be fulfilled primarily because they are the Will of the Creator, in the manner of *kabbalat ol* ["acceptance of the yoke"]; that is, in the same manner in which the commandments called *chukim*[125] [the supra-rational statutes] are fulfilled. (Nevertheless, it should be clear that those commandments which *do* contain a discernible reason, inasmuch as the Supernal Will within them has enclothed itself in reason—which is why they are called *in the Torah* by the name of *mishpatim*—must be fulfilled[126] for the sake of their intellectual reason as well.)[127]

---

123. *Lech 5666*, end [*Yom Tov Shel Rosh HaShana 5666*, p. 67]; and elsewhere. [There it explains that the rational is not the highest faculty of man; *ratzon* (will) precedes it.]

124. *Ve'ani Tefilati 5694 (Kuntres 27)*. [*Sefer Hamaamarim Kuntreisim*, vol. 2, p. 311. The term "abstractness" describes the primitive *ratzon*, before it is embodied in reason. See footnote 27.]

125. *L'maan Daat 5690*, ch. 5 [*Sefer Hamaamarim Kuntreisim* vol. 1 p. 84]; *Havaya Li Beozro 5691 (5687)* ch. 3 [ibid. p. 180]; *Sefer Hamaamarim Yiddish*, p. 46; and elsewhere.

[There are three categories of commandments in the Torah: 1) *Edut*; 2) *Mishpatim*; 3) *Chukim*. *Edut* (testimonials) commemorate the great events in Israel's history, such as *Pesach*, which commemorates the Exodus from Egypt. *Mishpatim* (judgments, ordinances) are laws that deal with man's just relation to man, and which are apprehensible through human reason. *Chukim* ("decreed statutes") are those *mitzvot* that are not comprehensible through reason, such as the laws of *Kashrut*.

Chasidus explains that the root of all these categories and their essence is G-d's Supernal Will, which transcends human reason, and thus *all* commandments must be performed with this awareness and intention.]

126. But the *foundation* and *basis* of their fulfillment must be in a manner of *kabbalat ol*, acceptance of G-d's Will, for *all* of the commandments are G-d's Supernal *Will*, as stated in the text. (It should be noted that also concerning *Mishpatim* our Sages said: "'Before them' [the Jewish courts]—and not before the non-Jewish courts... even if their law is the same as the Jewish law." [One is not allowed to take cases to the non-Jewish courts.] *Gittin* 88b; *Shulchan Aruch, Choshen Mishpat* beg. 26.

And furthermore: even the fact that the commandments of "*mishpatim*" must also be fulfilled for the sake of their reason is because G-d so *decreed* that His Will embodied in these commandments should also be enclothed in "reason."* See

---

* *Specifically through this [fulfillment of the rational commandments not just for the*

שֶׁיֵּשׁ עֲלֵיהֶם טַעַם, עִיקָרָם הוּא – רָצוֹן הָעֶלְיוֹן שֶׁלְּמַעְלָה
מֵהַטַּעַם‏צח (כִּי הָרָצוֹן, גַּם כְּשֶׁהוּא בָּא בְּטַעַם, נִשְׁאָר הוּא
בְּמַהוּתוֹ וּבִפְשִׁיטוּתוֹ‏צט). שֶׁלָּכֵן גַּם הַמִּצְוֹת דְּ"מִשְׁפָּטִים", צָרִיךְ
לְקַיְּימָם מִצַּד צִיוּוּי הַבּוֹרֵא בְּדֶרֶךְ קַבָּלַת עוֹל כְּמוֹ הַמִּצְוֹת
דְּ"חוּקִים"‏ק (אֶלָּא שֶׁהַמִּצְוֹת שֶׁיֵּשׁ עֲלֵיהֶם טַעַם, מִכֵּיוָן שֶׁרָצוֹן
הָעֶלְיוֹן שֶׁבָּהֶם נִתְלַבֵּשׁ גַּם בְּטַעַם (שֶׁלָּכֵן נִקְרָאִים הֵם בַּתּוֹרָה
בְּשֵׁם "מִשְׁפָּטִים"), צָרִיךְ לִהְיוֹת קִיּוּמָם גַּם‏קא מִצַּד הַטַּעַם שֶׁכְלִי
שֶׁבָּהֶם‏קב).

Likkutei Sichot vol. 8, pp. 130-31 at length.

127. Note *Shemonah Perakim L'ha-Rambam*, ch. 6 (quoted in *Derech Mitz-votecha* 84b), that concerning those evils that even logic dictates as evil, one must say, "I do not desire to do it."

Thus we can understand the Sages' statement (*Eruvin* 100b): "If He had not given the Torah (G-d forbid*) we would have learned modesty from the cat and laws of theft from the ant..." Seemingly, one might ask, what is the point of this saying [since the Torah already *has* been given]?

---

sake of their reason, but in submission to G-d's Will], Yechidah *is more revealed— even more than through fulfillment of* chu-kim, *which can only be performed amidst* kabbalat ol. *For it is specifically this that expresses that the fulfillment of the com-mandments is due to the essence of the soul, and hence one's intellect is also affected, since the "essence" is found in all the details, as will be explained in Chapter XVII below.*

* So Rabbi Shalom DovBer of Lu-bavitch used to add (in a whisper) when he would quote this saying of the Sages.

[That is, since the Torah already has been given, why do the Sages present us with a seemingly irrelevant and merely hypothetical case? The answer to this question is that even though the Torah lays down the laws of morality, we should nevertheless also use our own powers of reason in these areas and learn what we can from the behavior of animals and na-ture, thus fulfilling the Torah's laws for the sake of their logic as well.

This answer can be understood in light of *Shemonah Perakim L'haRambam*, ch. 6, where *Rambam* discusses the appar-ent contradiction between the point of view held by the philosophers and that held by the Sages, concerning the differ-ence between the saintly (or highly ethical man), and he who by struggle subdues his passions and practices self-restraint. The philosophers rank the former, who acts from a disposition to be moral without having any inclination to do evil, as su-perior to the latter, who has such in-clinations but must overcome his passions in order to act morally. For it would seem that one who by nature has no desire to do evil is far superior to one who does have such a nature.

The Sages say, however, that one who struggles and only with great difficulty

Now since the essence of all the commandments is G-d's Will, and He and His Will are one, therefore, just as it is impossible to say that G-d exists for the sake of some other purpose, G-d forbid, similarly His commandments do not exist for the sake of any other purpose. Their sole end and purpose is—themselves. In reference to our subject, the commandment to return an article given for safekeeping: The goal of the commandment is not (only) for the benefit of the depositor (that his article should be freely and completely returned to him), but the act of restoration itself is the end and purpose.

Therefore, even though the depositor owes money to the guardian and does not repay him this debt, there are still no grounds for maintaining that the guardian should withhold the object with which he has been entrusted, because he is obligated in the *mitzvah* of restoration.[128]

---

overcomes his evil inclination, is more praiseworthy than he who does not exert such efforts, and has a greater reward. Furthermore, the Sages forbid one to say, "I, by my nature, do not desire to commit such and such a transgression." Rather, one should say, "I do indeed want to commit the trangression, yet I must not, for my Father in heaven has forbidden it."

Rambam, however, further notes that in fact, the positions of the philosophers and the Sages really do not contradict each other at all. Both are correct and in agreement—but only in relation to those evils which the philosophers term evil through the use of reason, and of which it is commonly agreed that they are evil, such as murder, theft, robbery, fraud, etc. One who has no inclination to commit these types of evil is indeed superior to he who does desire to do them, but conquers his passions. In the Torah, this category of evil is prohibited by those commandments called *mishpatim* (the rational laws, as explained above in fn. 125).

However, when the Sages maintain that one who does have a desire for evil but overcomes his inclinations is superior to and has a greater reward than one who

does not, they are referring to the prohibitions in the category of laws called *chukim*, the non-rational statutes (such as mixing meat and milk, etc.). Were it not for the Torah's prohibitions against them, they would not rationally be considered transgressions. Regarding these, *Rambam* says, a man should allow himself to "retain" his natural inclination for them, but yet overcome it because of G-d's law. (It should be noted, however, that a *baal teshuvah*—one who has already had an experience with the transgression—should not allow himself such inclinations. —R. DovBer, the Maggid of Mezritch, cited in *Likkutei Torah, Va'etchanan* 9d.)

Concerning all that human reason dictates is evil, one of course must say, "I do not desire to do it"; one who does have such a desire is in this case (*mishpatim*) inferior. Regarding *chukim*, however, one who has such a desire but overcomes it is superior. This is also why the Sages state the seemingly irrelevant information that we would have learned the rules of morality from animals had the Torah (G-d forbid) not been given. They meant to convey the very practical message that we should still apply our own reason to these types of laws (*mishpatim*), and fulfill them

וּמִכֵּיוָן שֶׁכָּל הַמִּצְוֹת, עִנְיָנָם הוּא – רְצוֹן הַקָּדוֹשׁ בָּרוּךְ הוּא,
שֶׁהוּא יִתְבָּרֵךְ וּרְצוֹנוֹ אֶחָד, הֲרֵי כְּשֵׁם שֶׁבּוֹ יִתְבָּרֵךְ אֵין שַׁיָּיךְ
לוֹמַר שֶׁהוּא בִּשְׁבִיל אֵיזוֹ תַּכְלִית אַחֶרֶת חַס וְשָׁלוֹם, כֵּן גַּם
מִצְוֹתָיו אֵינָם בִּשְׁבִיל אֵיזוֹ תַּכְלִית אַחֶרֶת כִּי אִם כָּל תַּכְלִיתָם
הוּא – הֵם עַצְמָם. וּבַנּוֹגֵעַ לְעִנְיָנֵינוּ – מִצְוַת הַשָּׁבַת פִּקְדוֹן:
מַטְּרַת הַמִּצְוָה אֵינָהּ (רַק) בִּשְׁבִיל טוֹבַת הַמַּפְקִיד (שֶׁיּוּחֲזַר לוֹ
מָמוֹנוֹ בִּשְׁלֵימוּת), אֶלָּא הַהֲשָׁבָה עַצְמָהּ הִיא הַמַּטָּרָה וְהַתַּכְלִית.

וְלָכֵן, גַּם כְּשֶׁהַמַּפְקִיד חַיָּיב לוֹ מָמוֹן וְאֵינוֹ מַחֲזִיר לוֹ אֶת
חוֹבוֹ – אֵין מָקוֹם לוֹמַר שֶׁיְעַכֵּב אֶת פִּקְדוֹנוֹ, כִּי מְחוּיָּיב הוּא
בְּמִצְוַת הַהֲשָׁבָה[קיג].

---

for the sake of their intellectual reason—as well as for the reason that the Torah simply tells us to do so.]

128. In *K'tzot Hachoshen* sect. 4 on *Choshen Mishpat* 340, it is stated that as long as the deposited article is safe, there is no obligation upon the guardian to return it (and only through neglect—or if it is lost or stolen in the case of a *shomer sachar*—does he *then* have an obligation to return and compensate for it in full). However, in *Shulchan Aruch Harav* (443, *Kuntres Acharon* sub-para. 2) it states: "When the *shomer chinam* is liable for negligence, the obligation is not by reason of the negligence itself; but rather, from the moment the article is given to him, he is obligated to return it intact to the depositor at the proper time. If, however, within that time it is lost, not through the negligence of the guardian, the Torah has pity on him and releases him from his obligation." And on the basis of what is written in *Kuntres Acharon*, ibid., we can understand the words of *Yam Shel Shlomo* (quoted in *K'tzot Hachoshen*, ibid.), "As soon as one becomes a guardian, his case is identical as "I don't know if I returned it."

[To clarify, three of the four categories of the guardian (*shomer*) listed in the Talmud are relevant here: 1) *shomer chinam*—one who undertakes safekeeping without compensation and is responsible only for loss or damage incurred due to his negligence; 2) *shomer sachar*—one who is paid for guarding the object and is obligated to pay for its loss, theft, and his negligence (he is only exempted in the case of accident); 3) *shoel*—one who borrows the object and has to pay for whatever happens, except in the case of its "death" in the course of work.

The nature of the obligation to return the deposited article is the subject of a dispute: *K'tzot Hachoshen* maintains that the guardian has no obligation to return the object until something happens to it. *Shulchan Aruch Harav* maintains, however, that the obligation is incumbent upon him from the moment he receives it, regardless of whether or not something happens to it—simply because he has a *mitzvah* of returning it. This corresponds to the point which is made in the text: that there is no basis for maintaining that one can withhold the entrusted object for the debts of the depositor, for one is obligated in the *mitzvah* of restoration.

As explained earlier, one who bor-

The true feeling and genuine recognition of this [unembodied Will of G-d] comes solely through the *Yechidah*. For since the ties of the *NaRaNaCh* to their Creator are (relative to and) dependent upon *their* particular forms, their comprehension of the Supernal Will is also limited to the extent that it is embodied in some form. Only the *Yechidah*, which has no form or desires of its own whatsoever, and whose attachment to Divinity is from and for the sake of *Divinity* alone, comprehends within itself the true essence of the Supernal Will in its absolute simplicity—that its sole purpose is the Will itself.

XV

THE CHASIDIC ILLUMINATION OF KABBALAH

Everything explained previously regarding the illumination and vitality which Chasidus brings to the interpretations of *peshat, remez* and *drush* similarly applies to the "esoteric" level [*sod*] of *Modeh Ani*.

In the Kabbalistic interpretation, the words "living and eternal King" represent the attribute of *malchut* ["sovereignty," "kingship"] as it is united with the attribute of *yesod* ["foundation"], and it is from this level that the restoration of the soul comes. Chasidus proceeds to clarify and explicate this idea with rational explanations and elucidations. (And this is true of all the concepts of Kabbalah—their rationally comprehensible explanation comes solely through Chasidus, as discussed earlier in Chapter I.) Furthermore, through the explanations of Chasidus, the inner meaning of the interpretation is perceived, and the idea "lives" in a completely different manner.

---

rows an animal (*shoel*), unlike the other categories of guardians, is liable even for accidents. The Torah does, however, release him from his obligation to pay if the animal dies in the course of its work.

Now, in a case where the *shoel* is in doubt if the animal died in the course of its work or for other reasons, the authorities differ as to whether or not he is liable for compensation. *Nimukei Yosef* maintains that he is exempt since the obligation is of a doubtful nature. The owner of the animal can be compared to a creditor who claims money, and the debtor is in doubt if he had ever borrowed the money; in such a case, the debtor is exempt from payment. *Yam Shel Shlomo* takes issue and argues that the *shoel* is indeed liable, for this case is comparable to a different scenario, wherein the debtor replies in response to the creditor's claim, "I don't know if I *returned* the money or not"—a scenario where he would be obligated to pay (since he conceded the loan). Our situation, says *Yam Shel Shlomo*, is as if the *shoel* had said, "I don't know if I re-

וַאֲמִתִּית הָרֶגֶשׁ זֶה הוּא מִצַּד הַיְחִידָה דַּוְקָא. כִּי
נֶפֶשׁ-רוּחַ-נְשָׁמָה-חַיָּה, מִכֵּיוָן שֶׁהִתְקַשְּׁרוּתָם בַּהַבּוֹרֵא הוּא (כְּפִי
וּ)מִצַּד צִיּוּרָם הֵם, גַּם תְּפִיסָתָם בָּרָצוֹן הָעֶלְיוֹן הוּא כְּמוֹ שֶׁהוּא
מְלוּבָּשׁ בְּצִיּוּר. וְרַק הַיְחִידָה שֶׁאֵין בָּהּ צִיּוּר וּמְבוּקָּשׁ לְעַצְמָהּ
כְּלָל, וְהִתְקַשְּׁרוּתָהּ לֶאֱלֹקוּת הוּא מִצַּד **אֱלֹקוּת** – נִרְגָּשׁ בָּהּ
אֲמִתַּת מַהוּתוֹ שֶׁל רָצוֹן הָעֶלְיוֹן כְּמוֹ שֶׁהוּא בִּפְשִׁיטוּתוֹ, אֲשֶׁר
תַּכְלִיתוֹ הוּא הָרָצוֹן עַצְמוֹ.

טו.

עַל דֶּרֶךְ זֶה הוּא גַּם בְּחֵלֶק הַ"סוֹד" שֶׁבְּ"מוֹדֶה אֲנִי":

הַפֵּירוּשׁ שֶׁבְּקַבָּלָה שֶׁ"מֶלֶךְ" חַי וְקַיָּם" הוּא סְפִירַת
הַמַּלְכוּת כְּמוֹ שֶׁמְּיוּחֶדֶת עִם סְפִירַת הַיְסוֹד, וְשֶׁמִּבְּחִינָה זוֹ
בָּאָה הַחֲזָרַת הַנְּשָׁמָה, הִנֵּה נוֹסַף לָזֶה שֶׁחֲסִידוּת מְבָאֶרֶת
וּמַסְבִּירָה אוֹתוֹ בְּבֵיאוּרִים וְהֶסְבֵּרִים שִׂכְלִיִּים (כְּכָל הָעִנְיָנִים
שֶׁבְּקַבָּלָה, שֶׁבֵּיאוּרָם בְּשֵׂכֶל הוּא עַל יְדֵי הַחֲסִידוּת דַּוְקָא,
כַּנַּ"ל סוֹף סְעִיף א), הִנֵּה עוֹד זֹאת, שֶׁעַל יְדֵי הַבֵּיאוּר שֶׁל
חֲסִידוּת, נִרְגָּשׁ תּוֹכְנוּ הַפְּנִימִי שֶׁל הַפֵּירוּשׁ וְחַי הָעִנְיָן בְּאוֹפֶן
אַחֵר לְגַמְרֵי.

---

turned the object or not," and therefore he is obligated to pay.

The opinion of *Yam Shel Shlomo* can be understood in light of *Shulchan Aruch Harav's* perception that a guardian's obligation commences the moment he is entrusted with the article. Hence, any doubt that arises is comparable to the case where he claims, "I don't know if I *discharged* my obligation," since the guardian concedes that an obligation did exist. *K'tzot Hachoshen* maintains that the guardian has no obligation until something happens. Therefore, if there is a doubt concerning the nature of the accident, it is comparable to the situation where a doubt exists if there ever was an obligation. The position of *K'tzot* is entirely at odds with that of *Yam Shel Shlomo.*

Thus, we see that according to *Shulchan Aruch Harav* and *Yam Shel Shlomo* there is indeed an obligation upon the *shoel,* and consequently he is not permitted to withhold the object for payment of his debts, since the *mitzvah* of restoration would not be fulfilled without returning the article.]

Chasidus accomplishes this clarification of the Kabbalistic interpretation by explaining that the attribute of *malchut* is that level of Divinity which is related to the world; therefore, the boundaries of space and time issue from (and apply to) *malchut*. The attribute of *yesod*, conversely, is an aspect of Divinity which is above the realm of relation to the world. Thus, in *all* of the Divine attributes preceding *malchut*, the limitations of space and time do not exist.[129] (And as a result of the manifestation of those attributes, time and space are completely nullified.) The concept of the union of *malchut* with *yesod*, then, is the revelation of the light of the *Ein Sof* which *transcends* the worlds, within the level of G-dliness that is vested *in* the world.

This is the meaning of the statement that the restoration of the soul comes from the level of "living and eternal King": The restoration of the soul every morning means the making of a completely *new* being (as explained in Chapter XIII). Creation *ex nihilo* [*yesh me'ayin*—"something from nothing"] is actualized specifically through the attribute of *malchut* (for the attributes above *malchut* cannot give rise to any independent existence). Nevertheless, the power of *malchut* to create *ex nihilo* must come from the Essence of the *Or* [light of the] *Ein Sof*,[130] which transcends the realm of that which can relate to the worlds. For since the Essence of the *Or Ein Sof* is absolutely transcendent, it is consequently not restricted even to the categories of "nothing" and "something," and it therefore has the power to transform "nothing" into "something." That is not true, however, of the light that is relative of the worlds; it is confined, so to speak, within these limitations.

And this recognition [that creation *ex nihilo* comes from the Essence of G-d] comes to a person through his *Yechidah*. There are two concepts herein: 1) The apprehension of the Essence of the *Or Ein*

---

129. *Shaar Hayichud v'haEmunah*, ch. 7 (82a), and elsewhere.

[As explained in footnote 97, *malchut* is the last and "lowest" of the Divine attributes, or *Sefirot*, and is the instrument through which all that is latent and potential emerges into manifest reality, actuality, existence. As *Shaar Hayichud* explains further, *malchut* is the attribute which brings the world into existence and sustains it as a seemingly independent and separate entity. "World" refers here to that which possesses the dimensions of space and time, space and time themselves being creations *ex nihilo* from *malchut*.]

130. See *Igeret Hakodesh* epistle 20: "His Essence and His being... He alone..."

בֵּיאוּר פֵּירוּשׁ זֶה עַל פִּי חֲסִידוּת:

סְפִירַת הַמַּלְכוּת הִיא בְּחִינַת הָאֱלֹקוּת הַשַּׁיֶּכֶת לָעוֹלָם, וְלָכֵן נִמְשָׁכוֹת מִמֶּנָּה (וְשַׁיָּיכִים בָּהּ) גִּדְרֵי הַמָּקוֹם וְהַזְּמַן. וּסְפִירַת הַיְסוֹד הִיא בְּחִינַת הָאֱלֹקוּת שֶׁלְּמַעְלָה מִגֶּדֶר שַׁיָּיכוּת לָעוֹלָם, שֶׁלָּכֵן, בְּכָל הַמִּדוֹת שֶׁלְּמַעְלָה מִסְּפִירַת הַמַּלְכוּת אֵין שַׁיָּיךְ בָּהֶם גִּדְרֵי הַמָּקוֹם וְהַזְּמַן[קז] (וּמִצַּד גִּילּוּי מִדּוֹת אֵלּוּ, מִתְבַּטְלִים הַזְּמַן וְהַמָּקוֹם מִמְּצִיאוּתָם לְגַמְרֵי). וְעִנְיַן יִחוּד הַמַּלְכוּת עִם הַיְסוֹד הוּא – גִּילּוּי אוֹר אֵין סוֹף שֶׁלְּמַעְלָה מֵעוֹלָמוֹת בִּבְחִינַת הָאֱלֹקוּת הַמִּתְלַבֶּשֶׁת בָּעוֹלָם.

וְזֶהוּ מַה שֶּׁהַחְזָרַת הַנְּשָׁמָה בָּאָה מִבְּחִינַת "מֶלֶךְ חַי וְקַיָּים": הַחְזָרַת הַנְּשָׁמָה שֶׁבְּכָל בּוֹקֶר, הוּא עִנְיַן בְּרִיָּה חֲדָשָׁה (כַּנַּ"ל סָעִיף י"ג), וְהַחִידוּשׁ יֵשׁ מֵאַיִן, עִם הֱיוֹת שֶׁבְּפוֹעַל בָּא הוּא מִבְּחִינַת הַמַּלְכוּת דַּוְקָא (כִּי מִצַּד הַמִּדּוֹת שֶׁלְּמַעְלָה מִמִּדַּת הַמַּלְכוּת לֹא הָיָה מְצִיאוּת יֵשׁ כְּלָל), בְּכָל זֶה, הַכֹּחַ שֶׁבְּמַלְכוּת לְחַדֵּשׁ יֵשׁ מֵאַיִן הוּא דַּוְקָא מֵעַצְמוּת אוֹר אֵין סוֹף[קח] שֶׁלְּמַעְלָה מִגֶּדֶר שַׁיָּיכוּת לָעוֹלָמוֹת, וּבְמֵילָא אֵינוֹ בְּהַגְדָּרִים דְּ"אַיִן" וְ"יֵשׁ", וְלָכֵן בִּיכָלְתּוֹ לַעֲשׂוֹת אֶת הָ"אֵינוֹ" "יֶשְׁנוֹ". מַה שֶׁאֵין כֵּן בְּחִינַת הָאוֹר הַשַּׁיָּיךְ לָעוֹלָמוֹת, מוּגְדָּר הוּא כִּבְיָכוֹל בְּהַגְדָּרוֹת אֵלּוּ.

וְהַכָּרָה זוֹ בָּאָה לְהָאָדָם מִצַּד בְּחִינַת הַיְחִידָה שֶׁבּוֹ. וּשְׁנֵי עִנְיָנִים בָּזֶה: (א) הַהַכָּרָה בְּעַצְמוּת אוֹר אֵין סוֹף אֶפְשָׁרִית רַק

(130a ff.). There, however, the explanation is in a different manner.

[Rabbi Schneur Zalman explains creation of *yesh me'ayin* ("something from nothing") from the Essence of G-d thus: The feeling of a created being (*yesh*) that it is independent and self-existing, i.e., that it has no source, can come only as a result of a level which itself has no

source—"for the light is like its source, i.e., the nature and essence of the Emanator, whose Being is of His Essence, and He is not, G-d forbid, caused by some other cause preceding Himself. He alone, therefore, has it in His power and ability to create something out of absolute nothingness, without this 'something' having any other cause preceding it."]

Sof—the transcendent—is possible only through that level of the soul which itself is united with His Essence. (The four levels of *NaR-aNaCh*, in contrast, are related to the level of G-dliness which is manifest in the worlds.); 2) The true *recognition* of the meaning of creation *ex nihilo* is that one should deeply *realize* (and not simply understand intellectually) that there is utterly no possibility for any independent, separate existence, and that every existence is a completely new creation from Divinity—from which it necessarily follows that this creation *ex nihilo* comes from the Essence of the *Or Ein Sof.* Such recognition is possible only by virtue of the level of *Yechidah*, as explained previously in Chapter XIII.

XVI

CHASIDUS AS THE LINK BETWEEN ALL LEVELS OF INTERPRETATION

The Chasidic explanations of the four levels of *Pardes* in *Modeh Ani* are all interrelated:

A person's realization that the creation of "something from nothing" comes from the Essence of the *Or Ein Sof*, which transcends all the worlds—the explanation of the "esoteric" interpretation of *Modeh Ani*—intensifies his awareness that all the worlds are constantly being created from *utter nothingness*,[131] which is the in-

---

131. The recognition that creation comes from the Essence of *Or Ein Sof* derives from (and is compelled by) the recognition that the worlds are created *ex nihilo* (as explained above in Chapter XV). Nevertheless, since the realization of creation *ex nihilo* produces the realization that creation comes from the Essence of *Or Ein Sof*, this latter recognition in turn not only *intensifies* the understanding of creation *ex nihilo* but further adds to its depth. For the understanding of creation *ex nihilo* in itself [without the knowledge that it comes from the Essence of G-d] is (as explained above, Chapter XV) that "there is no possibility whatsoever for any *independent*, separate being of itself..." But this definition does not yet prove that there is also no basis for the world's existence even in relation to the "Light" that creates it (see next footnote). However, through the recognition that creation comes from the Essence of *Or Ein Sof* which transcends all the worlds, one subsequently realizes that even in relation to the Light that creates the world, the world is "nonexistent." And as a result, even after "it arose in the Divine Will to create...," the creation of the world at every instant is *totally new*.

[The question being addressed is this: How can it be said here in Chapter XVI that knowledge of creation from the Essence of G-d intensifies one's awareness of creation *ex nihilo*—when in Chapter XV we said just the opposite, that it was the recognition of creation as *ex nihilo* that leads one to realize that creation is from

מִצַּד בְּחִינָה זוֹ שֶׁל הַנְּשָׁמָה הַמְיוּחֶדֶת בְּעַצְמוּתוֹ יִתְבָּרֵךְ (מַה
שֶׁאֵין כֵּן ד' הַבְּחִינוֹת נֶפֶשׁ־רוּחַ־נְשָׁמָה־חַיָּה, שֶׁיִּכוּתָם הוּא
לִבְחִינַת הָאֱלֹקוּת שֶׁבָּעוֹלָמוֹת). **(ב)** גַּם אֲמִיתִּית **הַהַכָּרָה**
בְּהִתְחַדֵּשׁ דְּיֵשׁ מֵאַיִן, **שֶׁיַּכִּיר** (וְלֹא רַק שֶׁיָּבִין) שֶׁאֵין שׁוּם
נְתִינַת מָקוֹם לְהַיֵּשׁ מִצַּד עַצְמוֹ וְכָל מְצִיאוּתוֹ הוּא מְחוּדָּשׁ
מֵהָאֱלֹקוּת – הַמַּכְרִיחָה שֶׁהַהִתְחַדֵּשׁ בָּא מֵעַצְמוּת אוֹר אֵין סוֹף
– בָּאָה מִצַּד בְּחִינַת הַיְחִידָה דַּוְקָא, כַּנַּ"ל סְעִיף י"ג.

טז.

הַבֵּיאוּרִים שֶׁבַּחֲסִידוּת בְּד' חֶלְקֵי הַפְּשָׁט־רֶמֶז־דְּרוּשׁ־סוֹד
שֶׁבְּ"מוֹדֶה אֲנִי" – קְשׁוּרִים זֶה בָּזֶה:

הַכָּרַת הָאָדָם שֶׁהַהִתְחַדֵּשׁ יֵשׁ מֵאַיִן בָּא הוּא מֵעַצְמוּת אוֹר
אֵין סוֹף שֶׁלְּמַעְלָה מֵעוֹלָמוֹת – הַבֵּיאוּר בְּחֵלֶק הַ"סּוֹד"
שֶׁבְּמוֹדֶה אֲנִי – מְחַזֶּקֶת אֶת הַהַכָּרָה שֶׁכָּל הָעוֹלָמוֹת
מִתְחַדְּשִׁים תָּמִיד **מֵאַיִן וָאֶפֶס** הַמּוּחְלָט[טו] – הַבֵּיאוּר בְּחֵלֶק

---

the Essence of G-d.

To answer: there are two levels, so to speak, of one's understanding of the meaning of creation *ex nihilo*. The first level, the recognition that all creation is *ex nihilo*, leads one to realize that therefore creation must come from the Essence of G-d, and not from any "reflection" of His Light. But this recognition in turn casts new light on and gives one a deeper understanding of the meaning of creation *ex nihilo* in the following manner:

Without knowing that this creation *ex nihilo* comes indeed from the Essence of G-d, we only understand its meaning by saying that there is no basis for any separate existence *in itself*. However, in relation to its *source*—to that "Light" which created existence—we might perhaps believe that the world does have a prior basis; un-

til we realize that the source of all being is the very Essence of G-d, we do not know that existence has no basis even in regards to its source (which is *malchut*).

Before comprehending this latter fact, creation *ex nihilo* only meant that any separate, independent existence has to be created and does not have its own basis. With this understanding alone, though, we could assume that once brought into being, creation does possess an independent ground within its own source (*malchut*). However, since we now know that its source—the "Light" that created it—is also nothing in itself, and comes from the Essence of G-d, there is no basis for separate, independent existence whatsoever—neither in itself, nor in its source.

The result of this recognition is our new and deeper comprehension that even

terpretation of *remez* in *Modeh Ani*. For if the worlds had been
brought into being by the attribute of *malchut* alone [and not from
the Essence of *Or Ein Sof*], then since the worlds are of significance
to and have a relationship with *malchut* by its very nature, there
could not be this totally new creation of their *very* existence *ex nihilo*.[132] (The vivification of the worlds, were they to be brought into
existence from *malchut* alone, would rather be analogous to the way
in which the soul gives life to the body; for even without the life-
force of the soul, the body possesses its own existence.)[133] Since, how-

---

after G-d decided to create, He must re-
new the creation continuously, at every
instant. Had the creation come through
another level (or "Light"), and not from
His Essence itself, such a continuous creation of every aspect of existence would
not be necessary (as the text proceeds to
explain). Existence, instead, would attain
its own grounds for being. But since creation is from the Essence of G-d, then
even after the world is created, it still has
no basis for existence, and must be constantly and completely renewed at every
moment.]

132. [The worlds possess a pre-existing
basis and root within the attribute of
malchut, which is by definition that aspect of Divinity which is related to the
world. Hence *malchut*, while it actualizes
the creation, is not the aspect of Divinity
which creates from utter nothing—that
is, which can give rise to something totally new. *Malchut* is an activating channel, or instrument, for what it receives
from above. See footnote 97.]

133. See *Derech Mitzvotecha* (23a), that
the explanation in *Shaar Hayichud v'haE-
munah* ch. 6, concerning *Ein Od*
["There is nothing else besides
Him"]—that there isn't even any secondary or subordinate existence, in contradistinction to the manner in which
the body is subordinate to the soul—is
true in terms of *sovev kol almin* [Divine
transcendence] only. Hence, the nations

of the world, whose perception is only of
memalei kol almin [Divine immanence],
conceive G-d's relation to the world as
the relation of the soul to the body. See
there.

At first glance however, even in nations' systems of belief, aren't they compelled to recognize that G-d *creates* all be-
ings and does not simply vivify them?
The explanation: Since the Light of *memalei* allows for the existence of the
worlds, therefore, after the worlds were
created, their nullification to this Light is
similar to the subjugation of the body to
the soul (even though their entire existence and being is derived from the
Light, and not just their vivifying life-
force). This matter still requires clarification.

[To explain: The soul's relation to the
body as similar to G-d's relation to the
world is a frequently discussed topic in
Talmud and Chasidus. On one level, it is
quite simple to see that just as the soul
fills and vivifies the body, so does G-d fill
and vivify the world (*Berachot* 10a). Yet
the analogy is not absolute, as R. Schneur
Zalman explains in *Shaar Hayichud
v'haEmunah* ch. 6, because the soul and
body are two separate existences entirely,
and have different sources. The soul does
not create the body, as G-d creates the
world. The body is created from the seed
of the parents. In the case of heaven and
earth, however, "their very being and essence was brought into existence from absolute nothingness, solely through the

הָ"רֶמֶז" שֶׁבְּמוֹדֶה אֲנִי. כִּי בְּאִם הִתְהַוּוּת הָעוֹלָמוֹת הָיְתָה עַל
יְדֵי סְפִירַת הַמַּלְכוּת מִצַּד עַצְמָה, מִכֵּיוָן שֶׁהָעוֹלָמוֹת תּוֹפְסִים
מָקוֹם לְגַבָּהּ, לֹא הָיָה אָז הִתְחַדְּשׁוּת בְּכָל עִיקָּר מְצִיאוּתָם (כִּי
אִם עַל דֶּרֶךְ וְדוּגְמַת מַה שֶׁהַנְּשָׁמָה מְחַיָּה אֶת הַגּוּף, שֶׁגַּם בְּלִי
הַחַיּוּת שֶׁמֵּהַנְּשָׁמָה, יֵשׁ לוֹ מְצִיאוּת⁵י), אֲבָל מִכֵּיוָן שֶׁהַהִתְהַוּוּת
הִיא מֵעַצְמוּת אוֹר אֵין סוֹף בָּרוּךְ הוּא – שֶׁאֵין הָעוֹלָמוֹת

'word of G-d...' [which] still stands forever [in all created things], and flows into them continuously, and continuously brings them into existence from nothingness, just as, for example, the coming into existence of the light from the sun within the very globe of the sun." And just as in its source, the light of the sun is null, so also in relation to their source, which is G-d, all the worlds are considered as naught. The worlds only appear to be separate, independent existences because of G-d's "self-restriction" and concealment. Therefore, G-d does not fill and animate the worlds in the way that the soul animates the body, for the body has its own existence without the soul; whereas G-d constantly creates the worlds anew, and they are nullified completely to Him.

Now this constant creation *ex nihilo* cannot result from *malchut* alone, as the text explains—for *malchut* is already associated with the worlds in their finite, seemingly separate existences in space and time. *Malchut* vivifies the world as the soul vivifies the body, but it cannot create the world *ex nihilo*, just as the soul cannot create the body. That power comes from the Essence of G-d which transcends all the worlds. Chasidus clarifies this point, and thus intensifies one's realization that the worlds are as nothing in relation to G-d, and must constantly be created anew, from the Essence of G-d.

In Chasidus, these two levels of the creative force are called *sovev kol almin*

and *memalei kol almin*. *Sovev kol almin* is the Divine energy that transcends creation, while *memalei kol almin* is the Divine energy invested within the creation.

Sovev kol almin acts in a remote, imperative, unidirectional manner (i.e., solely from above to below, but not vice versa). An analogy: Sunlight shines into a room and illuminates it. However, the room itself is not changed thereby, since the light emanates from a source outside of the room; it is not the room itself that lights up. Even when the light illuminates the room, the walls of the room do not actually absorb the light. The light is merely there as light—an illumination from the luminary—but does not become part of that which it illuminates. Similarly, the energy of *sovev* is of an infinite order that cannot be confined within limited creatures. It therefore "encompasses" them in both a pervasive and transcending form. This is why it is called *makif*: it is "there," but remains remote from that which it illuminates.

Memalei kol almin, unlike *sovev*, is immanent Divine energy, measured and limited in accordance with that which is being animated. Since it is limited, it permeates all of creation and is mutually interactive and inter-responsive with the subject that it enlivens. By way of analogy, the life force from the soul is clothed within the body in a way that alters the body fundamentally. It is not simply lifeforce which enlivens the body; it is the life force *of the body*, that which trans-

ever, creation comes from the Essence of *Or Ein Sof,* in relation to which the worlds have no ground or significance whatsoever, there is hence utterly no basis for them at all,[134] and even their *elementary* existence must be constantly created anew from the light of the *Ein Sof.*

And consequently, one comes to realize and appreciate the Oneness [of G-d] in which "there is nothing else besides Him," that all the worlds "are complete nothingness in relation to the Holy One blessed be He, and are not called by any name at all, not even the name *od* [else] which is an expression indicating secondary, subordinate status."[135] One therefore senses as something obvious and elementary that the life of the flesh has no real existence at all (not even a secondary or subordinate kind of existence), and "existence" is only the connection to Divinity, as was discussed earlier in the Chasidic explanation of the "plain" meaning of *Modeh Ani.*

And from the realization that "there is nothing else besides Him," it becomes plainly evident to the person that in fulfilling the commandments of G-d it is not possible to inject (even as something secondary) any other reason or purpose; the entire observance of the commandments should be because they are the Will of the Creator. This is, as was explained earlier, the Chasidic explanation of the *drush* [the homiletic interpretation] of *Modeh Ani.*

---

forms a dead corpse into a live body. (See *Tanya,* chapters 46 and 48; *Sefer Ha-Maamarim 5703,* p. 31.)

In *Derech Mitzvotecha* (ibid.), it is stated that the belief that G-d relates to the world in the same manner that the soul vivifies the body is not called "faith" at all, for the nations of the world, who deal with intellectual and quantitative categories, grasp this concept and understand *memalei kol almin.* But the unique faith of the Jew in the Oneness of G-d is in the transcendent level of G-d, *sovev kol almin,* in His Essence which does not vest itself in the world, and in relation to which the world is completely nullified, like the light of the sun within its source in the sun. There is literally nothing else besides Him—not even anything subordinate, as the nations of the world believe. Other nations call Him the "G-d of gods," the First Power and Source of all other powers, but they still conceive the world as having a degree of independent and separate existence, similar to the relation of the body to the soul, wherein although the body is dependent on the soul, it still has a degree of independence. The truth is, however, that

תּוֹפְסִים מָקוֹם לְגַבֵּיהּ כְּלָל, הֲרֵי אֵין שׁוּם נְתִינַת מָקוֹם לְכָל עִנְיָנָם, וְכָל **עִיקַּר** מְצִיאוּתָם מִתְחַדֶּשֶׁת מֵאוֹר אֵין סוֹף בָּרוּךְ הוּא.

וּבְמֵילָא בָּא הוּא לְהַכָּרַת הָאַחְדוּת בְּאוֹפֶן שֶׁ״אֵין עוֹד מִלְּבַדּוֹ״, שֶׁכָּל הָעוֹלָמוֹת ״הֵן אַיִן וְאֶפֶס מַמָּשׁ לְגַבֵּי הַקָּדוֹשׁ בָּרוּךְ הוּא וְאֵינָן נִקְרָאוֹת בְּשֵׁם כְּלָל אֲפִילוּ בְּשֵׁם עוֹד שֶׁהוּא לְשׁוֹן טָפֵל״קח. וּמִכֵּיוָן שֶׁכֵּן, הֲרֵי נִרְגָּשׁ אֶצְלוֹ בִּפְשִׁיטוּת, שֶׁחַיּוּת בְּשָׂרִי אֵינוֹ שׁוּם מְצִיאוּת כְּלָל (גַּם לֹא מְצִיאוּת בְּדֶרֶךְ טָפֵל), וּ״מְצִיאוּת״ הִיא רַק – הִתְקַשְּׁרוּת בֶּאֱלֹקוּת, וְכַנַּ״ל בְּבֵיאוּר הַחֲסִידוּת בְּחֵלֶק הַ״פְּשַׁט״ שֶׁבִּמְמוּדָה אֲנִי.

וּמֵהַכָּרָה זוֹ שֶׁ״אֵין עוֹד מִלְּבַדּוֹ״, הֲרֵי פָּשׁוּט אֶצְלוֹ שֶׁבְּקִיּוּם צִיוּוֵי הַקָּדוֹשׁ בָּרוּךְ הוּא אִי אֶפְשָׁר לְעָרֵב (אֲפִילוּ לֹא כְּטָפֵל) שׁוּם טַעַם וְתַכְלִית אַחֵר, וְכָל קִיּוּמָם צָרִיךְ לִהְיוֹת מִצַּד רְצוֹן הַבּוֹרֵא. וְכַנַּ״ל בְּבֵיאוּר הַחֲסִידוּת בְּחֵלֶק הַ״דְּרוּשׁ״ שֶׁבִּמְמוּדָה אֲנִי.

He is completely transcendent—One—and there literally is nothing else.

Although "*nations of the world*" refers, of course, to "nations," the idea can be extended. The perspective of the created being allows for perceptions of the created world (nature), and from observing the world certain conclusions may be drawn. One of these is the existence of a Creator, described perhaps as a First Cause or Prime Mover, etc. Inferred *from* creation, the Prime Mover cannot *transcend* creation. He is bound by the laws of nature, by time and space, by "impossibility," and is subject to predictability. *Memalei*

kol almin as manifest in creation is termed *Elokim*, the Creator in action, and this name is numerically the equivalent of *hateva*, "nature." Acceptance of *Elokim*, the Creator, precluding a self-creating universe, is enjoined on all mankind, the "children of Noah."]

134. [That is, the worlds have no pre-existent basis or root in the Essence of *Or Ein Sof*, in relation to which they simply do not "exist" at all.]

135. *Shaar Hayichud v'haEmunah*, ch. 6 (80b).

XVII

THE CHASIDIC EMPHASIS ON THE RELATION OF ESSENCE TO DETAILS

Though *Yechidah* is an essence-state, it does not negate *NaRaNaCh*; on the contrary, *Yechidah* is the essence of each of these particular levels. (That itself is one of the differences between the terms "manifestation" [*gilui*] and "essence" [*etzem*]: "Manifestation" is particular, and therefore, whatever does not correspond to its own specific form of revelation is not "it." Since it is an outward revelation, "extension," it negates what is not consonant with itself. *Etzem*, in contrast, is the essence-state of any given subject.) Therefore, [because essence underlies all the particular forms that are manifest,] one of the fundamental emphases of Chasidus is the manner in which all of the individual particulars are united with the essence. This emphasis on the relation of the particulars to the essence will be even better understood by considering the way in which Chasidus infuses life and vitality into the four levels of *Pardes* in *Modeh Ani*.

In relation to the subject of the *sefirot* [Divine attributes], which is the "esoteric" level of interpretation of *Modeh Ani*, Chasidus emphasizes the way in which the attribute of *malchut* is united with the attribute of *yesod*, until they become one thing—"Living and Eternal King." Hence, the idea of Oneness expressed in "There is nothing else besides Him" does not negate the existence of the worlds, but means, rather, that even the worlds themselves as found within the limitations of their existences (and subject to the bounds of space and time) are still united in a perfect and complete unity with the Essence of the Light of the *Ein Sof.*

With regard to the subject of the *mitzvot*, which was discussed in the *drush* approach to *Modeh Ani*, Chasidus stresses that even those commandments which have a logical reason, and are called in the Torah of *truth* by the name *mishpatim* ["judgments"], (are united with and) their essential principle is the simple Will that transcends reason.

Concerning creation, in the *remez* view of *Modeh Ani*, Chasidus stresses that even in those aspects of the world in which it appears to our eyes that the Creation has attained its own separate and independent existence (and thus we do not *sense* and *feel* the continu-

יז.

בְּחִינַת הַיְחִידָה, לִהְיוֹתָהּ עַצְמִית, אֵינָהּ שׁוֹלֶלֶת אֶת הַנֶּפֶשׁ־רוּחַ־נְשָׁמָה־חַיָּה, אַדְּרַבָּה – הִיא הִיא הָ"עֶצֶם" שֶׁל כָּל מַדְרֵיגוֹת הַפְּרָטִיּוֹת (שֶׁזֶּהוּ אֶחָד הַחִילּוּקִים שֶׁבֵּין "גִּילּוּי" לְ"עֶצֶם": "גִּילּוּי" הוּא עִנְיָן פְּרָטִי, וְלָכֵן הָעִנְיָנִים שֶׁאֵינָם גִּילּוּי (שֶׁלּוֹ – אִיז דָאס נִיט עֶר, אֵינָם "הוּא", וְלִהְיוֹתוֹ גִּילּוּי וּמִתְפַּשֵּׁט) – הוּא שׁוֹלֵל אוֹתָם. מַה שֶּׁאֵין כֵּן "עֶצֶם" הוּא הָעַצְמִיּוּת שֶׁל כָּל עִנְיָן וְעִנְיָן). וְלָכֵן, מֵהַהַדְגָּשׁוֹת הָעִיקָּרִיּוֹת שֶׁבַּחֲסִידוּת הוּא – אִיחוּד הַפְּרָטִים עִם הָעֶצֶם. וְגַם הַדְגָּשָׁה זוֹ תּוּבַן יוֹתֵר מֵהַחַיּוּת שֶׁחֲסִידוּת מַכְנִיסָה בְּכָל ד' חֶלְקֵי הַפְּשַׁט־רֶמֶז־דְּרוּשׁ־סוֹד שֶׁבְּ"מוֹדֶה אֲנִי":

בְּעִנְיַן הַסְּפִירוֹת – חֵלֶק הַ"סּוֹד": גַּם בְּחִינַת הַמַּלְכוּת עַצְמָהּ מְיוּחֶדֶת עִם סְפִירַת הַיְסוֹד, עַד שֶׁנַּעֲשִׂים לְעִנְיָן אֶחָד – "מֶלֶךְ חַי וְקַיָּים". וּבְמֵילָא עִנְיַן הָאַחְדוּת שֶׁ"אֵין עוֹד מִלְּבַדּוֹ" אֵינוֹ שֶׁלֹּא יֶשְׁנָהּ מְצִיאוּת הָעוֹלָמוֹת, כִּי אִם שֶׁגַּם הָעוֹלָמוֹת עַצְמָם כְּמוֹ שֶׁהֵם נִמְצָאִים בִּמְצִיאוּתָם (וּמוּגְדָּרִים בְּגֶדֶר זְמַן וּמָקוֹם) מְיוּחָדִים הֵם בְּתַכְלִית הַיִּחוּד בְּעַצְמוּת אוֹר אֵין סוֹף בָּרוּךְ הוּא.

בְּעִנְיַן הַמִּצְווֹת – חֵלֶק הַ"דְּרוּשׁ": גַּם הַמִּצְווֹת שֶׁיֵּשׁ עֲלֵיהֶם טַעַם וְנִקְרָאִים בְּתוֹרַת אֱמֶת בְּשֵׁם "מִשְׁפָּטִים", (מִתְאַחֲדִים וְ)עִיקָּרָם הוּא הָרָצוֹן שֶׁלְּמַעְלָה מֵהַטַּעַם.

בְּעִנְיַן הַבְּרִיאָה – חֵלֶק הָ"רֶמֶז": גַּם בְּעִנְיְנֵי הָעוֹלָם כְּמוֹ שֶׁהֵם נִרְאִים לְעֵינֵינוּ שֶׁהַבְּרִיאָה נַעֲשֵׂית כְּבָר לִמְצִיאוּת בִּפְנֵי עַצְמָהּ (שֶׁלָּכֵן אֵין אָנוּ מַרְגִּישִׁים אֶת הַחִידּוּשׁ שֶׁבָּהּ בְּכָל

ously new creation of the world), indeed, the renewal of a person (and the world) every morning is a re-creation of the entire essence of his existence, just as in the Act of Creation in the Six Days.

Concerning human emotions, the subject of the plain meaning of *Modeh Ani* on the level of *peshat*, Chasidus emphasizes that even in the simple thanks one gives for his life (when he awakens from his sleep), it is implicit the feeling that his entire vitality and life consist in his being a Jew.

XVIII

"THE BEGINNING IS WEDGED IN THE END": ESSENCE IS FOUND IN ACTION

With all the foregoing in mind (the beginning of Chapter XVII), we can now understand the words of our Chasidic masters when they said that certain particular qualities of Chasidus constituted the essential idea of Chasidus (as discussed earlier at the beginning of this discourse). Though these specific qualities are only the ramifications of Chasidus (as explained there earlier), nevertheless, particularly through them is (the essence of) the nature of Chasidus expressed. For the indication of "essence" is that it "penetrates" and pervades and is found in all the particulars, to the smallest detail (as explained previously in the discussion of the difference between "manifestation" and "essence").

And according to the general principle that "the beginning is wedged specifically in the end,"[136] the more that Chasidus is extended and diffused into the lowest level, even to transforming the nature of the animal soul itself (which is the "outside" [*chutza*] within the person; and even lower—through the purifying [*birur*] of one's portion in the world, which is the "outside" that is external to a person)[137]—the more the essence of its nature is pointedly expressed.

---

136. *Sefer Yetzirah* 1:7.

[Only in the "end" is the first intention and purpose truly realized; just as, for example, man was created last, but was first in G-d's intent, and is the central purpose of all creation. Additionally, what is seemingly the lowest level contains the highest intent, and comes from the highest source. And, in particular, as the Rebbe proceeds to explain towards the end of the text, this lowest, unrefined physical world, and the lowest level within man are the true places for the most sublime revelations and intentions of G-d. For it is man's task and mission to transform this lowest world and the lowest element in himself into an abode for Divinity, "a dwelling place for G-d here

רֶגַע וָרֶגַע), הִנֵּה הִתְחַדְּשׁוּת הָאָדָם (וְהָעוֹלָם) שֶׁבְּכָל בּוֹקֶר הִיא הִתְחַדְּשׁוּת בְּכָל עֶצֶם מְצִיאוּתוֹ, כְּהַחִדּוּשׁ דְּמַעֲשֵׂה בְרֵאשִׁית.

בְּעִנְיַן רֶגֶשׁ הָאָדָם – חֵלֶק הַ"פְּשַׁט": גַּם בְּהוֹדָאַת הָאָדָם עַל חַיּוּתוֹ (שֶׁנִּיעוֹר מִשְּׁנָתוֹ) נִרְגָּשׁ שֶׁכָּל חַיּוּתוֹ הוּא – מַה שֶּׁהוּא יְהוּדִי.

חי.

עַל פִּי הַנַּ"ל (תְּחִלַּת סְעִיף י"ז) יוּבְנוּ דִּבְרֵי רַבּוֹתֵינוּ נְשִׂיאֵינוּ, שֶׁאָמְרוּ עַל כַּמָּה מַעֲלוֹת פְּרָטִיּוֹת שֶׁבַּחֲסִידוּת שֶׁזֶּהוּ עִנְיָנָהּ שֶׁל הַחֲסִידוּת (כַּנַּ"ל בִּתְחִלַּת הַשִּׂיחָה). כִּי אַף שֶׁמַּעֲלוֹת אֵלּוּ הֵן רַק מִסְתַּעֲפוֹת מִמַּהוּת הַחֲסִידוּת (כַּנַּ"ל שָׁם), מִכָּל מָקוֹם, עַל יָדָן דַּוְקָא מִתְבַּטֵּאת (עַצְמוּת) מַהוּתָהּ. כִּי הַהוֹרָאָה עַל עִנְיָן "עַצְמִי" הוּא שֶׁ"מְּפַעְפֵּעַ" וּמַחְדִּיר וְנִמְצָא בְּכָל הַפְּרָטִים, עַד לִפְרָט הַיּוֹתֵר קָטָן (וְכַנַּ"ל בְּעִנְיַן הַהֶפְרֵשׁ שֶׁבֵּין "גִּלּוּי" לְ"עֶצֶם").

וְעַל פִּי הַכְּלָל שֶׁנָּעוּץ תְּחִלָּתָן בְּסוֹפָן דַּוְקָא[137], הֲרֵי כָּל מַה שֶּׁהַחֲסִידוּת נִמְשֶׁכֶת בִּבְחִינָה תַּחְתּוֹנָה יוֹתֵר, עַד לַהֲפִיכַת טֶבַע נֶפֶשׁ הַבַּהֲמִית "חוּצָה" שֶׁבָּאָדָם. וּלְמַטָּה יוֹתֵר – בֵּירוּר חֶלְקוֹ בָּעוֹלָם, "חוּצָה" שֶׁמִּחוּץ לְהָאָדָם] – מִתְבַּטֵּא אָז בְּיוֹתֵר עֶצֶם מַהוּתָהּ.

---

below," through Torah study and the performance of mitzvot.]

137. [This exhortation also refers back to the expression explained in footnote 32, of the answer of Moshiach to the Baal Shem Tov—that he would come "when the wellsprings of Chasidus would be spread outside (chutza)" throughout the world, even to the lowliest place and person. Each person has his allotted "portion" in the world, which is his responsibility to refine and purify (birur), and restore to Holiness through Torah study and the performance of mitzvot.

Only through the dissemination to the "outside" is the essence of Chasidus revealed.]

Therefore, the Rebbe, my sainted father-in-law [R. Yosef Yitz-chak Schneersohn], stressed in so many of his talks that every idea which we learn in Chasidus must be carried out in action, because only through actual Divine service do we grasp the essential nature of Chasidus.

XIX

TORAH AND THE TRANSFORMATION OF THE EVIL INCLINATION

Now just as the infiniteness, the *Ein Sof* quality, that is found in Chasidus is *generally* also to be found in all parts of the Torah (as explained previously in Chapter III), similarly, the expression of *Ein Sof* through its extending to the lowest level—to transform and make even that a vessel for Divinity—is found generally throughout Torah (though it is primarily found in Chasidus).

And this is what our Sages meant when they said about G-d, "I created the *Yetzer Hara* [Evil Inclination] and I created the Torah to be as spices for it."[138] At first glance, though, this statement is perplexing: Of all the worlds, this material world is the very lowest—"there is none lower than it."[139] And within this lowly world of physical matter, the lowliest is the Evil Inclination, of which the Talmud observes, "G-d 'regrets' creating it."[140] Furthermore, all the worlds, even the Supernal Worlds, are utterly insignificant in relation to the Torah. (Therefore, when King David praised the Torah for the reason that all the worlds above and below depend on one minute commandment of it, he was punished).[141] How much more so, then, does there seem to be no meaning at all in the statement that the Torah was created to be "spices" for the Evil Inclination?

According to our earlier discussion, however, this statement can be understood: The essence of Torah—that it is united with the Essence of G-d—is expressed precisely in its being *spices* for the Evil Inclination, for the power to "spice" the *Evil* Inclination, and

---

138. *Kiddushin* 30b.
[The Talmud continues: "If you occupy yourself with Torah, then you will not fall into its [the Evil Inclination's] clutches... but if you do not occupy yourself with Torah, then you will fall into its

hands..." See further for the significance of "spices."]

139. This is the wording of Rabbi Schneur Zalman in *Tanya* ch. 36 (beg.).

140. *Sukkah* 52b.

וְלָכֵן הִדְגִּישׁ כְּבוֹד קְדֻשַּׁת מוֹרִי וְחָמִי אַדְמוֹ"ר בְּכַמָּה
וְכַמָּה מִשִּׂיחוֹתָיו, שֶׁכָּל עִנְיָן שֶׁלּוֹמְדִים בַּחֲסִידוּת צָרִיךְ
לַהֲבִיאוֹ בְּפוֹעַל, כִּי עַל יְדֵי הָעֲבוֹדָה בְּפוֹעַל דַּוְקָא תּוֹפְסִים
בְּמַהוּת הַחֲסִידוּת.

יט.

כְּמוֹ שֶׁבְּחִינַת הָ"אֵין סוֹף" שֶׁבַּחֲסִידוּת הוּא **בִּכְלָלוּת** גַּם
בְּכָל חֶלְקֵי הַתּוֹרָה (כַּנַּ"ל סְעִיף ג), כֵּן גַּם בִּיטוּי הָאֵין סוֹף עַל
יְדֵי הַמְשָׁכָתוֹ עַד לְהַתַּחְתּוֹן בְּיוֹתֵר – לַהֲפוֹךְ גַּם אוֹתוֹ
וְלַעֲשׂוֹתוֹ כְּלִי לֶאֱלֹקוּת, הוּא גַּם בִּכְלָלוּת הַתּוֹרָה (אֶלָּא
שֶׁעִיקַר הָעִנְיָן הוּא בַּחֲסִידוּת).

וְזֶהוּ מַה שֶּׁאָמְרוּ רַבּוֹתֵינוּ זִכְרוֹנָם לִבְרָכָה "בָּרָאתִי יֵצֶר
הָרָע בָּרָאתִי לוֹ תּוֹרָה תַּבְלִין"[קי]. דְּלִכְאוֹרָה תָּמוּהַּ: בְּכָל
הָעוֹלָמוֹת, עוֹלָם הַזֶּה הוּא הַיּוֹתֵר תַּחְתּוֹן "שֶׁאֵין תַּחְתּוֹן לְמַטָּה
מִמֶּנּוּ"[קיא]. וּבְעוֹלָם הַזֶּה גוּפָא – הַיֵּצֶר הָרָע מִתְחָרֵט עָלָיו
הַקָּדוֹשׁ בָּרוּךְ הוּא שֶׁבְּרָאוֹ[קיב]. וּמִכֵּיוָן שֶׁכָּל הָעוֹלָמוֹת, אֲפִילוּ
עוֹלָמוֹת הָעֶלְיוֹנִים הֵם כְּלֹא חָשִׁיב לְגַבֵּי הַתּוֹרָה (וְלָכֵן,
כְּשֶׁשִּׁיבַּח דָּוִד אֶת הַתּוֹרָה בָּזֶה שֶׁכָּל הָעוֹלָמוֹת עֶלְיוֹנִים
וְתַחְתּוֹנִים תְּלוּיִים בְּדִקְדּוּק מִצְוָה אַחַת שֶׁל תּוֹרָה, נֶעֱנַשׁ עַל
זֶה[קיג], הֲרֵי מִכָּל שֶׁכֵּן וְקַל וָחֹמֶר שֶׁלִּכְאוֹרָה אֵין שׁוּם מָקוֹם
לוֹמַר שֶׁבְּרִיאַת הַתּוֹרָה הוּא בִּכְדֵי שֶׁתִּהְיֶה תַּבְלִין לְהַיֵּצֶר הָרָע?

וְעַל פִּי הַנַּ"ל מוּבָן: עֶצֶם הַתּוֹרָה שֶׁמְּיוּחֶדֶת בְּעַצְמוּתוֹ
יִתְבָּרֵךְ, מִתְבַּטֵּא דַּוְקָא בָּזֶה שֶׁהִיא **תַּבְלִין** לְהַיֵּצֶר הָרָע, מִכֵּיוָן

---

141. See references in fn. 26—based an aphorism of our Sages (*Sotah* 35a).

[King David was punished for extolling the Torah with the praise that the entire vivifying force of all the worlds depends on one minute detail of it. For that is not the true recognition of the Torah's inner nature—which is its union with *Or Ein Sof*, in relation to which all the worlds are as naught and are utterly insignificant.]

moreover, transform it to *good*,[142] can come only from the Essence of G-d.

The explanation of this idea is that all the states of revelation, even the most sublime, are restricted by the limitations inherent in the forms of "light" and "revelation"; thus, the existence of evil, which is the opposite of "light," can stand in contrast and opposition to them.[143] Consequently, it is not within their power to transform the evil to good (but only, rather, to wage war against evil until it is completely destroyed). Since, however, the Essence of G-d is "Simple" with an absolute "Simplicity"[144] and exclusive of all forms, nothing can stand in contrast to and oppose Him; hence, He alone has the power to change evil and transform it to good.[145]

For this reason, too, the level of Torah which is united with the Essence of G-d is described as[146] "*a delight* before Him": Delight (and pleasure) above is caused by the purification and amelioration of *darkness*[147]—the transformation of darkness to light. And this is the meaning of "a delight before Him": Only through the transformation of darkness to light—the "delight" of Torah—is the innermost aspect [*pnimiyut*] of the Torah expressed, as it is united with

---

142. According to what is stated in the text, we can understand the expression: "I created the Torah as *spices* for it." At first glance, it would appear that the Evil Inclination must be *eliminated*. (This is also accomplished through Torah, as the Sages state (*Kiddushin* ibid.), "Drag it [the Evil Inclination] to the *House of Study*. If it is like a rock it will *dissolve*; if it is like iron it will be *shattered*)." Spices, however, do not destroy food but *on the contrary*, they flavor and season it.

It *is* necessary to destroy the Evil Inclination when "this disgraceful one meets you—[when] the Evil Inclination *incites* you." But the essence of the Evil Inclination, the essential power of craving *per se* (see *Likkutei Torah, Chukat* 56d; *Rosh Hashanah* 61d), must be *seasoned* and *flavored*, thus transforming this craving to good, as explained in the text.

This is the meaning of the saying, "*I*

created the Torah as *spices* for the Evil Inclination." The meaning of "I created...spices" refers to the *essence* of the Torah, i.e., the intention for which it was created. And the essence of the Torah expresses itself (not in the destruction of the Evil Inclination, but rather) in transforming it to good, as will be explained in the text.

[That is, there are two aspects to the Evil Inclination: 1) That which incites a person to do evil, and which, of course, must be destroyed; 2) The essence of the Evil Inclination itself, which is the power to desire and crave; this is not necessarily evil in itself, for this depends on to where this craving is directed. And this is precisely the aspect of the Evil Inclination which one has to "season" and not destroy, but rather direct it to "taste" the good.]

143. [Anything which is defined ex-

שֶׁהַכֹּחַ לְתַבֵּל אֶת יֵצֶר **הָרָע** וּלְהַפְּכוֹ **לְטוֹב**[קיד], הוּא מִצַּד עַצְמוּתוֹ יִתְבָּרֵךְ דַּוְקָא.

וְהַבִּיאוּר בָּזֶה: כָּל הַגִּילּוּיִים, גַּם הַיּוֹתֵר נַעֲלִים, לִהְיוֹתָם מֻגְדָּרִים בְּגֶדֶר אוֹר וְגִילּוּי, הֲרֵי מְצִיאוּת הָרָע – הֵיפֶךְ הָאוֹר – מְנַגֵּד אֲלֵיהֶם, וּבְמֵילָא, אֵין בִּיכָלְתָּם לְהַפְּכוֹ לְטוֹב (כִּי אִם לְהִלָּחֵם בּוֹ וְעַד – שֶׁיִּבָּטֵל לְגַמְרֵי). וְרַק עַצְמוּתוֹ יִתְבָּרֵךְ שֶׁהוּא פָּשׁוּט בְּתַכְלִית הַפְּשִׁיטוּת וּמוּשְׁלָל מִכָּל הַצִּיּוּרִים וְגַם אֵין שַׁיָּיךְ שׁוּם מְנַגֵּד אֵלָיו, וּבְמֵילָא – בִּיכָלְתּוֹ לְשַׁנּוֹתוֹ וּלְהַפְּכוֹ לְטוֹב[קטו].

וְזֶהוּ גַּם כֵּן מַה שֶּׁבִּבְחִינַת הַתּוֹרָה הַמְיוּחֶדֶת בְּעַצְמוּתוֹ יִתְבָּרֵךְ נֶאֱמַר[קטז] "**מְשַׂחֶקֶת** לְפָנָיו": שְׂחוֹק (וְתַעֲנוּג) שֶׁלְּמַעְלָה בָּא עַל יְדֵי בֵּירוּר וְתִיקּוּן **הַחֹשֶׁךְ**[קיז] – אִתְהַפְּכָא חֲשׁוֹכָא לִנְהוֹרָא. וְזֶהוּ "מְשַׂחֶקֶת לְפָנָיו": דַּוְקָא עַל יְדֵי בְּחִינַת אִתְהַפְּכָא חֲשׁוֹכָא לִנְהוֹרָא – "מְשַׂחֶקֶת" – שֶׁבַּתּוֹרָה, מִתְבַּטֵּאת

---

cludes whatever lies outside that definition. "Revelation" of G-d has definition, particularity, form, uniqueness; as a result, other "things" exist in a different framework. Evil, the subject at hand, is not only in a different framework, but in an opposing one. "Revelation" and evil struggle for supremacy, the supremacy over evil being in its destruction.

The Essence of G-d is "simple"—meaning undefined, formless, beyond categorization (even to call Him "good" is irrelevant), since He transcends all bounds. Evil does not stand in contrast to abstraction, and since Essence is the ultimate in abstraction, evil is not in opposition to Essence. When Essence is summoned into confrontation with evil, it does not just deal with the external, manifestation of evil, but its root, and can transform it to good.

This doctrine is well-based in Talmud

(*Berachot* 54a), which interprets to love G-d "with all your heart" as loving G-d with both your impulse to good and your impulse to evil; i.e., the latter impulse should also love G-d.]

144. [See footnote 27.]

145. See *Likkutei Sichot*, vol. 7, p. 23.

146. Proverbs 8:30. See also references in footnote 26, where it is stated that "delight *before Him*" refers to the inner aspect and essence of Torah. [I.e., its union with *Or Ein Sof*. As R. Schneur Zalman explains in *Kuntres Acharon* 6, this delight and pleasure of the Torah to G-d and man is beyond human comprehension—it is only before *Him*, G-d Himself. Man cannot truly appreciate this basic character of the Torah.]

147. See *Torah Or* 17d ff.

the innermost aspect of the *Or Ein Sof*—which is the meaning of "before *Him.*"

XX

THE LAW OF ACQUISITION IN A CHASIDIC PERSPECTIVE

These two special aspects of Chasidus (and of the Torah in general)

—namely: 1) its penetration into all the levels of *NaRaNaCh* until it also affects the animal soul and the world; 2) the expression of its essence only through its effects on the animal soul[148] and the world—

have parallels (as is true of all the subjects of Chasidus) in the revealed part of Torah,[149] and in *halachah* [Torah law]. Furthermore, this practical law will attain greater clarification and be better understood by considering it in light of the two foregoing aspects of Chasidus:

"The four cubits of a person acquire objects for him wherever he is":[150] in an alley, a side-street of a public domain[151] (and concerning divorce and marriage[152]—even in a public domain, according to several opinions).[153] This mode of acquisition was enacted by the Sages in order that "people should not come to quarrelling."[151]

Now even though the enactment stipulates only that an *object* located in the four cubits of a person belongs to him, nevertheless, to validate the act of acquisition, the Sages also appropriated to him the four cubits *themselves*, and made them as his own property [*chatzer*].[154] Hence, through this appropriation of property, the four cu-

---

148. [See footnote 7.]

149. [See footnote 65, and Chapter VIII.]

150. *Bava Metzia* 10a. [There are numerous manners by which on may legally acquire a moveable object (*Choshen Mishpat* 198): 1) Acquisition by lifting (*kinyan hagba'ah*); 2) Acquisition by property (*kinyan chatzer*), i.e., by the object being on one's property, as discussed in the text; 3) Acquisition with the four cubits of one's immediate territory (*kinyan arba amot*), i.e., were one to find an (ownerless) object in an alley or sidestreet, one needn't actually place his hands on it to acquire it; the mere fact that it is found within a four cubit radius around the person grants him ownership. The Sages arrived at the measurement of four cubits by taking into account the average height of man, which is three cubits, plus another cubit "in which one may spread, or stretch, his hands and feet." See *Eruvin* 48a and footnote 165, below.]

151. *Bava Metzia* 10b.

פְּנִימִיּוּתָהּ כְּמוֹ שֶׁהִיא מְיוּחֶדֶת בִּפְנִימִיּוּת אוֹר אֵין סוֹף בָּרוּךְ הוּא – "לְפָנָיו".

ב.

שְׁנֵי עִנְיָנִים אֵלּוּ שֶׁבְּתוֹרַת הַחֲסִידוּת (וְעַל דֶּרֶךְ זֶה בְּכָלְלוּת הַתּוֹרָה)

– (א) חֲדִירָתָהּ בְּכָל חֶלְקֵי נֶפֶשׁ-רוּחַ-נְשָׁמָה-חַיָּה וְעַד שֶׁפּוֹעֶלֶת גַּם בַּנֶּפֶשׁ הַבַּהֲמִית וּבָעוֹלָם, (ב) בִּיטּוּי עַצְמוּתָהּ הוּא דַּוְקָא עַל יְדֵי פְּעוּלָתָהּ בַּנֶּפֶשׁ הַבַּהֲמִית וּבָעוֹלָם –

יֵשׁ דוּגְמָתָם (כְּכָל הָעִנְיָנִים שֶׁבַּחֲסִידוּת) גַּם בַּנִּגְלֶה, וּבַהֲלָכָה. וְלֹא עוֹד, אֶלָּא שֶׁהֲלָכָה זוֹ בַּנִּגְלֶה נִיתּוֹסֵף בָּהּ בֵּיאוּר עַל יְדֵי עִנְיָנִים הַנַּ"ל שֶׁבַּחֲסִידוּת:

אַרְבַּע אַמּוֹת שֶׁל אָדָם קוֹנוֹת לוֹ בְּכָל מָקוֹם[קיח]: בְּסִמְטָא, בְּצִדֵּי רְשׁוּת הָרַבִּים[קיט] (וּבְנוֹגֵעַ לְגִיטִּין וְקִידּוּשִׁין – גַּם בִּרְשׁוּת הָרַבִּים, לְכַמָּה דֵיעוֹת[קכ]). וְקִנְיָן זֶה תַּקָּנַת חֲכָמִים הוּא, בִּכְדֵי "דְּלָא אָתֵי לְאַנְצוּיֵי"[קכא].

אַף שֶׁהַתַּקָּנָה הִיא שֶׁהַחֵפֶץ הַמּוּנָח בְּד' אַמּוֹתָיו שֶׁל אָדָם יוּקְנֶה לוֹ, מִכָּל מָקוֹם בִּשְׁבִיל קִנְיַן הַחֵפֶץ, הִקְנוּ לוֹ

---

152. [This refers to the law concerning the necessity of giving an object (a writ in the case of divorce, and an object of value or a contract in the case of marriage) into the hand, or domain of the woman, i.e., her four cubits.]

153. See *Beit Shmuel* 5 on *Even Ha'ezer* 30. *See further references there.* (And the opinion of Rav Pappa—*Bava Metzia*, ibid.—is that one may also acquire a lost object that is found in a public domain.)

154. *Avnei Miluim* 30:5 writes that according to the opinion of *Ramban* (*Gittin* 78a), the Sages did not appropriate the *place* of the four cubits themselves, but rather the *object* that is located in them. See there. However, see *Avnei Miluim* ibid., that according to the opinion of *Ran* (*Gittin*, ibid.) they also appropriated to him the four cubits *themselves*. (So it appears from *Ritva* (*Gittin*, ibid., his second answer) and the Responsa of R. Yosef Migash, ch. 106.)

Now the Sages' reason that "people should not quarrel" is only relevant to acquisition of the [actual] object [and not

bits automatically acquire for him the object located in them by the general rule of *kinyan chatzer* ["acquisition by property"].[155] (And therefore, a minor, who has no *chatzer*—i.e., who cannot acquire possessions through his property—also has no four cubits, i.e., cannot acquire possessions when the object is in his four cubits).[156] However, the Sages appropriated a person's four cubits to him only for the purpose of acquiring an object located in them, and not for any other purpose.[157]

Now even though the acquisition of objects through the mode of four cubits is based on the reason of *kinyan chatzer*, it is nevertheless superior to *kinyan chatzer*. In the law of *kinyan chatzer*, any property that is not enclosed or supervised (even when one stands so near the object that he could reach down and take it)[158] does not acquire the object for him until he declares, "My property acquires this object for me."[159] In acquisition through the four cubits, however, one does not have to say "My property acquires..." (even though they are not enclosed or supervised).[160] Furthermore, the four cubits acquire objects for a person even without his knowledge or desire.[161] But this superiority of the four cubits requires explanation: Since the entire mode of acquisition through four cubits is based on the reason of *kinyan chatzer*, (and concerning the four cubits themselves—they are even inferior to *chatzer* because, as explained before, they belong to him only for the purpose of acquiring the object,) how is it then possible that the acquisition through four cubits should be more powerful than *kinyan chatzer?*[162]

---

the four cubits themselves]. Why, then, did the Sages appropriate the four cubits themselves? One can answer that the Sages did not want to appropriate the object for the person in a manner which would be like "a law without a reason" completely. Therefore, they also appropriated the four cubits to the person, so that through them he may acquire the object.

155. [See footnote 150.]

156. *Bava Metzia* 11a. *Rambam, Hilchot G'zelah v'Avedah* 17:10. *Shulchan Aruch,*

Choshen Mishpat 243:23, and end of 268.

157. Therefore, *Tosfot* (s.v. *Arba*) and *Rosh* (*Bava Metzia* 10a) maintain that the four cubits do not acquire for theft, even though the Sages made them as his own property. (As for selling and giving—see *Shach* 9 on *Choshen Mishpat* 243.) They did not designate the four cubits as one's own property for *every* purpose, but only for the purpose of acquiring an object in certain situations (e.g., "for acquiring an object found," and the like).

חֲכָמִים אֶת ד' הָאַמּוֹת עַצְמָם וַעֲשָׂאוּם כַּחֲצֵירוֹקכֹּא, וְעַל יְדֵי
זֶה וּבְמֵילָא קוֹנוֹת לוֹ אֶת הַחֵפֶץ הַמּוּנָּח בָּהֶם בְּתוֹרַת קִנְיַן
חָצֵר (וְלָכֵן, קָטָן שֶׁאֵין לוֹ חָצֵר, אֵין לוֹ גַּם ד' אַמּוֹתקכֹּב).
— אֶלָּא, שֶׁזֶּה מַה שֶׁהִתְקִינוּ חֲכָמִים לְהָאָדָם אֶת ד' אַמּוֹתָיו —
הוּא רַק לְצוֹרֶךְ קִנְיַן חֵפֶץ הַמּוּנָּח בָּהֶם, וְלֹא לְעִנְיָן
אַחֵרקכֹּג.

וְעִם הֱיוֹת שֶׁהַקִּנְיָן דד' אַמּוֹת הוּא מִטַּעַם קִנְיַן חָצֵר,
בְּכָל זֶה עָדִיף הוּא מִקִּנְיַן חָצֵר. שֶׁחָצֵר שֶׁאֵינָהּ מִשְׁתַּמֶּרֶת
(גַּם כְּשֶׁעוֹמֵד בְּקֵירוּב לְהַחֵפֶץ בְּאוֹפֶן שֶׁיּוּכַל לִנְטוֹת עַצְמוֹ
וְלִיטְלוֹקכֹּד) אֵינָהּ קוֹנָה עַד שֶׁיֹּאמַר "זָכְתָה לִי שָׂדִי"קכֹּה.
וְאִילוּ ד' אַמּוֹת (אַף שֶׁאֵין מִשְׁתַּמְּרוֹת) אֵין צָרִיךְ לוֹמַר
"זָכְתָה כוּ'"קכֹּו, וְעַד שֶׁקּוֹנוֹת לוֹ לְאָדָם שֶׁלֹּא מִדַּעְתּוֹ וּרְצוֹנוֹ
כְּלָלקכֹּז. וְצָרִיךְ בֵּיאוּר: מִכֵּיוָן שֶׁכָּל הַקִּנְיָן דד' אַמּוֹת הוּא
מִטַּעַם קִנְיַן חָצֵר (וּבְנוֹגֵעַ לְד' הָאַמּוֹת עַצְמָם — גְּרוּעִים
הֵם מֵחָצֵר, כַּנַּ"ל שֶׁאֵינָן קְנוּיוֹת לוֹ כִּי אִם לְצוֹרֶךְ קִנְיַן
הַחֵפֶץ), אֵיךְ אֶפְשָׁר שֶׁהַקִּנְיָן דד' אַמּוֹת יִהְיֶה אַלִּים מִקִּנְיַן
חָצֵרקכֹּח?

---

158. See *D'rishah* 7 on *Choshen Mishpat* 268.

159. *Rambam, Hilchot G'zelah v'Avedah* ibid., law 8. And *Beit Yosef* on *Choshen Mishpat* ibid. (near the end) states that this is the final opinion.

160. See *Bava Metzia* 10a-b: "If he has not said it, it makes no difference."

161. See *Choshen Mishpat*, beg. 268: "And it [the law of *kinyan chatzer*] is not made inferior if he throws himself upon

it" (even though he thereby openly shows his intentions of not acquiring it through the method of four cubits).

162. This is the question of *Rashba* (quoted in *Maggid Mishneh* on *Rambam, Hilchot G'zelah*, ibid., and *Beit Yosef*, ibid.).

Beit Yosef answers there [why four cubits is superior to *chatzer* and does not require any proclamation], "that since the Sages enacted the law of acquisition through four cubits so that people should not come to quarrelling, they did not see

The explanation, however, is that one's *Yechidah* radiates and extends[163] throughout his four cubits; therefore, they [his four cubits] can acquire objects for him without either his declaration or knowledge, because on the level of *Yechidah*, knowledge and intelligence are immaterial. The extension of the *Yechidah* into the four cubits, however, is for the purpose of acquiring an object—acquiring a physical object that is *outside* the person. A person's faculties in all his *four* levels of *NaRaNaCh*, corresponding to the *four* cubits,[164] are themselves unable to elicit and reveal the level of the *Yechidah*. It is only when these powers are engaged in purifying some physical object which is outside the person—which corresponds to the acquisition of the object into one's domain (in order to refine and purify it through using it for the sake of Heaven)—then, and only then, does the aspect of *Yechidah* reveal and manifest itself in these faculties.[165]

---

any reason to distinguish between the case of one who says 'My property acquires this object for me' and one who does not, for it would still lead to quarrelling." This answer, however, requires explanation, for since ultimately they enacted the law of four cubits through the mode of designating them as *his own chatzer* (see fn. 154), it does not therefore appear to be possible that they should acquire for him in any manner that property itself (*chatzer*) does not acquire.

[That is, the answer of *Beit Yosef* does not appear sufficient, for if the four cubits are synonymous with *chatzer*, why then is the saying of these words necessary for *chatzer* and not for the four cubits?]

163. *Imrei Binah, Shaar Hakriyat Shema*, ch. 42.

164. Note *Eruvin* 48a: "One's *body* is three cubits and one cubit in order to..." The levels of the soul which are clothed in the physical body are only the three levels of *Nefesh, Ruach*, and *Neshamah* [and correspond to the 3 cubits]. The fourth cubit, which is *in addition* to the length of the body, but is connected to

it (for the idea of this cubit is "in order to extend arms and legs" or "in order to pick up an object which is under his feet and place it under his head"), is the category which is "in addition" to the *Nefesh, Ruach*, and *Neshamah*—the (close) encompassing level, *Chaya*.

[Based on Exodus 16:29 that on Shabbat, "Let every man remain in his place; let no man leave his place on the seventh day," the Sages decreed that one is allowed to walk no more than 2,000 cubits from his "place" (as defined by his home) on Shabbat. He may walk this 2,000 cubits in any one, or in several, directions, and even walk back and forth several times up to the 2,000 cubit line. Once he passes beyond this 2,000 cubit point, however, he is only allowed another four cubits. He can neither walk backwards nor forwards further than these four cubits. The Talmud gives two reasons for this allowance of four cubits: 1) His body occupies a space of three cubits, and one additional cubit is allotted in order that he may extend his arms and legs; 2) The additional cubit is allotted so that he may pick up an object which is under his feet and place it under his head.

וְהַבֵּיאוּר בָּזֶה: בְּד' אַמּוֹתָיו שֶׁל אָדָם מִתְפַּשֶּׁטֶת בְּחִינַת
הַיְּחִידָה שֶׁבּוֹקכט. וְלָכֵן קוֹנוֹת לוֹ לָאָדָם שֶׁלֹּא בַּאֲמִירָתוֹ וְדַעְתּוֹ, כִּי
בִּבְחִינַת הַיְּחִידָה אֵינוֹ נוֹגֵעַ עִנְיַן הַדַּעַת וְהַשֵּׂכֶל. אֶלָּא
שֶׁהִתְפַּשְּׁטוּת הַיְּחִידָה בְּד' אַמּוֹתָיו הוּא בִּשְׁבִיל קִנְיַן חֵפֶץ –
הַקְנָאַת דָּבָר גַּשְׁמִי **שָׂמֵחוּץ** לָאָדָם: הַכֹּחוֹת שֶׁל הָאָדָם עַצְמוֹ,
בְּכָל **ד'** הַבְּחִינוֹת נֶפֶשׁ-רוּחַ-נְשָׁמָה-חַיָּה שֶׁבּוֹ – **אַרְבַּע** אַמּוֹתקל,
אֵין בִּיכָלְתָּם לְהַמְשִׁיךְ וּלְגַלּוֹת אֶת בְּחִינַת הַיְּחִידָה. וְרַק
כְּשֶׁהַכֹּחוֹת בָּאִים לְבָרֵר אֵיזֶה דָּבָר גַּשְׁמִי שֶׂמֵחוּץ לְהָאָדָם –
הַקְנָאַת חֵפֶץ לִרְשׁוּתוֹ שֶׁל הָאָדָם (בִּכְדֵי לְבָרְרוֹ וּלְזַכְּכוֹ עַל יְדֵי
שֶׁיִּשְׁתַּמֵּשׁ בּוֹ לְשֵׁם שָׁמַיִם) – אָז דַּוְקָא מִתְגַּלֵּית בָּהֶם בְּחִינַת
הַיְּחִידָהקלא.

The Rebbe explains that this additional fourth cubit corresponds to the fourth level of the soul—*Chaya*. *Chaya* and *Yechidah* are both "transcendent" aspects of the soul, and not enclothed in the physical body. *Chaya*, however, is called *makif hakarov*, a transcendent level which is nevertheless still "close," and related to the other three levels of the soul (*Nefesh, Ruach, Neshamah*). *Yechidah*, on the other hand, is *makif harachok*—so "distant" from *NaRaNaCh* that it is utterly transcendent, and cannot even be classed as their "source," as was explained in Chapter V. In Chasidus, these two levels of transcendence, *makif hakarov* and *makif harachok*, are explained through an analogy to the difference between the encompassing nature of a garment and that of a house. A garment is *makif*, i.e., it is not part of but rather surrounds a person, yet it is also *karov*, "close" to him, moulding itself to the contours of his body. A house is *makif harachok*—it entirely surrounds and encompasses him, but has no relation to his body whatsoever. For further explanation of the four cubits, see *Likkutei Sichot*, vol. 16, p. 192 ff. (esp. fn. 46., p. 197).]

165. And then *Yechidah* manifests itself (not only in the purification of the physical object which is outside the person, but also) in the various levels of the soul itself, the four levels of *Nefesh, Ruach, Neshamah*, and *Chaya*. Only through them does *Yechidah* affect the physical object that is outside the person (though the arousal of *Yechidah* comes solely because of the purification [*birur*] of the physical object).

(A parallel of this phenomenon can be seen in the power of the Essence of G-d, "Whose Existence comes from Himself" [i.e., the Essence of G-d does not derive its origin and sustenance from anything other than itself—it is its own source]. Though this power is specifically expressed through the creation of a physical being, nevertheless, eliciting this power of Essence into an independent being comes only through the Light [*Or*], for "the Light is that which mediates between True Being and created being. Thus, through the mediation of the Light, the power of Essence is enabled to bring about the existence of a 'thing' from complete and utter nothingness." (*Yechayenu 5694*, ch. 14 [*Sefer Hamaamarim 5711* p.

XXI

CHASIDUS: MORE THAN A PRELUDE TO MOSHIACH

Considering all we have discussed, it is most fitting that the preparation and "vessel"[166] for the "coming of the Master" is precisely the "dispersal of the fountains [of Chasidus] abroad." For

—(the revelation of Moshiach will be not only throughout all aspects of the world, until "all flesh will see...[the word of G-d...],"[167] and hence, the preparation and vessel for this revelation is the dissemination of the fountains outwards into *everything*—down to the very lowest level, the *outside* [*chutza*], but also)—

the essential nature of the fountains of Chasidus is expressed specifically when they are spread and extended to the "outside."

Indeed, for as long as the wellsprings are found only "inside," their true nature is not yet expressed. And since the preparation and vessel for the coming of Moshiach is [the revelation of] the *essence* of Chasidus, it is therefore imperative to disseminate the fountains specifically outwards—until the "outside," too, will be transformed into wellsprings—for through this, the essential nature of the fountains is manifested; and then "the Master comes," that is King Moshiach.

And in the words of the Alter Rebbe,[168] "then the *dross* of the body and of the *world* will be purified (indicating that there will be physicality, but it will be purified)... (and the light of G-d will shine forth to Israel 'without any garment') and from the overflow of the illumination on Israel, the darkness of the nations will also be illuminated,[169] as it is written 'and *all* flesh shall see *together*'... 'and

---

39]; see also *Igeret Hakodesh*, epistle 20.) [See fn. 130, that the power of Essence expresses itself in the creation of an independent, physical being. *Or* is the medium, however, which brings Essence (*atzmut*) to the world.]

The same is true in one's Divine service: Though the manifestation of Essence comes specifically through the actual performance of *mitzvot*, nevertheless, the manner of eliciting the Essence into the performance of *mitzvot* is only through the inner faculties (one's intellectual and emotional faculties). (See *Likkutei Sichot*, vol. 3, p. 956, that for this reason love and fear [of G-d] are called "the paths of G-d." See there further at length.)

And therefore (for the purpose of acquiring an object) the four cubits themselves (*Nefesh, Ruach, Neshamah, Chaya*) are also appropriated to the person; and it is specifically through this that the *four cubits* acquire the object for him, as ex-

כא.

עַל פִּי כָל הַנַּ"ל יוּמְתַּק מַה שֶׁהַהֲכָנָה וְהַ"כְּלִי"קלב לְ"אָתֵי מַר" הוּא הֲפָצַת הַמַּעְיָנוֹת חוּצָה דַּוְקָא. כִּי

(נוֹסָף לָזֶה, שֶׁמֵּכֵיוָן שֶׁגִּלּוּי הַמָּשִׁיחַ יִהְיֶה בְּכָל עִנְיְנֵי הָעוֹלָם עַד אֲשֶׁר "וְרָאוּ כָל בָּשָׂר גו'", וּבְמֵילָא, גַּם הַהֲכָנָה וְהַכְּלִי לָזֶה הִיא הֲפָצַת הַמַּעְיָנוֹת בְּכָל – עַד הַתַּחְתּוֹן בְּיוֹתֵר, חוּצָה)

בִּיטּוּי מַהוּת מַעְיָנוֹת הַחֲסִידוּת הוּא כְּשֶׁהֵם מִתְפַּשְּׁטִים "חוּצָה" דַּוְקָא:

כָּל זְמַן שֶׁנִּמְצָאִים הַמַּעְיָנוֹת רַק בְּהַ"פְּנִים", אֵין מִתְבַּטֵּא עֲדַיִין אֲמִיתִית מַהוּתָם. וּמֵכֵיוָן שֶׁהַהֲכָנָה וְהַכְּלִי לְבִיאַת הַמָּשִׁיחַ הוּא – מַהוּת הַחֲסִידוּת, לָכֵן מֵהַהֶכְרַח הוּא לְהָפִיץ אֶת הַמַּעְיָנוֹת חוּצָה דַּוְקָא – וְעַד שֶׁיֵּהָפְכוּ אֶת הַ"חוּצָה" לְמַעְיָנוֹת – שֶׁעַל יְדֵי זֶה מִתְבַּטֵּא מַהוּת הַמַּעְיָנוֹת, וְאָז "אָתֵי מַר" – דָּא מַלְכָּא מְשִׁיחָא.

וּבִלְשׁוֹן רַבֵּנוּ הַזָּקֵןקלג "שֶׁאָז יִזְדַּכֵּךְ גַּשְׁמִיּוּת (הַיְינוּ שֶׁיִּהְיֶה גַּשְׁמִיּוּת, אֶלָּא שֶׁיִּזְדַּכֵּךְ) הַגּוּף וְהָעוֹלָם . . (וְיָאִיר אוֹר ה' לְיִשְׂרָאֵל "בְּלִי שׁוּם לְבוּשׁ") וּמִיתְרוֹן הַהֶאָרָה לְיִשְׂרָאֵל יַגִּיהַּ חֹשֶׁךְקלד הָאוּמּוֹת גַּם כֵּן כְּדִכְתִיב כו' כָּל בָּשָׂר יַחְדָּיו כו' כָּל

---

plained in the text.

One can further say that this is also the inner explanation of why the Sages did not want to appropriate the object in a manner which would be completely like "a law without a reason" (see fn. 154)—for even the purification of the physical, etc., must specifically flow from *sechel* (reason).

166. The preparation and vessel also *elicit* (and are not only passive receptacles for) the effusion and light. As stated in Tanya, beg. ch. 37 (and quoted further in the text), they *cause* the reward of the *mitzvah*.

167. Isaiah 40:5.

168. Tanya ch. 36 and beg. ch. 37.

169. Perhaps one can understand his meaning through the explanation in *Shaarei Orah* (end of *Ki Atah*) of the

all the inhabitants of the world…'"[170] (As the Alter Rebbe explains there,) "This culminating fulfillment of the Era of Moshiach and of the Resurrection of the Dead…is contingent on our works and service[171] throughout the duration of the Exile; for what causes the reward of a commandment is the commandment itself."

With the true and complete redemption, may it be speedily in our days.

---

verse "G-d will *illuminate my darkness*" [II Samuel 29:29], that this refers to the *transformation* of darkness to light (in the manner explained previously in the text—i.e., evil itself will be positively transformed).

170. Liturgy, High Holiday *Amidah.*

171. My father, teacher and master [R. Levi Yitzchak Schneersohn] explained:

"The two expressions *maasenu v'avodatenu* ('our works and our service') can be understood from what is stated further in *Igeret Hakodesh* epistle 12, s.v., '*And the act of tzedakah…,*' see there. It can be said that '*maasenu*' refers to the Era of Moshiach,* and '*avodatenu*' to the

---

* *See also* Igeret Hakodesh, *ibid. (118a), explaining the term* maaseh: *"In*

יוֹשְׁבֵי תֵבֵל אַרְצֶךָ וגו' (וּמְבֹאָר שֶׁ)וְהִנֵּה תַּכְלִית הַשְּׁלֵימוּת הַזֶּה שֶׁל יְמוֹת הַמָּשִׁיחַ וּתְחִיַּת הַמֵּתִים . . תָּלוּי בְּמַעֲשֵׂינוּ וַעֲבוֹדָתֵינוּ‎קלה כָּל זְמַן מֶשֶׁךְ הַגָּלוּת כִּי הַגּוֹרֵם שְׂכַר הַמִּצְוָה הִיא הַמִּצְוָה בְּעַצְמָה",

בִּגְאוּלָה הָאֲמִיתִית וְהַשְּׁלֵימָה, בְּקָרוֹב מַמָּשׁ.

Resurrection of the Dead" (*He'arot l'Tanya—Likkutei Levi Yitzchak*, p. 15).

[R. Schneur Zalman distinguishes between "*maaseh*" and "*avodah*" by defining "*maaseh*" as that level of man's deeds from "below" which arouse a manifestation of G-d from "Above." This level of action, however, does not entirely separate good from evil, nor take the vitality out of evil. "*Avodah*," on the other hand, applies to that which man does with great effort, and that which is contrary to his natural inclination. By this self-abnegation of his body, and his subordination to the will of G-d, he subdues the evil to such an extent that it can no longer awaken itself, and thus, falls away.]

his goodness He renews the act of creation every day," and *"They are new every morning..."*

APPENDIX

APPENDIX

EXCERPT FROM A TALK BY THE LUBAVITCHER REBBE
LAST DAY OF PASSOVER, 5730 (1970)

1.

It is written in the *Zohar*:[1] "In the sixth century of the sixth
millenium,[2] the portals of wisdom above, and the fountains of
wisdom below will be opened... This is alluded to in the words,
'In the six hundredth year of the life of Noah... all the fountains
of the great depths burst forth.'"[3] The *Zohar* plainly means that
the gates to the "wisdoms," or sciences in general, and of more
essential import, the gates to the wisdom of Torah in particular,
will be opened at that time. Indeed, we have seen this fulfilled in
the development of knowledge in the sciences which occurred in
that period. And in regards to the wisdom of Torah—it was also
in those days that we merited the revelation of the inner aspect
of Torah, that part of Torah which until then had been concealed.[4]

Originally, this knowledge had been revealed and known only
"to a select few, and even then, discreetly and not publicly."[5] They
withheld these studies from the discussions and examinations of the
majority of the people of Israel. The dissemination of the inner part
of Torah began only with the *Arizal*,[6] who said, "It is only in these

---

1. *Zohar* I:117a.

2. [The "sixth century of the sixth millennium" (5600-5700) corresponds to the
years 1740-1840. See *Likkutei Sichot*, vol.
5 p. 42 ff., where the Rebbe elaborates on
the significance of this period of time in
relation to the dissemination of Chasidus.
At the end of the sixth century of the
sixth millennium, two Chasidic classics,
Torah Or and *Likkutei Torah*, were first
published—*Torah Or* in 5597 (1837) and

Likkutei Torah in 5608 (1848). These
two works were great breakthroughs in
the process of articulating Chasidus in rational and intellectual terms.

The Rebbe cites further the remark of
Rabbi Menachem Mendel, the *Tzemach
Tzedek*, that the predictions of the coming of Moshiach in the year 5608 alluded
to the publication of *Likkutei Torah*. This
work was an immense contribution to the
"knowledge of G-d," and hence an important preparation for the Era of Mo-

הוספה

קטע משיחת אחרון של פסח, ה׳תש״ל

רשימת אחד השומעים

א.

אִיתָא בְּזוֹהַרא ״וּבְשִׁית מְאָה שְׁנִין לִשְׁתִיתָאָה יִתְפַּתְּחוּן
תַּרְעֵי דְּחָכְמְתָא לְעֵילָא וּמַבּוּעֵי דְּחָכְמְתָא לְתַתָּא וכו׳ וְסִימָנָךְ
בִּשְׁנַת שֵׁשׁ מֵאוֹת שָׁנָה לְחַיֵּי נֹחַ וגו׳ נִבְקְעוּ כָּל מַעְיְנוֹת תְּהוֹם
רַבָּה״. וְכַוָּונַת הַזּוֹהַר הַקָּדוֹשׁ בְּפַשְׁטוּת הִיא, כִּי בִּזְמַן הַהוּא
יִפָּתְחוּ שַׁעֲרֵי הַחָכְמוֹת בִּכְלָל וְשַׁעֲרֵי חָכְמַת הַתּוֹרָה בְּעִיקָר
וּבִפְרָט. וְכֵן רָאִינוּ בְּאוֹתוֹ הַזְּמַן בַּנּוֹגֵעַ לְחָכְמוֹת בִּכְלָל.
וּבְחָכְמַת הַתּוֹרָה – זָכִינוּ בְּאוֹתָם הַיָּמִים לְגִילּוּיָהּ שֶׁל פְּנִימִיּוּת
הַתּוֹרָה – חֵלֶק הַתּוֹרָה שֶׁהָיָה כָּמוּס וְסָתוּם עַד אָז,

שֶׁהֲרֵי בַּתְּחִלָּה הָיְתָה חָכְמָה זוֹ גְּלוּיָה וִידוּעָה רַק ״לִיחִידֵי
סְגוּלָה וְאַף גַּם זֹאת בְּהַצְנֵעַ לֶכֶת וְלֹא בָּרַבִּים״ב כִּי הֵם הָעֲלִימוּהָ
מֵעֵינָם וְעִיּוּנָם שֶׁל רוֹב עַם יִשְׂרָאֵל. וְרַק מַתְחִיל מֵהָאֲרִיז״ל –
הֲרֵי אָמַר ״דְּדַוְקָא בְּדוֹרוֹת אֵלּוּ הָאַחֲרוֹנִים מוּתָּר וּמִצְוָה לְגַלּוֹת
זֹאת הַחָכְמָה״ב. אָמְנָם גַּם אָז טֶרֶם בָּאָה לִידֵי גִילּוּי וְהִתְפַּשְּׁטוּת

---

shiach, an essential aspect of which will be, as Isaiah 11:9 states, that "the earth will be filled with the knowledge of G-d...."

The "revelation" of these works at the *end* of the sixth century of the sixth millennium, was a crucial step in the process of bringing to fruition the attempts to disseminate the Baal Shem Tov's teachings; and the Baal Shem Tov's emergence as a leader of Israel coincided with the *beginning* of the sixth century of the sixth

millennium, ca. 1740.]

3. Genesis 7:11.

4. [See *Likkutei Sichot,* ibid.]

5. *Iggeret HaKodesh* epistle 26 (142b).

6. [ARIZAL (lit., "the lion of blessed memory"): acronym for R. Isaac Luria (1534-1572); universally accepted father of modern kabalistic thought.]

latter generations that it is permitted and a duty to reveal this wisdom."[5] Even then, however, its revelation was not widespread, nor was it diffused in such a manner[7] that "it will sustain and nourish"[8]—until the appearance of the Baal Shem Tov. Upon his arrival, and through his efforts, the extensive and all-embracing dissemination of this wisdom to all Israel began. This was in accordance with the response of the King Moshiach (to the question of the Baal Shem Tov, "When will the Master come?"): "When your wellsprings are *dispersed* abroad."[9] And it was especially after the revelation of Chabad Chasidus through Rabbi Schneur Zalman[10] that it attained the level of "nourishment," for then Chasidus was articulated in terms of man's intellectual understanding and in rational language ("food").[11] From that point on, this knowledge was disseminated in a mode of continuous progression and increasing light."

At first glance, however, this matter is difficult to understand:

The period of the latter generations is the "advent of Moshiach,[12] as the *Sukkah of David* has fallen to a level of 'feet' and 'heels.'"[13] Fur-

---

7. [That is, revelation both to large numbers of people, and "revelation" in terms of ordinary intellectual comprehensibility.]

8. This is implied by the expression used in *Tikkunei Zohar* (*Tikkun* 6, end), in the words of Eliyahu the prophet announcing the redemption from our present exile (to R. Shimon bar Yochai): "Many people in the world will be *sustained and nourished* from this work of yours [the *Zohar*], when it is revealed below in the last generation, at the end of days, and on *its account* 'you will proclaim freedom in the land...'"

Kisay Melech there explains and emphasizes: "In the last generation only, near the coming of Moshiach... (even though) several hundred years have passed since it [the *Zohar*] has been revealed... (because the learning of it must be in such a manner that) it sustains and nourishes... wherein its [*Zohar's*] profound statements will be *clearly explained*

by the introductions of the *Arizal...* so *they will understand...* for although one who studies it superficially has a good reward... nevertheless the virtue on whose account 'you will proclaim freedom' is when it will sustain and nourish, and is studied with the explanatory discourses..." See also introduction by R. Chaim Vital to *Shaar Hahakdamot.*

9. This story is recorded by the Baal Shem Tov in his well-known letter concerning the matter of the ascension of his soul on Rosh Hashanah, 5507 (1746). (The letter is printed at the end of *Ben Porat Yosef,* and in a book of letters by the Baal Shem Tov and his students (Lwow 1923, wherein the publisher notes that he copied this letter from the one written by R. Yechiel, the Baal Shem Tov's son-in-law, and signed by the Baal Shem Tov). It is also printed in *Ginzei Nistarot* (Jerusalem, 1924) part 1 ch. 65, and in part at the beginning of *Keter Shem Tov* and the

בְּהַרְחָבָה – בְּאוֹפֶן דְּ"יִתְפַּרְנְסוּן"ᵍ, עַד שֶׁהוֹפִיעַ כְּבוֹד קְדֻשַּׁת הַבַּעַל שֵׁם טוֹב, וּבוֹ וְעַל יָדוֹ הִתְחִילָה חָכְמָה זוֹ לְהִתְגַּלּוֹת וּלְהִתְפַּשֵּׁט בְּהַרְחָבָה בֵּין כָּל יִשְׂרָאֵל – בְּהֶתְאֵם לִתְשׁוּבָתוֹ שֶׁל מֶלֶךְ הַמָּשִׁיחַ (עַל שְׁאֵלַת הַבַּעַל שֵׁם טוֹב "אֵימָתַי אָתֵי מַר", **לִכְשֶׁיָּפוּצוּ** מַעְיְנוֹתֶיךָ חוּצָה"ᶜ. וּבִפְרָט לְאַחַר הִתְגַּלּוּתָהּ שֶׁל חֲסִידוּת חַבַּ"ד עַל יְדֵי כְּבוֹד קְדֻשַּׁת אַדְמוֹ"ר הַזָּקֵןʰ, עַד הֱיוֹתָהּ בִּבְחִינַת "יִתְפַּרְנְסוּן", הַיְינוּ שֶׁתּוֹרַת הַחֲסִידוּת נִתְלַבְּשָׁה בִּלְבוּשֵׁי הֲבָנָה וְהַשָּׂגָה (מָזוֹן) שֶׁל הַשֵּׂכֶל הָאֱנוֹשִׁי, וּמִנִּי אָז הִיא מִתְפַּשֶּׁטֶת בְּאוֹפֶן דְּ"מוֹסִיף וְהוֹלֵךְ מוֹסִיף וְאוֹר".

וְלִכְאוֹרָה תָּמוּהַּ הַדָּבָר:

הֲרֵי דּוֹרוֹת הָאַחֲרוֹנִים הוּא זְמַן שֶׁל "עִקְּבוֹת מְשִׁיחָא שֶׁנָּפְלָה סֻכַּת דָּוִד עַד בְּחִינַת רַגְלַיִם וַעֲקֵבַיִם"ⁱ וַהֲרֵי הוּא

Maggid of Mezritch's *Likkutei Amarim*.) For an explanation of the Baal Shem Tov's question and Moshiach's answer according to Chasidus, see *Likkutei Dibburim* vol. 2, chapters 16-18. [Main text, fn. 32.]

10. And especially after Rabbi Schneur Zalman's release from imprisonment in Petersburg, Russia in 5559 (1798)—*Torat Shalom*, p. 112 ff.

[See A.C. Glitzenstein, *The Arrest and Liberation of Rabbi Schneur Zalman of Liadi: The History of Yud-Tes Kislev*, (Kehot, 1999); and Mindel, *Rabbi Schneur Zalman of Liadi* (Kehot, 2002).]

11. See *Tanya*, end of ch. 5: ["Since, in the case of knowledge of the Torah, the Torah is clothed in the soul and intellect of a person and is absorbed in them, it is called "bread" and "food" of the soul. For just as physical bread nourishes the body as it is absorbed internally, in his very inner self, where it is transformed into blood and flesh of his flesh, whereby he lives and exists—likewise, it is with the knowledge of the Torah and its comprehension by the soul of the person who studies it well, with a concentration of his intellect, until the Torah is absorbed by his intellect and is united with it and they become one."]

12. [ADVENT OF MOSHIACH. Lit., "heels of Moshiach," an expression used in Psalms 89:52 and in the *Mishnah* on *Sotah* (49b) to mean the "footsteps" of Moshiach. Rashi explains the *Mishnah's* expression to mean "the end of the Exile, before the coming of Moshiach," i.e., his imminent coming. The "heels of Moshiach" in its literal sense expresses the lowliness of these latter generations, in contrast to earlier generations, which were described with the epithet "generation(s) of intelligence."]

13. *Iggeret hakodesh* epistle 9.

thermore, it is a bereaved generation,"[14] because its darkness is "doubled and redoubled."[15] How is it possible that precisely these generations will merit the most sublime revelations, the like of which the earlier generations did not merit, not even the generations of the *Tannaim, Amoraim,* the *Geonim,* and *Rishonim,*[16] etc?

We find this same question, however, in regard to the Torah in general.

Our Sages, of blessed memory, have said:[17] "All that a distinguished scholar will introduce into Torah in the future was already given to Moshe at Sinai." It would seem that this idea, too, is difficult to understand: since all the creative contributions of the scholar were already "given" to Moshe at Sinai, why then were they not revealed to all of the generations which preceded the arrival of this distinguished scholar and his introduction of the idea?

The explanation to these questions is as follows:

It is written in the Torah,[18] "He has made everything beautiful in its time." The Sages commented on this verse: "By rights the Torah should have been given through Adam... The Holy One, blessed be He, reconsidered the matter and said... I will give it to his descendants," for the Holy One, blessed be He, appoints a time for everything He does; and this is what is meant by "the beautiful time," the time which is appropriate, relevant, and necessary for this matter. Thus it can be understood that until the arrival of that time in which the idea came to be introduced into Torah by a distinguished scholar, there was as yet no need for the concept, and therefore it was not revealed.

Torah is derived from the word *hora'ah* ("teaching"),[19] because its purpose is to teach the Jewish people "the path in which they should walk,"[20] and the service by which they should strive to pur-

---

14. *Iggeret Hateshuvah* epistle 10.

15. See *Tanya,* ch. 36.

16. [TANNAIM. "Teachers"—the Sages of the *Mishnah* who lived between the era of the Men of the Great Assembly and R. Yehudah Hanassi (ca. 350 B.C.E. to 150 C.E.).

AMORAIM. Sages of the Talmud who

lived between the redaction of the *Mishnah* until the completion of the Talmud (ca. 150-500 C.E.).

GEONIM. Heads of the leading rabbinic academies in Babylon between the 6th and 12th centuries.

RISHONIM. Early authorities who lived between the 11th and 15th centuries, and who wrote commentaries on the Talmud, Codes of Law, etc. Rashi, Rambam, and

"דּוֹר יָתוֹם"[א], כִּי הַחֹשֶׁךְ בּוֹ הוּא כָּפוּל וּמְכוּפָּל – וְאֵיךְ יִתָּכֵן
שֶׁדַּוְקָא דּוֹרוֹת הַלָּלוּ יִזְכּוּ לְגִלּוּיִם נַעֲלוּיִם כָּאֵלּוּ שֶׁלֹּא זָכוּ לָהֶם
הַדּוֹרוֹת הַקּוֹדְמִים, אַף לֹא דּוֹרוֹת הַתַּנָּאִים וְאָמוֹרָאִים,
הַגְּאוֹנִים וְרִאשׁוֹנִים וְכוּ'?

אָמְנָם כְּגוֹן דָּא אָנוּ מוֹצְאִים גַּם בְּעִנְיָן כְּלָלֵי בַּתּוֹרָה:

אָמְרוּ רַבּוֹתֵינוּ זִכְרוֹנָם לִבְרָכָה[ט] "כָּל מַה שֶׁתַּלְמִיד וָתִיק
עָתִיד לְחַדֵּשׁ בַּתּוֹרָה הַכֹּל נִתַּן לְמֹשֶׁה מִסִּינַי". וְלִכְאוֹרָה גַּם
בָּזֶה יֵשׁ לִתְמוֹהַּ: מִכֵּיוָן שֶׁחִידוּשָׁיו שֶׁל הַתַּלְמִיד כְּבָר נִתְּנוּ
לְמֹשֶׁה מִסִּינַי, לָמָה לֹא נִתְגַּלּוּ כָּל אוֹתָם הַדּוֹרוֹת, עַד כִּי יָבוֹא
תַּלְמִיד וָתִיק זֶה וִיחַדֵּשׁ עִנְיָן זֶה?

וְהַבֵּיאוּר הוּא:

כָּתוּב בַּתּוֹרָה: "אֶת הַכֹּל עָשָׂה יָפֶה בְעִתּוֹ" וְאָמְרוּ חֲכָמֵינוּ
זִכְרוֹנָם לִבְרָכָה רָאוּי הָיָה אָדָם הָרִאשׁוֹן שֶׁתִּנָּתֵן הַתּוֹרָה עַל יָדוֹ
כוּ' חָזַר וְאָמַר (הַקָּדוֹשׁ בָּרוּךְ הוּא) כוּ' אֲנִי נוֹתֵן לְבָנָיו – שֶׁכָּל
דָּבָר שֶׁהַקָּדוֹשׁ בָּרוּךְ הוּא עוֹשֵׂהוּ בִּזְמַן מְסוּיָּם, הֲרֵי זוֹ הִיא
הָעֵת הַ"יָּפָה", הַמַּתְאִימָה וּזְקוּקָה לַדָּבָר הַזֶּה. מִזֶּה מוּבָן אֲשֶׁר
עַד שֶׁיַּגִּיעַ הַזְּמַן שֶׁבּוֹ נִתְחַדֵּשׁ עִנְיָן זֶה בַּתּוֹרָה עַל יְדֵי הַתַּלְמִיד
וָתִיק, עֲדַיִין לֹא הָיוּ זְקוּקִים לְהָעִנְיָן הַזֶּה, וְלָכֵן לֹא נִתְגַּלָּה,

כִּי הֲלֹא תּוֹרָה הוּא מִלְּשׁוֹן הוֹרָאָה[א], שֶׁתַּכְלִיתָהּ לְהוֹרוֹת
לִבְנֵי יִשְׂרָאֵל אֶת הַדֶּרֶךְ יֵלְכוּ בָהּ וְאֶת הָעֲבוֹדָה אֲשֶׁר יַעֲבוֹדוּ

---

the Tosefists are among them.]

17. See *Megillah* 19b; Jerusalem Talmud, *Peah* 2:4; *Shemot Rabbah*, beg. 47; *Vayikra Rabbah*, beg. 22; *Kohelet Rabbah* 1:9; 5:8; Responsa *Radach* 5:3; *Torat Ha'olah* 3: 55; introduction of *Shach* to the Torah; *Or Torah* of the Maggid, beg. *Toldot*; *Iggeret Hakodesh, Kuntres Acharon* s.v. "*Lehavin Pratei Hahalachot.*"

18. Ecclesiastes 3:11. *Kohelet Rabbah*, ibid. See also the beginning of the portion on the verse (3:1), "To everything there is a season and a time to every purpose."

19. *Zohar* III:53b. *Gur Aryeh*, beg. of *Bereishit* in the name of *Radak*.

20. [Exodus 18:20.]

ify and refine the world—which indeed is the very purpose of the soul's descent to this world.[21] Hence, since the world as yet had no need for the purification which would be accomplished through the teaching of the new idea, the innovation was not revealed.[22] And thus the arrival of that time specifically in which the scholar introduces the idea into Torah itself demonstrates that this is the "beautiful" time for the idea—for the condition of the world is such that it urgently needs the instruction flowing from the scholar's innovation.[23]

The same explanation applies to our subject. All the revelations of the future with the coming of Moshiach "depend on our actions and service throughout the duration of the Exile."[24] This statement refers not only to the service of this final Exile—but in light of the saying of our Sages[25] that "A mitzvah is ascribed only to he who completes it," it is understood that when the service and the purifications of this Exile are completed then the aim and purpose of all the Exiles will be fulfilled and consummated (for the Redemption from this Exile is a Redemption after which there will be no more exile).[26] It follows accordingly that our service which brings to a conclusion the fourth Exile and inaugurates the succeeding redemption—thus affects and elevates the three preceding Exiles.

Thus, it is precisely inasmuch as these latter generations are the "heels of Moshiach"—for in them is to be found the purification and culmination of the fourth and last Exile—that these generations are charged with a greater responsibility, and their service must be of higher quality, and undertaken with greater strength and effort than the service of the preceding generations and periods

---

21. *Tanya*, ch. 37 (48b).

22. Nonetheless, this "innovation" was always a part of Torah. This is similar in concept to the entire Torah, which "preceded the world" (*Pesachim* 54b; *Nedarim* 39b), and there were a select few who studied and fulfilled the whole Torah in its entirety even before it was given (*Kiddushin* 82a; *Yoma* 28b). To all of

Israel however, it was given only after twenty six generations.

23. This is also a reason why my sainted father-in-law, Rabbi Yosef Yitzchak, revealed certain teachings and customs, etc., only in the recent past—and some of them in the United States, the "lower hemisphere" of the world [i.e., in relation to Israel, the "upper hemisphere"],

לְבָרֵר וּלְזַכֵּךְ אֶת הָעוֹלָם – תַּכְלִית הַיְרִידָה לָעוֹלָם הַזֶּה‏‏ ‏.
וּמֵכֵּיוָן שֶׁהָעוֹלָם לֹא הָיָה זָקוּק עֲדַיִין לְהַבֵּירוּר שֶׁל הוֹרָאָה זוֹ
הַבָּאָה בְּהָעִנְיָן שֶׁמִּתְחַדֵּשׁ עַל יְדֵי הַתַּלְמִיד – לֹא **נִתְגַּלָּה**
הַחִידּוּשׁ‏‏‏‏‏‏. וּבְבוֹא הַזְּמַן שֶׁבּוֹ הַתַּלְמִיד וָתִיק מְחַדֵּשׁ אֶת הָעִנְיָן
בַּתּוֹרָה הֲרֵי זֶה גּוּפָא הוֹכָחָה שֶׁהוּא הוּא הָעֵת הַ"יָפֶה" לָזֶה;
וְהַיְינוּ לְפִי שֶׁמַּצַּב הָעוֹלָם הוּא כָּזֶה, שֶׁנֶּחוּצָה וּמוּכְרַחַת
הַהוֹרָאָה הַנּוֹבַעַת מֵחִידּוּשׁוֹ שֶׁל הַתַּלְמִיד וָתִיק‏‏.

וְעַל דֶּרֶךְ זֶה הוּא בְּעִנְיָן דִּידָן: כָּל הַגִּילוּיִים דִּלְעָתִיד,
בְּבִיאַת הַמָּשִׁיחַ, הֲרֵי הֵם דָּבָר הַ"תָּלוּי בְּמַעֲשֵׂינוּ וַעֲבוֹדָתֵינוּ כָּל
מֶשֶׁךְ הַגָּלוּת"‏‏. וְאֵין הַכַּוָּונָה רַק לְהָעֲבוֹדָה שֶׁל גָּלוּת זוֹ
הָאַחֲרוֹנָה, אֶלָּא מֵאַחַר שֶׁאָמְרוּ רַבּוֹתֵינוּ זִכְרוֹנָם לִבְרָכָה‏‏ "אֵין
הַמִּצְוָה נִקְרֵאת אֶלָּא עַל שֵׁם גּוֹמְרָהּ". הֲרֵי מוּבָן שֶׁבְּגֶמַר
הָעֲבוֹדָה וְהַבֵּירוּרִים שֶׁל גָּלוּת הַלָּזוֹ, יוּגְמַר וְיִסְתַּיֵּים גַּם עִנְיָן
וְתַכְלִית כָּל הַגָּלוּיוֹת שֶׁהֲרֵי הַגְּאוּלָה מִגָּלוּת זוֹ הִיא גְּאוּלָה שֶׁאֵין
אַחֲרֶיהָ גָּלוּת"‏‏‏‏. מוּבָן עַל פִּי זֶה, אֲשֶׁר עֲבוֹדָתֵנוּ זוֹ, הַמְּבִיאָה
לִגְמַר הַגָּלוּת הָרְבִיעִית וְהַגְּאוּלָה שֶׁלְּאַחֲרֶיהָ – פּוֹעֶלֶת עִילּוּי
גַּם בְּשָׁלֹשׁ הַגְּאוּלוֹת הַקּוֹדְמוֹת.

הַיּוֹצֵא מִזֶּה, אֲשֶׁר דַּוְקָא וְכֵיוָן שֶׁדּוֹרוֹת אֵלּוּ הָאַחֲרוֹנִים הֵם
"עִקְּבְתָא דִמְשִׁיחָא" שֶׁבָּהֶם הוּא בֵּירוּר וּגְמַר גָּלוּת הָרְבִיעִית
וְהָאַחֲרוֹנָה – מוּטֶּלֶת עֲלֵיהֶם אַחְרָיוּת יוֹתֵר גְּדוֹלָה, וַעֲבוֹדָתָם
צְרִיכָה לִהְיוֹת יוֹתֵר נַעֲלֵית וּבְהִתְחַזְּקוּת וְהִתְגַּבְּרוּת יוֹתֵר מִזוֹ

---

even though he had heard them many years before—because "for everything there is a time," and the time had then come when the world needed them. (See his letter in *Sefer Hamaamarim* 5708, p. 232.)

24. *Tanya*, beg. ch. 37.

25. *Sotah* 13b. Quoted in *Tanchuma* and Rashi's commentary on Deuteronomy 8:1.

26. See *Mechilta* on Exodus 15:1: "The Future Redemption will not be followed by any enslavement" (quoted in *Tosfot* s.v. *Venomar, Pesachim* 116b). Similarly in *Shemot Rabbah* 23:11 (see Rashi on *Erchin* 13b s.v. *b'nevel*).

of Exile. For our service is the final preparation for the complete and perfect Redemption: to transform the "doubled and redoubled" darkness to doubled and redoubled light.[27]

Since "the Holy One blessed be He is not a tyrant to His creatures"[28] and demands of them only according to the measure of the powers He has given them, it is therefore specifically in these generations that the most sublime and inner portions of Torah are revealed (to which earlier generations were not privileged). And through these revelations, special powers flow from above for this elevated work—for the Torah is "strength and might";[29] it gives power for achievement in the service of G-d.

Furthermore: in addition to the fact that this great task in itself demands special powers, it is known that the more necessary the service, and the closer it is to its desired end and purpose, the *kelipah*[30] and the Evil Inclination exert themselves more vigorously in order to oppose and hinder it.[31] And since the service of the *latter* generations literally reaches to the culminating end of the entire process of purifying the world, the opposition of the Evil Inclination becomes greater and more intense, in order to prevent the person from fulfilling the duty with which he is charged. Hence it is also for this reason that we in this generation most urgently require special powers, in order that through our service we be able to fulfill and perfectly realize the will of the Holy One, blessed be He, for "the Holy One blessed be He desired to have for Himself (may He be blessed)[32] a dwelling place in the lower worlds."[33]

2.

It can be said, in light of all the above, that just as this general difference exists between the latter generations and the earlier generations, so does it also exist amongst the latter generations themselves.

---

27. See *Tanya* ch. 36, *Iggeret Hateshuvah*, end of ch. 9.

28. *Avodah Zarah* 3a.

29. See *Torah Or*, beg. *Yisro*.

30. [*Kelipah*, or "shell" is the symbol frequently used in Kabbalah to denote "evil" and the source of sensual desires in human nature. See Schochet, *Mystical Concepts in Chassidism*, ch. 10 (*Kelipot*), Kehot, 1988.]

אֲשֶׁר בְּדוֹרוֹת וְגָלֻיּוֹת הַקּוֹדְמִים. כִּי הֲלֹא עֲבוֹדָתֵנוּ זוֹ הִיא הַכָנָה אַחֲרוֹנָה לַגְּאוּלָה הַשְּׁלֵימָה: לְהַפֵּךְ אֶת הַחֹשֶׁךְ כָּפוּל וּמְכוּפָּל – לְאוֹר כָּפוּל וּמְכוּפָּלֵ"ח.

וְכֵיוָן שֶׁ"אֵין הַקָּדוֹשׁ בָּרוּךְ הוּא בָּא בִּטְרוּנְיָא עִם בְּרִיּוֹתָיו"ֵ"ט, וְאֵינוֹ מְבַקֵּשׁ אֶלָּא לְפִי הַכֹּחוֹת שֶׁנִּיתְּנוּ לָהֶם, לָכֵן בַּדּוֹרוֹת הָאֵלֶּה דַּוְקָא מִתְגַּלִּים חֶלְקֵי הַתּוֹרָה הַנֶּעֱלָמִים עַד עַתָּה וְהַפְּנִימִיִּים (מַה שֶׁלֹּא זָכוּ לָהֶם בַּדּוֹרוֹת הָרִאשׁוֹנִים), וּבָהֶם וְעַל יָדָם נִשְׁפָּעִים מִלְמַעְלָה כֹּחוֹת מְיוּחָדִים לַעֲבוֹדָה נַעֲלֵית זוֹ – שֶׁהֲרֵי הַתּוֹרָה הִיא "**עוֹז** וְתוּשִׁיָּה"ֵ, הִיא הַנּוֹתֶנֶת כֹּחַ לַעֲשׂוֹת חַיִל בַּעֲבוֹדָה.

יוֹתֵר מִזֶּה: נוֹסָף עַל זֶה שֶׁעֲבוֹדָה גְדוֹלָה זוֹ מִצַּד עַצְמָהּ דּוֹרֶשֶׁת כֹּחוֹת מְיוּחָדִים – הֲרֵי יָדוּעַ, שֶׁכָּל שֶׁהָעֲבוֹדָה מוּכְרַחַת יוֹתֵר וּקְרוֹבָה יוֹתֵר לַתַּכְלִית הַנִּרְצָה שֶׁבָּאָה עַל יָדָהּ, מִתְגַּבֶּרֶת יוֹתֵר הַקְּלִיפָּה וְהַיֵּצֶר הָרָע לְנֶגֶד וְלִמְנוֹעַ וכּוֹ'ֵ. וֶהֱיוֹת שֶׁעֲבוֹדַת דּוֹרוֹת **הָאַחֲרוֹנִים** נוֹגַעַת מַמָּשׁ לִגְמַר וְהַשְׁלָמַת כָּל הַבֵּירוּרִים, הֲרֵי הִתְנַגְדוּת הַיֵּצֶר הָרָע נֶגְדָּהּ הוּא בְּיֶתֶר תּוֹקֶף וָעוֹז – לִמְנוֹעַ הָעוֹבֵד לַעֲשׂוֹת אֶת הַמוּטָל עָלָיו – וְאִם כֵּן גַּם בִּגְלַל זֶה מוּכְרָחִים בַּדּוֹרוֹת אֵלּוּ לְכֹחוֹת מְיוּחָדִים, כְּדֵי שֶׁעַל יְדֵי עֲבוֹדָתֵנוּ נוּכַל לְקַיֵּים וּלְהַשְׁלִים אֶת רְצוֹנוֹ שֶׁל הַקָּדוֹשׁ בָּרוּךְ הוּא, שֶׁ"נִּתְאַוֶּה הַקָּדוֹשׁ בָּרוּךְ הוּא לִהְיוֹת לוֹ (יִתְבָּרֵךְֵ) דִּירָה בַּתַּחְתּוֹנִים"ֵ.

ב.

עַל פִּי הַנִּזְכָּר לְעֵיל יֵשׁ לוֹמַר שֶׁכְּמוֹ שֶׁהוּא בִּכְלָלוּת, בַּהֶפְרֵשׁ שֶׁבֵּין דּוֹרוֹת הָאַחֲרוֹנִים לְבֵין הַדּוֹרוֹת שֶׁלְּפָנֵיהֶם, כֵּן הוּא הָעִנְיָן גַּם בַּדּוֹרוֹת הָאַחֲרוֹנִים עַצְמָם – שֶׁבְּכָל דּוֹר וָדוֹר

---

31. See *Tanya* ch. 28; *Likkutei Sichot* vol. 3 p. 747 ff.

32. This expression was frequently added by Rabbi Shalom DovBer. See *Likkutei*

Sichot vol. 19, pp. 27-28.

33. *Tanchuma, Naso* 16; *Bamidbar Rabbah* 10:6; *Tanya* ch. 36.

Just as the responsibility of each generation nearer to the coming of Moshiach greatly increases[34]—likewise, the revelation of the most sublime ideas of Torah greatly increases, in relation to the earlier generations. We have seen this to be true in regard to the revelation of the inner part of Torah: from generation to generation it becomes more *revealed*, and further expresses itself in terms of rational understanding and intellectual form.

An example of such greatly increased exposition is especially prominent in the *maamarim* [Chasidic discourses] of Rabbi Shalom DovBer.[35] Here the concepts of Chasidus are articulated more broadly and clearly, in terms of rational understanding and intellectual comprehension, more so than (is apparent even to people on our level) in the *maamarim* of the Rebbes who preceded him.

There is a well-known[36] saying of the early Chasidim concerning Rabbi Shalom DovBer that he is "the Rambam [Maimonides] of Chasidus," for in his *maamarim* the concepts of Chasidus were formulated in a highly ordered and systematic way, with step-by-step explanations and clarifying illustrations, etc. We can understand the nature of the *maamarim* of Rabbi Shalom DovBer from what the Rambam writes[37] concerning his work the *Yad Hachazakah,* "I decided to put together the results… all in plain language and terse style, so that thus the entire Oral Law might become systematically

---

34. Note *Sotah* 49a: "Every single day [of Exile] the curse becomes greater than the day before."

[In *Likkutei Sichot* vol. 4, p. 1226 it is explained that although this generation is the "lowest," i.e., the "heels of Moshiach," Moshiach's advent is specifically in this generation—for in this generation, the entire plan and purpose for which previous generations strove will be completed. Just as in the body, the feet are lowest yet support the head, likewise our generation is compared to the "feet" which support the previous generations. In this respect, every succeeding period (of Jewish history) has a certain distinction and advantage over the preceding ones, even though generally speaking, the latter periods are of lower quality and in a greater "exile." This is true of the entire *seder hishtalshelut* (see main text footnote 51) which is analogous to a chain wherein the top of the lower ring is higher than the bottom of the upper ring. The same is true of the chain of generations—the beginning of the succeeding generation is greater than the end of the preceding one.]

35. See *Chanoch L'naar* (p. 8, and see *Hayom Yom* p. 106) that the *Tzemach Tzedek* said regarding Rabbi Shalom DovBer: "He was born on the 20th of *Cheshvan* 5621 (1860). In this date the Hebrew letter *chaf* (כ) is found twice, an allusion to the Supernal *keter*." It is known that two

שֶׁמִּתְקָרֵב יוֹתֵר לְבִיאַת הַמָּשִׁיחַ, כְּמוֹ שֶׁהָאַחֲרָיוּת הוֹלֶכֶת וּגְדֵלָהּ²ⁿ – כֵּן הוֹלֶכֶת וְרַבָּה הִתְגַּלּוּת הָעִנְיָנִים הַנַּעֲלִים דְּתוֹרָה, לְגַבֵּי הַדּוֹרוֹת שֶׁקָּדְמוּם. וּכְמוֹ שֶׁאָנוּ רוֹאִים שֶׁכֵּן הוּא הַדָּבָר בְּעִנְיַן גִּילּוּי פְּנִימִיּוּת הַתּוֹרָה – מִדּוֹר לְדוֹר הִיא **מִתְגַּלֵּית** יוֹתֵר וְיוֹרֶדֶת וּמִתְלַבֶּשֶׁת יוֹתֵר בִּלְבוּשֵׁי הֲבָנָה וְהַשָּׂגָה וּתְפִיסָא.

גִּילּוּי בְּתוֹסֶפֶת רַבָּה כָּזוֹ נִיכָּר וּבוֹלֵט בִּמְיוּחָד בְּמַאֲמָרָיו שֶׁל כְּבוֹד קְדֻשַּׁת אַדְמוֹ"ר (מהורש"ב) נִשְׁמָתוֹ עֵדֶן²ⁿ, אֲשֶׁר בָּהֶם בָּאִים עִנְיְנֵי הַחֲסִידוּת בְּבֵיאוּר יוֹתֵר רָחָב וּבַהֲבָנָה וְהַשָּׂגָה שִׂכְלִית יוֹתֵר, מִכְּמוֹ שֶׁהֵם (בְּגָלוּי – גַּם לַאֲנָשִׁים כְּעֶרְכֵּנוּ) בְּמַאֲמָרֵי רַבּוֹתֵינוּ שֶׁקָּדְמוּ.

וַהֲרֵי יָדוּעַ²ⁿ הַפִּתְגָּם שֶׁל חֲסִידִים הָרִאשׁוֹנִים שֶׁכְּבוֹד קְדֻשַּׁת אַדְמוֹ"ר (מהורש"ב) נִשְׁמָתוֹ עֵדֶן הוּא "הָרַמְבַּ"ם דְּתוֹרַת הַחֲסִידוּת", לְפִי שֶׁעִנְיְנֵי תּוֹרַת הַחֲסִידוּת בָּאוּ בְּמַאֲמָרָיו בְּסֵדֶר־מְסוּדָּר, בְּהַסְבָּרָה מוּדְרֶגֶת וּבִמְשָׁלִים הַמְבָרְרִים וכו'. וּמוּבָן, אֲשֶׁר עַל דֶּרֶךְ שֶׁהָרַמְבַּ"ם כּוֹתֵב²ⁿ אוֹדוֹת סִפְרוֹ יַד הַחֲזָקָה "וְרָאִיתִי לְחַבֵּר דְּבָרִים הַמִּתְבָּרְרִים וכו' בְּלָשׁוֹן בְּרוּרָה בְּדֶרֶךְ קְצָרָה עַד שֶׁתְּהֵא תּוֹרָה שֶׁבְּעַל פֶּה סְדוּרָה בְּפִי הַכֹּל כו'

---

chafs allude to the two levels of *keter, arich* and *atik* (*Likkutei Torah, Shir Hashirim* 35c). This means that he is connected not only to *arich* (which though above *hishtalshelut*, is nevertheless connected to *hishtalshelut*) but also to *atik*, which completely transcends *hishtalshelut*.

Another related fact is thus: Rabbi Shalom DovBer's circumcision was on the second day of Chanukah, since it was on the second day of Chanukah that the miracle of Chanukah was openly revealed (a miracle emanating from a level transcending *hishtalshelut*), not as on the first day when the miracle was not yet apparent, and concerning which there is discussion

of this in Torah which requires a particular explanation. (See *Taz* beg. *Hilchot Chanukah* ch. 670, and elsewhere.) And indeed, all of this is related to the Redemption, for the Redemption also results from a level higher than *hishtalshelut*.

[For an explanation of the terms *keter, arich, atik,* and *hishtalshelut,* see main text footnotes 16 and 51.]

36. *Likkutei Dibburim* (Eng. Ed.) vol. 2, p. 243. See also *Sefer Hasichot* 5701, p. 160.

37. In his introduction to his work *Yad Hachazakah*.

known to all... statements clear, accessible, and correct...." In his *maamarim*, Chasidus was formulated (in revealed rather than arcane form, as mentioned above) into "plain language... consisting of statements accessible and correct."

3.

The *maamarim* of the year 5666 (1905) were a series about which Rabbi Shalom DovBer spoke with unusual praise. All the distinctive qualities elaborated above in praise of his *maamarim* are expressed in a particularly outstanding manner in this series.

Furthermore, it is not only in these *maamarim* that Chasidus is revealed and articulated in broader and more widely comprehensible rational form, but also the connection of "this wisdom" to the future Redemption (as explained above, this is the very reason why the inner part of Torah is revealed more and more from generation to generation) is more readily apparent in this series.

As it is known, Rabbi Shalom DovBer associated his discourses of this year (5666—1905-6) with the predictions of the *ketz*[38] found in several works in reference to that year[39] (and also with the fact that at that time there were pogroms in Russia, and that it was the year *after* a leap year).[40]

In practical terms: as explained previously, it is clear that we have been endowed with powers from Above in order to transform the "doubled and redoubled" darkness. It is written, "The *Shechinah* went into exile in Edom with them,"[41] and is called by the name *She-*

---

38. [KETZ. Lit., "end." This term generally refers to the specific years in which it is especially likely for Moshiach to come.]

39. It can be said that this was the reason he instituted the drinking of the Four Cups on the last day of Passover in that year (*Hayom Yom* p. 47)—because the last day of Passover, and its central meaning, is associated with the future Redemption, as indicated in the content of the *Haftarah*. (See *Likkutei Sichot* vol. 4, p. 1299).

One can suggest a special association to

wine, because wine represents "revelation of the concealed." For at first, the liquid was concealed within the grapes, and afterwards it comes out. Hence, it *effects* the revelation of the hidden, as it is written (Judges 9:13), "It gladdens G-d and men," since it reveals the concealed states of G-d and men (*Likkutei Torah, Drushim L'sukkot* 79d).

40. [A leap year in the Jewish calendar contains an extra month. According to Chasidus, a leap year therefore requires

דְּבָרִים בְּרוּרִים קְרוֹבִים נְכוֹנִים כו'" – הוּא הַדָּבָר בַּנּוֹגֵעַ
לְמַאַמְרֵי כְּבוֹד קְדֻשַּׁת אַדְמוּ"ר (מהורש"ב) נִשְׁמָתוֹ עֵדֶן, אֲשֶׁר
בָּהֶם בָּאָה תּוֹרַת הַחֲסִידוּת (בְּגִלּוּי כְּנִזְכָּר לְעֵיל) "בִּדְבָרִים
הַמִּתְבָּרְרִים, בְּלָשׁוֹן בְּרוּרָה . . דְּבָרִים קְרוֹבִים נְכוֹנִים" וְכוּ'.

ג.

מִבֵּין מַאֲמָרָיו גּוּפָא דִּבֶּר כְּבוֹד קְדֻשַּׁת אַדְמוּ"ר
(מהורש"ב) נִשְׁמָתוֹ עֵדֶן בִּמְיֻחָד בְּשֶׁבַח הַהֶמְשֵׁךְ תרס"ו. כִּי כָּל
מַעֲלוֹת הַנִּזְכָּרִים לְעֵיל, בָּהֶן נִשְׁתַּבְּחוּ מַאֲמָרָיו, יֶשְׁנָן בְּמִדָּה
מְרוּבָּה וּמְיֻחֶדֶת בְּהֶמְשֵׁךְ זֶה.

וְלֹא רַק שֶׁבְּהֶמְשֵׁךְ זֶה בָּאָה תּוֹרַת הַחֲסִידוּת לִידֵי הִתְגַּלּוּת
יוֹתֵר וּבְהַשָּׂגָה לְמַטָּה יוֹתֵר, אֶלָּא שֶׁגַּם שַׁיָּיכוּתָהּ שֶׁל "חָכְמָה
זוֹ" לִגְאוּלָה הָעֲתִידָה (וְכַנִּזְכָּר לְעֵיל, שֶׁהִיא הִיא הַסִּבָּה מַה
שֶּׁפְּנִימִיּוּת הַתּוֹרָה מִתְגַּלֵּית יוֹתֵר מִדּוֹר לְדוֹר) נִרְאֵית יוֹתֵר
בְּהֶמְשֵׁךְ זֶה,

וְכַיָּדוּעַ אֲשֶׁר כְּבוֹד קְדֻשַּׁת אַדְמוּ"ר (מהורש"ב) נִשְׁמָתוֹ
עֵדֶן קִישֵּׁר אֲמִירָתוֹ שֶׁל הַהֶמְשֵׁךְ בְּשָׁנָה זוֹ (תרס"ו) עִם הַ"קֵּץ"
הַנִּמְצָא בְּכַמָּה סְפָרִים עַל שָׁנָה הַהִיא[מ] (וְגַם עִם זֶה שֶׁבִּזְמַן
הַהוּא הָיוּ פְּרָעוֹת בִּמְדִינַת רוּסְיָא לֹא עָלֵינוּ וְשֶׁהָיְתָה **מוֹצָאֵי**
שְׁנַת הָעִיבּוּר).

וּבְנּוֹגֵעַ לַפּוֹעַל: עַל פִּי כָּל הַנִּזְכָּר לְעֵיל שֶׁנִּיתְנוּ וְנִמְשְׁכוּ
הַגִּלּוּיִים וְהַכֹּחוֹת מִלְמַעְלָה לַהֲפוֹךְ אֶת הַחֹשֶׁךְ כָּפוּל וּמְכוּפָּל,
וְי"גָלוּ לֶאֱדוֹם **שְׁכִינָה** עִמָּהֶם"[מט] שֶׁנִּקְרֵאת "בְּשֵׁם שְׁכִינָה עַל שֵׁם

---

greater spiritual forces.]

41. *Sifri Massei* 35:34. (See *Megillah*,
29a: "The *Shechinah* went into exile in
Babylon with them" and note also the
difference: In *Tanya* ch. 17; *Iggeret Hak-*
odesh epistle 25 (and elsewhere in Chasidus)—"to Edom." In *Iggeret Hakodesh* 4
(and elsewhere)—"to Babylon." In several places where the same topic is discussed and the above statement of the
Sages is not quoted at all.)

chinah because "it dwells and clothes itself in all the worlds,"[42] which means that even though we find ourselves in a very humble condition, nevertheless He, may He be blessed, dwells with us; even unto, "And I will dwell within them, '*within* every single one.'"[43] He gives us the ability to conclude the Exile, to purify the "small jars"[44] that as of yet have not been purified, and to merit that He will "set an end to darkness,"[45] an end to the Exile, and afterwards—bring the beginning of the Redemption, followed by the complete, perfect, and true Redemption through our righteous Moshiach, speedily in our days.

---

42. *Tanya* ch. 41.

43. *Reshit Chochmah* (*Shaar Ha'ahavah* ch. 6 near beg.); *Shalah* (*Shaar Ha'otiyot, Lamed. Taanit* s.v. *Me'inyan Ha'avodah. Trumah*, sect. of *Torah Or*—325b, 326b—and elsewhere).

44. [The purpose of Exile, as seen in Kabbalah and Chasidic literature, is to purify the world by releasing the "sparks of holiness" from their spiritual bondage (in the *kelipot*). In the course of the long Exile, almost all have been released, and all that is left are the "small jars," i.e., the few final remaining "sparks." See Rashi's commentary on Genesis 32:25. See

שֶׁשּׁוֹכֶנֶת וּמִתְלַבֶּשֶׁת תּוֹךְ כָּל עָלְמִין"ל, הַיְינוּ שֶׁגַּם כַּאֲשֶׁר נִמְצָאִים אָנוּ בִּשְׁפַל הַמַּצָּב, מִכָּל מָקוֹם הֲרֵי הוּא יִתְבָּרֵךְ הוּא הַשּׁוֹכֵן אִתָּנוּ וְעַד אֲשֶׁר "וְשָׁכַנְתִּי בְּתוֹכָם בְּתוֹךְ כָּל אֶחָד וְאֶחָד"לא, הֲרֵי הוּא הַנּוֹתֵן לָנוּ כֹּחַ לְסַיֵּים הַגָּלוּת, לְבָרֵר "הַפַּכִים קְטַנִּים" שֶׁעֲדַיִין לֹא נִתְבָּרְרוּ, וְלִזְכּוֹת לְקֵץ שָׁם לַחוֹשֶׁךְלב, קֵץ הַגָּלוּת, וְאַחַר כַּךְ – לְהָאִתְחַלְתָּא דִגְאוּלָה וְאַחַר כַּךְ לִשְׁלֵימוּת הַגְּאוּלָה הָאֲמִתִּית עַל יְדֵי מָשִׁיחַ צִדְקֵנוּ – בִּמְהֵרָה בְּיָמֵינוּ מַמָּשׁ, אָמֵן כֵּן יְהִי רָצוֹן.

---

also Schochet, *Mystical Concepts in Chassidism*, ch. 11 (*Birur* and *Tikun*), op. cit.]

45. Job 28:3. *Or Hatorah, Miketz* (340a). And as in the explanation of *Midrash Rabbah* quoted there—likewise in *Tanya* ch. 33)—he also references to *Zohar*

I:194a. And ibid., on the verse, "To everything there is a season and a time to every purpose" (explained in *Likkutei Levi Yitzchak* on the *Zohar*.), "Come and see: For everything G-d does below, He appoints a time, and a set period. He sets the time for light…" [Hence, G-d will set an end to the darkness.]

HEBREW NOTES

HEBREW NOTES
ON THE ESSENCE OF CHASIDUS

*) קטע משיחת חג גאולת אדמו"ר הזקן – י"ט כסלו ה'תשכ"ו. וראה להלן הערה מו.

א. ראה ג"כ קונטרס תורת החסידות וקונטרס לימוד החסידות (לכ"ק מו"ח אדמו"ר).

א*. בכת"י שהבהערה ב, שישראל היו בהתעלפות. ומכיון שהעולם "נתן בלבם", הרי כשהם בהתעלפות, במילא העולם במצב זה (ראה לקו"ת במדבר ה' רע"ב). [הערת כ"ק אדמו"ר זי"ע על גליון קונטרס ענינה של תורת החסידות].

ב. נמצא בכת"י דא"ח ישן (לא נודע למי). וראה גם קובץ יו"ד שבט ע'ד סה. סו.

ג. ד"ה פדה בשלום העת"ר (תשכ"ו) שבהמשך בששה"ק תער"ב (סעיף שעו) – ברוקלין, תשל"א.

ד. נדה יז, א ותוספות שם. וראה לקו"ד ח"א סח, א.

ה. לקו"ד שם נו, א.

ו. שם ע"ב. ונתבאר ב"התמים" ח"ג ע' סו ואילך.

ז. תורת שלום ע' 117.

ח. איוב יט, כו. וראה לקו"ד ח"ב שלב, ב ואילך.

ועיין בתורת שלום ע' 185, שמצד ענין זה [שנתחדש בתורת החסידות שע"י הכחות שבאדם משיגים את הענינים שלמעלה], נעשים הכחות אלקות. עיי"ש. ועפ"ז יש לקשר ענין זה עם ענין הג'.

ט. ראה ס' השיחות קיץ ה'ש"ת ע' 26 ואילך. ובכ"מ.

י. אלא שמ"מ, ע"י מעלות אלו דוקא תופסים במהות החסידות, כדלהלן סעיף חי.

יא. ד"ה פדה בשלום הנ"ל.

יב. שם (סעיף שעג).

יג. שם (סעיף שעד. שעו).

יד. תנחומא פקודי ג. ת"ז תס"ט (ק, א). ועייג"כ אדר"נ פל"א. קה"ר א, ד. זח"א קלד, ב. מו"נ ח"א פע"ב. לקו"ת במדבר רד"ה והי' מספר.

טו. ראה פירוש הרע"ב ריש מס' אבות.

*טו. כי כל עניני העולם ברא אלקים לעשות ולתקן (ראה ב"ר פי"א, ו. וברש"י שם. זח"א מז, ב ואילך. אוה"ת עה"פ (ע' תקיד וע' תשיז)) ולאחרי חטא עה"ד מעורבים הם טו"ר (תו"א ס"פ תולדות. תו"ח תולדות יד, ב. ובכ"מ) ואין טוב בלא כו' (ראה לקו"ד ח"א פז, א).

טז. במכתבו מד' טבת תרח"ץ (י"ל בקופיר).

יז. דברים ד, ו.

יח. קו"א בתניא ד"ה דוד זמירות קרית להו. דרמ"צ מא, א-ב. ובכ"מ.

יט. תהלים קב, כז. וכידוע דב' סוגים בלבושים, דיש שא"א להחליפם (וכהלבוש דעור ובשר תלבישני).

כ. סעיף ח' ואילך.

כא. תניא פל"ט (נג, א).

כב. הדיוק בהפצת המעינות דוקא, ראה להלן סעיף כא.

כג. מענה המשיח שאז יבא – וכמ"ש הבעש"ט באגרתו הידועה על דבר עליית הנשמה שלו בר"ה שנת תק"ז, נדפסה: בסוף הספר בן פורת יוסף: בספר המכתבים מהבעש"ט ז"ל

ותלמידיו (לבוב תרפ"ג, וכותב המו"ל שהעתיקה מן המכתב – כת"י חתנו של הבעש"ט הרה"צ וכו' ר' יחיאל – החתום בעצם כי"ק של הבעש"ט): בספר גנזי נסתרות (ירושלים ת"ו תרפ"ד) ח"א סי' סה. – וחלק ממנה בתחלת חלק ספר כתר שם טוב, וספר לקוטי אמרים להה"מ ממעזריטש.

ביאור שאלת הבעש"ט ומענה המשיח ע"פ חסידות – ראה לקו"ד ח"ב ליקוט טז-יח.

כד. ראה גם ד"ה פדה בשלום הנ"ל (סעיף שעה ואילך), שההמשכה ד"חסידות" היא דוגמת ההמשכה דלעתיד.

כה. כמרז"ל (מגילה כט, א) הקב"ה שב עמהן מבין הגליות.

כו. רמב"ם סוף הל' מלכים. – שגם בזמן ביהמ"ק לא היתה מלאה הארץ דעה את הוי' גו'.

כז. ראה רמב"ם שם דלא יהי' קנאה כו' וכל המעדנים כו' – אף לדעתו (שם ר"פ) ד"וגר זאב גו'" משל הוא. ועאכו"כ להדעה (וכן היא הכרעת תורת הקבלה והחסידות) – דהדברים כפשוטם. ועייג"כ ראב"ד (הל' תשובה פ"ח ה"ב). עבוה"ק ח"ב פמ"א. ובכ"מ.

ואואפ"ל לחומר הענין (עכ"פ בדוחק), דגם לרמב"ם ב' תקופות לאחרי שודאי משיח הוא, ו"מלאה הארץ גו'" יהי' בתקופה הראשונה דגאולה, וכל הפרק שברמב"ם שם מדבר בתקופה זו. וכמ"ש בהל' תשובה פ"ט שמ"ש ומלאה הארץ דעה גו' מיירי בהתקופה שעולם כמנהגו הולך.

עפי"ז יש לתרץ קושיית הלח"מ (הל' תשובה פ"ח ה"ז), כי מ"ש "אין בין כו' אלא שעבוד מלכיות בלבד" הוא רק בתחילת הגאולה. (וא"ש תירוץ הכ"מ (הל' מלכים רפי"א) על השגת הראב"ד (שם), שהרמב"ם אזיל לטעמי, כי בתחלת הגאולה, אין מלך המשיח צריך לעשות אותות ומופתים ולא יוצרך להיות מורה וראין). אבל אח"כ, גם הרמב"ם מודה שיהי' חידוש בעולם, ומ"ש (ישעי' ב, ד) וכתתו חרבותם לאתים הוא כפשוטו, ולא דרך משל בלבד. ומכיון שהם בטלים בתקופה השני' (עכ"פ) של הגאולה, הרי זה מוכיח שאינן כתשיטין.

כח. ברכות לד, ב. וש"נ. רמב"ם הל' תשובה ספ"ט. הל' מלכים פי"ב ה"ב.

כט. ראה זח"א קלט, א. וראה לעיל הערה כז.

ל. זח"ג קכה, א. נתבאר באגה"ק סכ"ו.

לא. וכפשוטו (וראה ג"כ אגה"ק סי"ט (קכח, א). לקו"ת ויקרא (ו, ד). שה"ש (לא, ג)) שקרי הו"ע גילוי וכתיב – העלם.

לב. פסחים נ, א.

לג. זח"ג רנז, סע"ב. שעהיוה"א פ"ז (פב, א).

לד. אבל נעלה יותר מהגילוי שבזמן המקדש, שלכן יהי' אז גילוי שם הוי' בכל העולם (וע"ד המבואר בלקו"ת דרושי ר"ה (נז, סע"ג) מעלת בית ראשון על בית שני, שבב"ר דוקא האיר גם בגבולין).

לה. ראה ר"ה ח, ריש ע"ב. ירושלמי ר"ה פ"א ה"ג. תנחומא (באבער) בא יג.

לו. ד"ה וידבר אלקים אכה"ד תרצ"ט (השני) ס"ד בשם הרמ"ז. עיין שער (וספר) הגלגולים בתחלתו ובכ"מ. ואכ"מ.

לז. ראה ב"ר (פי"ד, ט) דב"ר (פ"ב, לז): חמשה שמות נקראו לה, נפש רוח נשמה חי' יחידה. – בכמה דפוסים במדרש שם הוא בשינוי הסדר וכן בפיוטים וכו', אבל בכהאריז"ל (ע"ח שמ"ב בתחלתו. שער הגלולים בתחלתו. ובכ"מ) ובדא"ח מובא ובדיוק בסדר זה. ועייג"כ זח"א פא, א. שם רו, א.

לח. ראה אמ"ב שער הק"ש פ"ח. וראה גם לקו"ת בלק ע, א.

לט. ראה סנהדרין עב, סע"א (וראה גם מדרש הנעלם (וירא קיד, ב)): צדיקים אין חוזרין לעפרן כו' לעולם קיימי. וידוע דיעות הרמב"ם והרמב"ן בזמן עיקר השכר וההכרעה בזה (לקו"ת צו טו, ג. שש"ה סה, סע"ד. דרמ"צ יד, ב).

מ. כי רק מצד סדר ההשתלשלות שבתורה ישנה הגבלה זו, שחלקי הפשט רמז ודרוש

שבתורה יהיו בגילוי וחלק ה"סוד" יהי' בהעלם. אבל מצד עצם מהות התורה, בחי' יחידה, אין חילוק בין חלק הסוד שבה לשאר החלקים, וגם הסוד יכול להיות בגילוי.

מא. מצד בחי' נרנ"ח, האדם הוא במציאותו עדיין, אלא שעובד הוא את בוראו. ומכיון שהוא במציאותו, הרי (א) כוונתו בעבודתו הוא בשביל הגילויים (שבכללות זהו"ע ההנהגה ע"פ דין, כמבואר בד"ה פדה בשלום הנ"ל סעיף שער), כי גם בבחי' חי' ישנו איזה מבוקש (ד"ה וזאת התרומה עת"ר. קונט' העבודה פ"ה). (ב) לא נשתנה טבע מדותיו, ורק שממצל את מדותיו לאהבת ה' וכו', משא"כ מצד בחי' יחידה, מתבטל הוא ממציאותו לגמרי, ולכן (א) אין שום מבוקש בעבודתו – ההנהגה דלפנים משורת הדין. (ב) נשתנה גם טבע מדותיו (מגבורה לחסד ומחסד לגבורה וכו').

מב. כי ההתעלפות היא רק בנוגע לגילויים ולא בעצם הנשמה, בחי' יחידה, שלכן אפשר להעירו.

מג. ראה ד"ה וידבר תרצ"ט שם, שפנימיות התורה שילמד משיח הוא מצד בחי' היחידה שבו. ולהעיר מה שאחי' השלוני – רבו של הבעש"ט, מייסד תורת החסידות [פנימיות התורה, מעין פנימיות התורה שתתגלה לעתיד] – נקרא בשם "בעל חי' יחידה" (סה"ש ה'ש"ת ע' 159). וכן ראשי אלפי ישראל שבכל דור – הנשיאים שגילו תורת החסידות, הם בחי' יחידה הכללית של כלל ישראל (ד"ה פדה בשלום (בשעה"ת לאדמוהאמ"צ) פי"ב).

מד. שבתורת החסידות גופא, בזה שהביא את החסידות להבנה והשגה דחב"ד, גילה את עצם פנימיות התורה (ד"ה פדה בשלום תרפ"ה, בשם אדמו"ר (מהורש"ב) נ"ע בי"ט כסלו עטר"ת. וראה גם לקו"ש ח"ד ע' 1138).

מה. סה"ש תש"ה ע' 127 ואילך. וראה לקו"ת שה"ש (נ, א) בפירוש ענין נשמות חדשות. וש"נ.

מו. ולהעיר מזה אשר חג הגאולה י"ט כסלו [שאז הי' עיקר ענין התלבשות החסידות בשכל (תו"ש ע' 114. וראה לקו"ד ח"א כב, א ואילך), שע"י התלבשות זו, מתבטא העצם דפנימיות התורה כבהערה 44] הוא "ראש השנה לחסידות", שענינו של ר"ה הוא בחינה כללית, ובו נמשך "עומק ופנימיות כו' מבחי' פנימיות ועצמות אוא"ס ב"ה" (אגה"ק של אדמו"ר (מהורש"ב) נ"ע לי"ט כסלו תרס"ב, נדפסה – פאקסימיליא – במבוא לקונטרס ומעין ע' 17).

מז. ובפרט לאחרי גאולת י"ט כסלו ("לאחרי פטרבורג") וכידוע פתגם כ"ק אדמו"ר (מהורש"ב) נ"ע בזה: "מה הזית הזה כשכותשין אותו הוא מוציא את שמנו כו' כן ע"י הקטרוגים שהיו בפטרבורג נתגלה הפנימיות דוקא כו'" (תורת שלום ע' 26).

מח. אמ"ב שער הק"ש פנ"ד ואילך. ועיי"ש ההפרש בין יין (רזין) לשמן (רזין דרזין), שהיין ע"י עיכובו בהעלם בענבים הולך ומתגבר בכחו, משא"כ השמן, עיכובו בזית אין מוסיף כח כלל. והיינו, שיין הוא בחי' העלם – יין בגימטריא "סוד" (ולכן מיתוסף כחו ע"י עיכובו בהעלם), משא"כ שמן הוא למעלה מגדר ענין העלם וגילוי (שלכן העיכוב בהעלם אינו מוסיף כח). ומזה מובן, שגם תורת החסידות שנמשלה לשמן, היא למעלה מגדר העלם וגילוי (ולכן, ביכולתה לעשותה מהעלם – גילוי, כנ"ל הערה 40).

מט. ראה תו"א לט, א. קי, א. ד. לקו"ת נשא כז, ד. אמ"ב שם פנ"ו (נד, ב).

נ. טבול יום פ"ב מ"ה. רמב"ם הל' טומאת אוכלין פ"ח ה"י. (וגם לדעת ריב"נ ש"שניהן חיבור", אי"ז שהשמן מתערב ביין, ורק לפי שנוגע ודבוק בו – ראה אמ"ב שם רפנ"ו). וראה גם שמו"ר פל"ו, א.

נא. ראה חולין צז, רע"א. שו"ע יו"ד סק"ה ס"ה.

נב. זח"ב קסא, א. וראה גם ב"ר בתחלתו.

נג. ראה תו"ש ריש ע' 172: די וועלט מיינט אז חסידות איז א ביאור אויף קבלה, דאָס איז א טעות כו'.

ומה שמסיים שם "קבלה איז אַ ביאור אױף חסידות" – י"ל: החסידות ענינה ידיעת האלקות כו' (יחידה – מקבלת מיחיד. ולהעיר מע"ח שמ"ב רפ"א: ניצוץ כו' מתלבשת בכח ניצוץ כו' הנק' יחידה) ע"י כמה משלים דוגמאות הסברות וכו', והקבלה מבארת "המקום" בגופא דמלכא, בספירות וכו'. כן להעיר אשר "גילוי" הכתר (חשך) – הוא בחכמה: קוצו של יו"ד – ביו"ד; יחידה – בחי'; הרצון – בחכמה וכו'. אבל תוקף ועצמות הכתר וכו' – מתבטא דוקא במעשה וכו'.

נד. יומא לב, סע"ב. וש"נ. וראה צפע"נ (להרגצובי) עה"ת ר"פ קרח.

נה. וכ"ה בנוגע להתפלות דיי"ט (שתפלות כנגד קרבנות תקנום – ברכות כו, ב): הסיבה שהביאה להוספת תפלת נעילה (שבה הוא עיקר גילוי בחי' החמישית – בחי' יחידה), פועלת גם בשאר ד' התפלות שביום זה (אף שישנם גם בשאר ימי השנה) – נרנ"ח, וכהלשון (לקו"ת ס"פ פנחס): יום שנתחייב בחמש תפלות (ראה לקו"ש ח"ד ע/ 1154).

נו. ראה לקו"ת דרושי יו"כ בסופם, ש"שבת שבתון" הוא בחי' אוא"ס המלובש ברדל"א. וזוהי מדריגת תורת החסידות, כנ"ל סעיף ב'.

נז. מקור הנוסח ד"מודה אני" הוא ב"סדר היום". הובא בעט"ז ריש שו"ע או"ח. שו"ע אדה"ז ס"א ס"ה (ובמהדו"ת שם ס"י). סידור אדה"ז בתחלתו.

נח. שו"ע אדה"ז מהדו"ת שם. ובסידור: יזכור כו' הנצב כו'.

נט. ירמי' כג, כד.

ס. סידור אדה"ז שם.

סא. שו"ע אדה"ז מהדו"ק שם ס"ב. וראה ד"מ בטור שם (ממו"נ ח"ג פנ"ב).

סב. שו"ע אדה"ז מהדו"ת שם ס"ה. ועיי"ש כמה שינויים ממהדו"ק. ואכ"מ.

סג. אואפ"ל אשר בת"ת שחיובו תמידי (והוא המביא לידי מעשה – עבודת כל היום כולו) יש תמיד מעין ניעור משינתו. כי הידיעה בתורה שהאדם מגיע אלי' אפשרית היא ע"י (לקו"ת שלח מד, א) שמקודם לזה – כשהוא בבטן אמו, מלמדין אותו כל התורה כולה אלא שבא מלאך וסטרו על פיו (נדה ל, ב), וע"י לימודיו חוזר ויודע מה שידע לפני זה ונשכח (ונסתלק) ממנו.

סד. הל' תשובה פ"ג ה"ד.

סה. אלא שבנדו"ד, מכיון שאין שייך לברך על החזרת הנשמה טרם (שהחזירה) שנהנה, מחוייב הוא לברך עכ"פ מיד כשניעור. וכמו (ובמכ"ש מ)ברכת הטבילה, דאף שא"א לברך עלי' עובר לעשייתה כי "אכתי גברא לא חזי", אינו דוחה את הברכה על לאחר זמן, כ"א מברך מיד בעלייתו (פסחים ז, ב. וראה גם שו"ע אדה"ז ס"ו ס"ה: כל מה דאפשר לקרב הברכה כו').

סו. שהרי אסור לו לאדם שיהנה כו' בלא ברכה (ברכות לה, א).

סז. ברכות ס, ב. שו"ע אדה"ז שם ס"ז.

סח. ראש בברכות שם. שו"ע אדה"ז סמ"ו ס"ג.

סט. ברכות מ, ב. שו"ע אדה"ז סרי"ד ס"א.

ע. מפני שהיו קדושים והיו יכולים לברך בנקיות מיד כשניערו משנתם (רבינו יונה בברכות ס, ב – ד"ה כי שמע).

עא. ברכות נז, ב. זח"א קסט, ב. ח"ג קיט, א.

עב. ראה איכ"ר עה"פ (ג, ח) חדשים לבקרים רבה אמונתיך. וש"נ.

עג. זח"ג שם. בניצוצי זהר (לח"ג שם וקצ"ח, ב) מציין להספרים: ספרי האזינו לב, ד. ז"ח בראשית (יח, ב). רות (פח, ד). מרדכי ב"מ סי' ת"י (וכ"ה בכל בו סי' קטז) – מתשובות ותקנות ר"ת. שם סי' ת"ח – מירושלמי. רדב"ז ח"א סי' תפג. בעה"ט תצא כד, יד. רמ"א בחו"מ סע"ב סי"ז. ש"ך בחו"מ סרצ"ב סק"ב – מתשובת מהר"א ששון. קצוה"ח חו"מ ס"ד פ"ת בחו"מ שם אות ג' – מברכי יוסף בשם הרמ"ע מפאנו.

עד. סידור האריז"ל (קול יעקב) בתחלתו.

עה. ראה הערה עח.

עו. היום יום ע׳ יט.

עז. לקו״ת פנחס פ, ב. וראה זח״ג רנז, ב.

עח. בפשטות, מה שב״מודה אני״ לא נזכר שום שם, ושלכן אפשר לאומרו גם קודם נט״י (ראה שו״ע אדה״ז ס״א ס״ה (ובמהדו״ת – שם ס״ו). סידור אדה״ז בתחלתו), – היינו לפי שהוא למטה מבחי׳ השמות. אבל בפנימיות הענינים, מה שאין בו שום שם (וכן מה שאומרים אותו קודם נט״י), הוא לפי שהוא למעלה מבחי׳ השמות כבפנים*. (ולהעיר מהביאור בהא דמגלת אסתר אין בה ״שם״ – תו״א ק, ב. קכא, ב).

ואי״ז סותר למה ״שאין בו קדושה״ (שו״ע מהדו״ק שם) – כי זהו בדוגמת תיבת ״אנכי״ (ה׳ אלקיך)״, דאף שמורה על העצמות שלמעלה מכל השמות (כנ״ל בהנסמן בהערה הקודמת), מ״מ (מצד זה גופא) אין בו קדושה (כי תיבת ״אנכי״ אינה כלי להעצמות, כ״א מרמזת עליו בלבד).

* וזה שבזמן הש״ס לא אמרו ״מודה אני״; אף שע״פ פנימיות הענינים (משא״כ ע״פ נגלה, כנ״ל סעיף יו״ד) יש בזה מעלה שאינה בברכת ״אלקי נשמה״; יש לומר בדרך אפשר, לפי שהתעוררות וביטוי היחידה הוא דוקא כאשר גם מי שהוא טמא וכו׳ ומ״מ הוא מודה כו׳ (וע״ד המבואר לקמן סעיף חי ואילך). וע״ד הידוע (ד״ה קול דודי תש״ט. ובכ״מ) שכח המס״נ (הבא מצד יחידה) הוא בגילוי יתר בזמן הגלות ובפרט בעקבתא דמשיחא; מבזמן הבית. ולהעיר שכ״ה גם בנוגע לחסידות; בחינת יחידה; שנתגלתה בדורות האחרונים דוקא, וכשהעולם הי׳ במצב של התעלפות, כמובא בתחילת השיחה.

עט. אף שנזכר במדרש – נסמן לעיל הערה לז. וכן בזהר – ח״ב קנח, ב. ובהשמטות לזהר (מספר הבהיר) ח״א (רסז, א) וכו׳. (ולהעיר, שבחי׳ יחידה שבזח״ב שם הוא בחי׳ ״בכל נפשך״, ולא ״בכל מאדך״ – שמזה משמע, שאי״ז אמיתית בחי׳ יחידה).

פ. ח״א עט, ב. פא, א. (וכן הובא באוה״ח אמור כב, יב).

הל׳ נשמה לנשמה (וכיו״ב), נזכר גם בזח״ג קנב, א. ז״ח רות עח, ג.

פא. משא״כ בע״ח וכו׳. וראה ההג״ה בע״ח שמ״ב (דרושי אבי״ע) רפ״א ובהגהות וביאורים שם.

פב. ראה שו״ע אדה״ז סמ״ו ס״ד.

פג. יבמות סא, רע״א.

פד. קהלת ג, כא.

פה. בנוגע לעבד – יבמות סב, א. וש״נ.

פו. בנוגע לנכרי – יחזקאל כג, כ. וראה שבת קנו, א. יבמות צח, א (ותוד״ה לדרוש – כתובות ג, ב) ועוד.

פז. בראשית א, כט־ל. ובדרז״ל שם.

פח. נח ט, ה־ז. ובדרז״ל שם.

פט. שבת סז, א. יתרה מזו נתבאר בפנימיות התורה (זח״ב כו, ריש ע״ב. הקדמת תקו״ז בתחלתו) דמלכים הם (בפנימיות).

צ. היום יום ע׳ קב.

צא. ב״ר פכ״ח, ג. זח״ב כח, ב. והוא שונה לגמרי משאר הגוף (עיי״ש ובמפרשים).

צב. ילקו״ש תהלים רמז תשב. שו״ע אדה״ז ס״ו ס״א. וראה גם מד״ר שבהערה עב.

צג. ראה שער היחוד והאמונה בתחלתו.

צד. ראה לקו״ת אחרי כו, א: מחדש . . מאין המוחלט, אך אין נמצא משל כמוהו ודוגמתו למטה כלל להראות בחוש רק אפס קצהו שבכל יום מאיר מחשך הלילה . . והרי הוא כמו יש מאין.

צה. שער הגלגולים בתחלתו. ובכ״מ.

צו. אין לזה סתירה מהנזכר בכ״מ (ראה ד״ה בסוכות תשבו (פכ״ז), מי יתן תש״ו. ועוד) ש(גם) באצילות אלקות הוא בפשיטות ועולמות בהתחדשות — כי בפרטיות מציאות העולמות מתחילה מבריאה, אבל בכלל — הרי גם אצילות נקרא עולם האצילות. — וראה ד״ה ויהי הענן והחשך — תרע״ה דחילוק זה (אלקות בפשיטות כו׳) הוא: לפני הצמצום ולאחריו כו׳ אדה״ר בג״ע כו׳ ועד בצדיקים גדולים כו׳. וכן יהי׳ לעת״ל. הרי שכו״כ דרגות בזה.

צז. אלא שכלפי הלוקח ישנו (איסור אחר:) האיסור דלפני עור (סמ״ע חו״מ סקמ״ו סקל״ט). אבל בנוגע להוציא חפצו מהגזלן, אין בזה איסור.

צח. סד״ה לך תרס״ו. ובכ״מ.

צט. ד״ה ואני תפלתי תרצ״ד (קונט׳ כז).

ק. ד״ה למען דעת תר״ץ פ״ה. הוי׳ לי בעוזרי תרצ״א (תרפ״ז) פ״ג. סה״מ אידיש ע׳ 46. ובכ״מ.

קא. אבל עיקר קיומם צ״ל בדרך קב״ע, שהרי כל המצות הם רצון העליון, כבפנים [ולהעיר דגם במשפטים אמרו "לפניהם ולא לפני עו״כ ואפי׳ . . דנין אותו כדיני ישראל" (גיטין פח, ב. שו״ע חו״מ ר״ס כו)].

ויתירה מזו: גם זה עצמו מה שהמצות ד"משפטים" צריכים לקיימם גם מצד הטעם, היינו לפי שכן גזר הקב״ה שהרצון דמצות אלו יתלבש גם ב"טעם"*. וראה באריכה לקו״ש ח״ח ע׳ 130 ואילך.

*) וע״ז דוקא מתגלה יותר ענין היחידה מאשר ע״י קיום המצות ד"חוקים" שהוא רק בדרך קב״ע. כי בזה דוקא מתבטא שקיום המצות הוא מצד עצם נפשו, שלכן פעל זה גם על שכלו, כי ה"עצם" נמצא בכל הפרטים, כדלקמן סעיף יז.

קב. להעיר מח״פ להרמב״ם פ״ו (הובא בדרמ״צ פד, ב) שהרעות שהן רע גם מצד השכל צריך לומר ע״ז "אי אפשי".

ובזה יובן מה שאמרו (עירובין ק, סע״ב): "אלמלי לא ניתנה תורה (ח״ו*) היינו למדים צניעות מחתול וגזל מנמלה כו׳" — דלכאורה, למאי נפקא מינה.

*) כן הי׳ מוסיף (בלחש) כ״ק אדמו״ר (מהורש״ב) נ״ע כשהי׳ מביא מרז״ל זה.

קג. בקצוה״ח סש״מ סק״ד, שכל זמן שהפקדון בעין, אין חיוב השבה על השומר [ורק כשפשע (או שנגנב ונאבד — בשומר שכר), אז נעשה עליו חיוב תשלומין]. אבל בשו״ע אדמוה״ז (סתמ״ג בקו״א סק״ב): "דמה שש״ח חייב על הפשיעה אין חיובו בא מחמת הפשיעה עצמה, אלא משעה שנמסר לו הפקדון נשתעבד ונתחייב להחזיר לו בשלימות כשיגיע הזמן, אלא שאם בתוך הזמן נאבדה ממנו ע״י פשיעתו חסה עליו התורה ופטרתו". וע״פ מ״ש בקו״א שם, יובנו דברי היש״ש (הובאו בקצוה״ח שם) "כיון שנעשה שומר ה״ל איני יודע אם החזרתיו".

קד. שער היחוה״א פ״ז (פב, א). ובכ״מ.

קה. עיין אגה״ק ס״ך "מהותו ועצמותו כו׳ הוא לבדו כו׳" (קל, סע״א ואילך) — אלא שהביאור שם באוא״א.

קו. ואף שההכרה שהחידוש בא מעצמות אוא״ס באה (ומוכרחת) מההכרה שהעולמות הם מחודשים יש מאין (כנ״ל סט״ו), בכל זה, לאחרי שההכרה בהחידוש יש מאין מביאה את ההכרה שהחידוש בא מעצמות אוא״ס, הנה הכרה זו — לא רק שמחזקת את ההכרה בהחידוש יש מאין, אלא שמוסיפה בה גם עומק. כי ההכרה בהחידוש יש מאין שמצד עצמה, היא (כנ״ל סט״ו) "שאין שום נתינת מקום להיש מצד עצמו כו׳", אבל אי״ז מוכיח עדיין שאין לו נתינת מקום גם מצד בחי׳ האור המהווה אותו (ראה הערה הבאה), אבל ע״י ההכרה שהחידוש בא מעצמות אוא״ס שלמעלה מעולמות, הוא בא לידי הכרה, שגם מצד בחי׳ האור המהווה אותו, אין לו שום תפיסת

מקום, ולכן גם לאחרי שעלה ברצונו להוות כו', ההתהוות בכל רגע היא התחדשות גמורה.

קיז. ראה דרמ"צ (כג, א), שמה שמבואר בשער היחוה"א פ"ו בענין "אין עוד", שאין אפילו דבר טפל, ולא כהגוף שהוא טפל לנשמה – הוא לגבי בחי' הסובב דוקא. שלכן, אוה"ע שכל ידיעתם הוא רק בבחי' הממלא, מחשיבים אותו כנשמה לגוף. עיי"ש. ולכאורה: הרי גם לשיטתם, בהכרח שיודו שהקב"ה בורא את הנבראים ולא רק מחי' אותם בלבד? והביאור, דמכיון שאר הממלא נותן מקום לעולמות, הרי לאחרי שנבראו העולמות ביטול העולמות לאור זה (אף שכל מציאותם הוא ממנו, ולא רק חיותם) הוא דוגמת ביטול הגוף לנפש. ועצ"ע.

קיח. שער היחוה"א פ"ו (פ, סע"ב).

קיט. ספר יצירה פ"א מ"ז.

קי. קידושין ל, ב.

קיא. לשון אדה"ז בתניא פל"ו (בתחילתו).

קיב. סוכה נב, ב.

קיג. ראה הנסמן בהערה יח – ע"פ מרז"ל (סוטה לה, א).

קיד. ע"פ מ"ש בפנים, יובן הלשון "בראתי לו תורה תבלין" – דלכאורה: את היצה"ר הרי צריך לבטל [וגם זה נעשה ע"י התורה, כמרז"ל (קידושין שם) "משכהו לבית המדרש אם אבן הוא נימוח ואם ברזל הוא מתפוצץ"] ואילו התבלין אינו מבטל את התבשיל, כ"א אדרבה מתבל אותו ונותן בו טעם.

– ומה שצריך לאבדו, הוא כש"פגע בך מנוול זה – יצה"ר מתגרה בך". אבל עצמיות היצה"ר, והוא עצם כח המתאווה (ראה לקו"ת חקת נו, ד. ר"ה סא, ד), צריך לתבלו ולהפכו לטוב, כבפנים.

וזהו שאמרו "בראתי לו תורה תבלין" – כי הכוונה ב"בראתי" . . תבלין" היא לעצם התורה, היינו הכוונה שבשבילה נבראת. ועצם התורה מתבטא (לא באיבוד היצה"ר כ"א) בהפיכתו לטוב, כדלקמן בפנים.

קטו. ראה לקו"ש ח"ז ע' 24-23 ובהנסמן שם.

קטז. משלי ח, ל. וראה בהנסמן בהערה יח, ש"משחקת לפניו" קאי על פנימיות ועצמיות התורה.

קיז. ראה תו"א יז, ד ואילך.

קיח. ב"מ יו"ד, א.

קיט. שם, ע"ב.

קכ. ראה בית שמואל אה"ע ס"ל סק"ה. וש"נ. (ולדעת ר"פ – ב"מ שם – קונות ברה"ר גם במציאה).

קכא. באבני מילואים ס"ל סק"ה כתב, שלדעת הרמב"ן (גיטין עח, א) לא הקנו חכמים את מקום הד"א עצמם, כ"א – את החפץ המונח בו. עיי"ש. אבל ראה באב"מ שם שלדעת הר"ן (גיטין שם) הקנו את הד"א עצמם (וכ"מ בריטב"א (גיטין שם – בתירוץ הב'). שו"ת הר"י מיגש סק"ו).

ומה שהקנו את הד"א עצמם – אף שמצד הטעם "דלא אתי לאנצויי" נוגע רק שהחפץ יהי' קנוי – י"ל, שלא רצו להקנות את החפץ באופן שיהי' כ"הלכתא בלא טעמא" לגמרי, ולכן הקנו את הד"א שעל ידם יקנה את החפץ.

קכב. ב"מ יא, רע"א. רמב"ם הל' גזילה ואבידה פי"ז ה"י. שו"ע חו"מ סרמ"ג סכ"ג. סו"ס רסח.

קכג. שלכן ס"ל להתוס' (ד"ה ארבע) והרא"ש (ב"מ יו"ד, א) שד"א אינן קונות בגניבה (ובמכירה ומתנה – ראה ש"ך חו"מ סרמ"ג סק"ט) – אף שעשאום חכמים כחצירו – כי לא עשאום כחצירו לכל דבר, כ"א לצורך קנין החפץ באופנים מסויימים (מציאה וכיו"ב).

קכד. ראה דרישה חו״מ סרס״ח סק״ז.

קכה. רמב״ם הל׳ גזילה ואבידה שם ה״ח. ובב״י חו״מ שם (קרוב לסופו) – דהכי נקטינן.

קכו. ראה ב״מ י, א״ב: ״כי לא אמר מאי הוי״.

קכז. ראה חו״מ ר״ס רס״ח: ולא גרע משום דנפל עלי׳ (אף דגלי דעתי׳ דלא ניחא לי׳ לקנות בתורת קנין ד׳ אמות).

קכח. וכקושיית הרשב״א (הובא במ״מ הל׳ גזילה שם ובב״י שם).

ומה שתירץ הב״י שם ״דכיון דמשום דלא אתי לאנצויי תקינו רבנן דליקני לא ראו לחלק בין אמר ללא אמר דא״כ אכתי הוו אתי לאנצויי״ – צריך ביאור: מכיון שסוף סוף מה שתיקנו שד׳ אמות יהיו קונות הוא ע״י שעשאום כחצירו (ראה לעיל הערה קכא), הרי א״א לכאורה שיהיו קונות באופן שחצר עצמו אינו קונה.

קכט. אמרי בינה שער הק״ש פמ״ב.

קל. להעיר מעירובין מח, א: גופו שלש אמות ואמה כדי כו׳ – והרי בחינות הנשמה המתלבשות בגוף האדם הם רק ג׳ הבחי׳ דנר״ן, ואמה הרביעית שיתירה מאורך גופו אבל שייכת אליו (שהרי ענינה של אמה זו היא ״כדי לפשוט ידיו ורגליו״ או ״כדי שיטול חפץ מתחת מרגלותיו ומניח תחת מראשותיו״) – בחי׳ ״היתירה״ על נר״נ – מקיף (הקרוב), חי׳.

קלא. ואז היא מתגלית (לא רק בירור הדבר גשמי שמחוץ להאדם, אלא גם) בהבחינות של הנשמה עצמה, ד׳ הבחינות נרנ״ח, ועל ידם דוקא היא נמשכת ופועלת בדבר הגשמי שמחוץ להאדם (אף שההתעוררות היחידה באה מצד בירור דבר הגשמי דוקא)

[כדוגמת מה שכח העצמות שמציאותו מעצמותו, עם היותו מתבטא בהתהוות היש הגשמי דוקא, מ״מ המשכת כח העצמות בהיש הוא ע״י האור דוקא ״שהאור הוא ממוצע בין יש האמיתי ליש הנברא, והיינו דע״י אמצעות האור בא כח העצמות, ווערט אראפגעטראגען דער כח העצמות להוות יש מאין ואפס המוחלט״ (ד״ה יחיינו תרצ״ד פי״ד. וראה גם אגה״ק סי׳ כ׳)

ועד״ז בעבודת האדם, שעם היות שגילוי העצמות הוא בקיום המצות מעשיות דוקא, בכל זה, אופן המשכת העצמות במעשה המצות הוא ע״י הכחות פנימיים (שכל ומדות) דוקא (ראה לקו״ש ח״ג ע׳ 956 שמטעם זה נקראים אהוי״ר בשם ״דרכי הוי׳. עיי״ש בארוכת)]

שלכן (לצורך קנין החפץ), גם הד״א (נרנ״ח קנויים להאדם, ועי״ז דוקא, הד״א קונות לו את החפץ, כנ״ל בפנים.

ויש לומר, שזהו גם הביאור בפנימיות הענינים מה שלא רצו להקנות את החפץ באופן שיהי׳ כ״הלכתא בלא טעמא״ לגמרי (ראה לעיל הערה קכא) – כי גם בירור הגשמי דוקא צ״ל נמשך ע״י השכל (טעמא) דוקא.

קלב. הכנה וכלי שהם גם ממשיכים (לא רק – מקבלים) את ההשפעה והאור וכמש״כ ע״ז בתניא רפל״ז (הובא לקמן בפנים) הגורם שכר המצוה.

קלג. תניא פל״ז ורפל״ז.

קלד. י״ל שכוונתו עפמש״כ בשערי אורה (סד״ה כי אתה) בפי׳ והוי׳ יגי׳ חשבי שזהו אתהפכא חשוכא לנהורא (ע״ד הנ״ל בפנים – שהרע עצמו נהפך לטוב).

קלה. מדייק אאמו״ר ומבאר: הב׳ לשונות, מעשינו ועבודתינו, יובן ממ״ש לקמן באגרת הקדש פי״ב המתחיל והי׳ מעשה הצדקה כו׳ ע״ש. וי״ל מעשינו קאי על ימות המשיח* ועבודתינו קאי על תחה״מ (הערות לתניא – ליקוטי לוי יצחק).

* וראה באגה״ק שם (קיח, סע״א) בביאור מעשה ״בכל יום ויום בטובו מחדש מע״ב וחדשים לבקרים כו׳״.

HEBREW NOTES
APPENDIX

א. ח"א קיז, א.

ב. אגה"ק סי כו (קמב, ב).

ג. בדיוק הל' בתקוני זהר (ת"ז בסופו) דברי אליהו הנביא מבשר הגאולה מגלותנו זה (לרשב"י): כמה ב"נ לתתא יתפרנסון מהאי חיבורא דילך כד אתגלי לתתא כדרא בתראה בסוף יומיא ובגינא וקראתם דרור בארץ גו'. ובכסא מלך שם ביאר והדגיש: בדרא בתראה דוקא קרוב לימות המשיח כו' (אף אשר) זה כמה מאות שנים שנתגלה כו' (כי הלימוד צ"ל דוקא באופן של) יתפרנסון כו' יפורשו מאמריו העמוקים בהקדמות שגילה האר"י זלה"ה כו' שיבינו כו' כי הלומד גירסא בעלמא הגם שיש לו שכר טוב כו' עכ"ז הסגולה דבגיני' וקראתם דרור הוא כשיתפרנסון וילמדו פירושי המאמרים כו'. — ראה גם כן הקדמת הרח"ו לשער ההקדמות.

ד. הבעש"ט באגרתו הידועה על דבר עליית הנשמה שלו בראש השנה שנת תק"ז (נדפסה בסוף הספר בן פורת יוסף, בספר המכתבים מהבעש"ט ז"ל ותלמידיו (לבוב תרפ"ג, וכותב המו"ל שהעתיקה מן המכתב — כת"י חתנו של הבעש"ט הרה"צ וכו' ר' יחיאל — החתום בעצם כי"ק של הבעש"ט). בספר גנזי נסתרות (ירושלים ת"ו תרפ"ד) ח"א סי' סה. — וחלק ממנה בתחלת ספר כתר שם טוב, וספר לקוטי אמרים להה"מ ממעזריטש. — ביאור שאלת הבעש"ט ומענה המשיח ע"ד החסידות ראה לקו"ד ליקוט טז-יח.

ה. ובפרט לאחרי פעטערבורג (תקנ"ט) (תורת שלום ס"ע 112 ואילך).

ו. ראה תניא ספ"ה.

ז. אגה"ק סי' ט.

ח. אגה"ת פ"י.

ט. ראה מגילה יט, ב. ירושלמי פאה פ"ב, ה"ד. שמו"ר רפמ"ז. ויק"ר רפכ"ב. קה"ר פ"א, פ"ה ח. שו"ת רד"ך בית ה' חדר ג'. תורת העולה ח"ג, פנ"ה. הקדמת הש"ך עה"ת. אור תורה להה"מ ר"פ תולדות. אגה"ק קו"א ד"ה להבין פרטי ההלכות.

י. קהלת ג, יא. ובקה"ר שם. ועיי"ג"כ שם ר"פ עה"פ לכל זמן ועת לכל חפץ.

יא. זח"ג נג, ב. גו"א ר"פ בראשית בשם הרד"ק.

יב. תניא פל"ז (מח, ב).

יג. אף שהיתה גם אז חלק בתורה — וכמו כל התורה ש"קדמה לעולם" (פסחים נד, ב. נדרים לט, ב), ויחידי סגולה למדו וקיימו כל התורה כולה עד שלא ניתנה (קידושין פב, א. יומא כח, ב) אבל לכל ישראל ניתנה לכ"ו דור.

יד. וזהו גם הטעם לזה שכ"ק מו"ח אדמו"ר גילה כמה הוראות והנהגות וכו' בזמן האחרון דוקא, וכמה מהם — בארצוה"ב, בחצי כדור התחתון (ראה מכתבו בסה"מ תש"ח ע' 232), אף ששמעם כמה שנים לפנ"ז — כי "לכל זמן" ואז בא הזמן שהעולם הוצרך להם.

טו. תניא רפל"ז.

טז. סוטה יג, ב. הובא בתנחומא ובפירש"י עקב (ח, א).

יז. ראה מכילתא עה"פ אז ישיר: התשועה העתידה להיות אין אחרי' שעבוד (הובאה תוד"ה ונאמר פסחים קטז, ב). ועד"ז שמו"ר פכ"ג, יא (וראה רש"י ערכין (יג, ב) ד"ה בנבל).

יח. ראה תניא פל"ו, אגה"ת ספ"ט.

יט. ע"ז ג, א.

כ. ראה תו"א ר"פ יתרו.

כא. עיין תניא פכ"ח. – ראה לקו"ש ח"ג פ' בראשית.

כב. כן הי' מוסיף (פעמים רבות) כ"ק אדמו"ר (מהורש"ב) נ"ע – נתבאר בשיחת ש"פ וישלח תשכ"ט.

כג. תנחומא נשא טז. עד"ז במדב"ר פי"ג, ו. – ראה תניא פל"ו.

כד. להעיר מסוטה (מט, א): בכל יום ויום כו'. ראה לקו"ש ע' 1226, ובהערה 32 שם.

כה. וראה חנוך לנער (ע' 8. וראה היום יום ע' קו) אשר הצ"צ אמר בנוגע לכ"ק אדמו"ר (מהורש"ב) נ"ע: "נולד כ' חשוון תרכ"א, שיש בזה שני כפי"ן שהוא רומז לכתרא עילאה" – וידוע (לקו"ת שה"ש לה, ג) אשר שני הכפי"ן רומזים לב' הבחינות שבכתר אריך ועתיק, היינו שהוא שייך לא רק לאריך (שאף שהוא למע' מהשתל', מ"מ ה"ה שייך להשתל') אלא גם לעתיק שלמע' מהשתל' לגמרי.

ויש לקשרו עם זה שהתהבר"מ שלו היתה בנר ב' דחנוכה (שם), לפי שביום ב' דחנוכה נראה הנס דחנוכה (הבא מלמעלה מהשתל') בגלוי, לא כמו ביום א' שבגלוי אין נראה הנס ושקו"ט בזה בתורה וזקוקים לביאור מיוחד כו' (ראה ט"ז ריש הלכות חנוכה סי' תרע. ועוד).

והרי כ"ז שייך לענין הגאולה, דהרי גם ענין הגאולה בא מבחי' שלמע' מהשתל'.

כו. לקו"ד ח"ב ע' רצו. וראה ספה"ש תש"א ע' 160.

כז. בהקדמתו לספרו יד החזקה.

כח. ויש"ל אשר לכן התחיל ענין שתיית ד' כוסות באחש"פ בשנה ההיא דוקא (היום יום ע' מז), כי אחש"פ וענינו – ה"ה שייך להגאולה העתידה וכתוכן ההפטורה וכו' (ראה לקו"ש ח"ד ע' 1299).

ויי"ל שייכות מיוחדת ליין דוקא, כי ענינו של יין הוא גילוי העלם, דהרי מתחילה הוא טמון בענבים ואח"כ יוצא לגילוי, ולכן הוא פועל גילוי העלם, כמ"ש (שופטים ט, יג) "המשמח אלקים ואנשים", היינו שמגלה ההעלם דאלקים ואנשים (לקו"ת דברים עט, ד).

כט. ספרי מסעי לה, לד. (וראה מגלה (כט, א): לבבל כו'. ולהעיר מהשינוי: בתניא פי"ז, אגה"ק סכ"ה (ובכ"מ בחסידות) לאדום, באגה"ק ס"ד (ובכ"מ) לבבל ובכ"מ שמדובר אותו הענין ולא הובא מרז"ל בכלל).

ל. תניא פמ"א.

לא. ר"ח (שער האהבה פ"ז קרוב לתחלתו). בשל"ה (שער האותיות אות ל. מס' תענית רד"ה מענין העבודה. פ' תרומה חלק תו"א – שכה, ב. שכו, ב. – ועוד).

לב. איוב כח, ג. ובאוה"ת פ' מקץ (שם, א. וכפי' המד"ר שהובא שם – כ"כ בתניא פל"ג) – מציין גם לזח"א (קצד, א). ושם הוא עה"פ לכל זמן ועת לכל חפץ (ונת' בלקוטי לוי יצחק על הזהר): ת"ח כל מה דעבד קוב"ה לתתא לכלא שוי זימנא וזמן קצוב שוי לנהורא כו'.

GLOSSARY

GLOSSARY

The words explained here are either those that have not been translated as they appeared in the text, or appear more than once. Where terms are explained in the text or footnotes, the reader is directed to refer to them in this glossary. Italicized words are explained in the glossary.

Adam: The first man. Of the four Hebrew words for "man," "Adam" is the highest. The etymology of the word is both "Earth" (*adamah*), and "I shall *resemble* the One Above" (*ad-ameh l'elyon*—Isaiah 14:14).

Ad-nay: "L-rd."

Alter *Rebbe*: lit. "Old Rabbi." Among *Chabad Chasidim*, the term *Alter Rebbe* refers to R. Schneur Zalman of Liadi. It was first used during the time of R. Menachem Mendel of Lubavitch (third generation *Chabad* leader), to differentiate between the incumbent *Rebbe* (always known as the "the *Rebbe*"), the previous *Rebbe* ("the *Mitteler Rebbe*"), and the first *Rebbe* ("the *Alter Rebbe*").

Arich Anpin: lit. "Long Image." See fn. 16 to main text.

Arizal: Acronym formed from the Hebrew words for "Our Master Rabbi Isaac [Luria] of blessed memory" (1534-1572); the founder and head of the most prominent school of *Kabbalah*. His intricate *Kabbalistic* teachings were received by his pupils orally, and were posthumously recorded by his pupil R. Chaim Vital.

Asher Yatzar: lit. "Who has formed." Blessing of thanksgiving for physical health.

Atik: See fn. 16 to main text.

Atzilut: See fn. 45 to main text.

Atzmut: Essence; the Essence of G-d.

Baal Shem Tov: "Master of the Good Name"; applied to R. Israel, founder of *Chasidus* (1698-1760).

Baal Teshuvah: A penitent; one who returns to Judaism after going astray.

Beracha: A blessing.

Beriah: See fn. 45 to main text.

Birur: lit. "Refining." One of the basic doctrines of *Kabbalah* is the idea of refining the "sparks" of holiness which are to be found in everything. This is accomplished by every *mitzvah*.

Chabad: Acrostic of *chochma* (wisdom), *binah* (understanding), *da'at* (knowledge). The branch of the *Chasidic* movement based on an intellectual approach to the service of G-d, and founded by R. Schneur Zalman of Liadi

Chochmah: "Wisdom; concept." One of the three primary intellectual powers *chochma* is the first and highest of the ten *sefirot*.

Chaf: Hebrew letter; numerical equivalent of 20.

Chasid: (pl. *Chasidim*) lit. "Pious man." Term applied to followers of the *Chasidic* movement; follower of a *Chasidic Rebbe*. See fn. 5 to main text.

Chasidic: Appertaining to *Chasidus*.

Chasidism: Movement founded by R. Yisrael *Baal Shem Tov* (1698-1760).

Chasidus: Movement founded by R. Yisrael *Baal Shem Tov*; the philosophy of the *Chasidic* movement.

Chatzer: Property.

Chaya: One of the soul's five levels. See fn. 48 to main text.

Chukim: "Statutes"; commandments for which no reason is given; supra-rational commandments, e.g., the prohibition against wearing wool and linen.

Drush: The homiletic, expounded meaning of the *Torah*; one of the four levels of interpretation known as *Pardes*.

Echad: "One." See fn. 50 to main text.

Edom: Esau (Gen. 36:1). The destruction of the second Sanctuary by the Romans, who were the descendents of Esau, marked the beginning of the fourth and final exile, known as the Exile of *Edom*.

Eliyahu: The Prophet Elijah.

Elokai Neshama: "O, my G-d, the soul…"; morning blessing that mentions the various stages of the soul's descent, and expresses gratitude to G-d for restoring it every morning after sleep.

Gaon: "Genius;" title given to the exceptionally brilliant Talmudist. Originally the title of the heads of the leading rabbinic academies in Babylon between the sixth and twelfth centuries.

Hey: Hebrew letter; numerical equivalent of five. Comprises two of the letters of the Tetragrammaton.

Halachah: The Jewish legal system; also any practical *Torah* law.

Halachic: Appertaining to *halachah*.

Hamotzi: "Who brings forth." Blessing before eating bread.

Havaya: See fn. 42 to main text.

Hishtalshelut: See fn. 51 to main text.

Kabbalah: lit. "Received Tradition." Esoteric Jewish wisdom; Jewish Mysticism; inner interpretation of the *Torah*.

Kabbalat Ol: lit. "Acceptance of the Yoke." Subordination to the Will of G-d.

Kabbalistic: Appertaining to *Kabbalah*.

Keter: See fn. 16 to main text.

Kinyan Chatzer: Acquisition by property. See fn. 150 to main text.

Kislev: A winter month in the Hebrew calendar (third from *Tishrei*).

Lubavitch: "Town of Love" in White Russia. It became the residence of the *Chabad* movement in 1814, when R. Dovber, son and successor of R. Schneur Zalman, settled there. For over a century (until 1916) and through four generations of *Chabad* leaders, it remained the center of the movement. Hence, the leaders of *Chabad* became known as the "*Lubavitcher Rebbes*" and their *Chasidim* as "*Lubavitcher Chasidim*."

Lubavitcher Rebbe: The leader of the *Chabad Chasidim*.

Maamar: (pl. *maamarim*) lit. "word" or "article." In *Chabad* circles, the term refers to a formal discourse by a *Chabad Rebbe*, in which a topic of *Chasidus* is expounded.

Maggid of Mezritch: The "preacher" of Mezritch, R. DovBer, was the leading disciple and successor of the *Baal Shem Tov*. He passed away on the nineteenth of *Kislev* 5533 (1772). R. Schneur Zalman, the founder of *Chabad*, was one of the Maggid's leading disciples.

Maimonides: See *Rambam*.

Malchut: "Kingship." See fn. 97 to main text.

Megillah: lit. "Scroll." The Book of Esther is popularly referred to by this name; also title of a *Talmudic* tractate.

Middot: Attributes; character traits.

Midrash: Rabbinic homiletical literature, exegesis. *Midrash Rabbah* and *Midrash Tanchuma* are two of the most famous *Midrashim*.

Mishnah: The codification of the Oral law by R. Yehudah HaNassi (ca. 150 C.E.).

Mishpatim: Judgments; rational commandments. See fn. 125 to main text.

Mitteler Rebbe: R. DovBer Schneuri, son of R. Schneur Zalman (the founder of *Chabad*), was popularly known as the *Mitteler Rebbe* ("intermediate *Rebbe*"), i.e., the "middle one" of the first three generations of the "fathers" of *Chabad*.

Mitzvah: (pl. *mitzvot*). Commandment(s); religious obligation(s); good deed(s).

Modeh Ani: "I give thanks unto You..." First prayer recited upon arising, thanking G-d for restoring the soul.

Moshe: Moses.

Moshiach: The Messiah.

Nachmanides: See *Ramban*.

NaRaNaCh: Acronym for: *Nefesh, Ruach, Neshama, Chaya*.

Nefesh: One of the five levels of the soul. See fn. 48 to main text.

Ne'ilah: "Closing" prayer on *Yom Kippur*.

Neshama: One of the five levels of the soul. See fn. 48 to main text.

Nissan: Name of a Hebrew month in the spring. Passover begins on the fifteenth of *Nissan*.

Or Ein Sof: "Infinite Light." Light is used in *Kabbalisitic* and *Chasidic* literature as a metaphor for the manifestations of the Essence of G-d. Light, though only a reflection of its source, is also Infinite.

Pardes: Acronym for: *peshat, remez, drush, sod*—the four levels of *Torah* interpretation.

Peshat: The plain, straightforward meaning of the *Torah*; one of the four levels of interpretation known as *Pardes*.

Radla: Acronym for *Reisha d'Lo Ityada*. See footnotes 19 to the main text.

Rambam: The popular name by which R. Moses ben Maimon (Maimonides; 1135-1204) is known. Among his numerous writings, his two greatest works are his code *Mishneh Torah* (or *Yad HaChazakah*) and his philosophical work *Moreh Nevuchim* ("Guide for the Perplexed"). Rambam's works, especially the *Mishneh Torah*, are distinguished for their clarity and comprehensiveness.

Ramban: The popular name by which R. Moses ben Nachman (Nachmanides; 1194-1270) is known. One of the greatest Talmudists, Bible commentators, Kabbalists, and Jewish leaders of his age.

Rashi: Acronym for Rabbi Shlomo Yitzchaki. Rabbi Shlomo ben Yitzchak lived in Troyes, France and Worms, Germany (1040 – 1105). His commentary is printed in practically all editions of the Torah and Talmud, and is the subject of some two hundred commentators.

Raya Mehemna: A part of the *Zohar*.

Reb: An honorary and affectionate title used before a man's Hebrew name.

Rebbe: Rabbi and teacher; leader of a *Chasidic* group.

Remez: The allusion or intimated meaning of the *Torah*; one of the four levels of interpretation known as *Pardes*.

Rosh Chodesh: First day of a Hebrew month.

Rosh Hashanah: lit. "Head of the Year." The two day festival marking the beginning of the Jewish year.

Ruach: One of the five levels of the soul See fn. 48 to main text.

Sefirah: (pl. *sefirot*). Divine attribute(s), emanation(s) or manifestation(s). There are ten *sefirot*.

Shema: lit. "Hear." Passage of the *Torah* recited daily, in the morning and evening (Deut. 6:4-9).

Shevat: Name of a Hebrew month in the winter.

Shulchan Aruch: lit. "Set Table." Standard code of Jewish law compiled by R. Joseph Karo (1488-1575). R. Schneur Zalman's revision of this code carries the same name, otherwise known as the *Shulchan Aruch Admor HaZaken*, or *Shulchan Aruch HaRav*.

Sod: The esoteric meaning of the *Torah*; one of the four levels of interpretation known collectively as *Pardes*.

Sukkah: A hut or booth in which the autumn festival of Sukkot is observed.

Talmud: lit. "Teaching, learning." Applies to the compilation of the Oral *Torah* that includes the *Mishnah* and *Gemara*. The Jerusalem *Talmud* was compiled about the end of the third century C.E., while the larger and more popular Babylonian *Talmud* was compiled and edited about the end of the fifth century C.E.

Talmudic: Appertaining to the *Talmud*.

TaNaCH: Popular name and acronym for *Torah* (Pentateuch), *Nevi'im* (Prophets), and *Kesuvim* (Writings, Hagiographa).

Tanya: Primary work of *Chabad Chasidus* written by R. Schneur Zalman of Liadi, the founder of *Chabad Chasidism*. The name is derived from the initial word of this work. Also called *Likkutei Amarim* and *Sefer Shel Benonim* (The Book of the Intermediates).

Tevet: A winter month in the Hebrew calendar.

Torah: lit. "Teaching." In the narrow sense, the Five Books of Moses

(Pentatuech), and in the comprehensive sense, the entire body of Jewish knowledge and literature (Bible, *Talmud, Kabbalah,* etc.).

Tosfot: "Additions." The name of a standard and major *Talmudic* commentary. The authors known as the *Baalei Tosfot,* were the leading *Torah* authorities in France and Germany from about the twelfth to the fourteenth century C.E.

Tzemach Tzedek: "Seed of Righteousness." Famous work of responsa and Halacha by R. Menachem Mendel, third generation *Chabad* leader (1789-1866). The author is usually referred to as the "*Tzemach Tzedek*" after the name of his great work.

Tzimtzum: "Contraction"; a *Kabbalistic* doctrine that explains the creative process by means of the so-called "self-limitation" of the Infinite Light (*Or Ein Sof*).

Vav: Hebrew letter; numerical equivalent of 6; one of the four letters of the Tetragrammaton.

Yachid: "Sole, only one."

Yad Hachazakah: "The Powerful Hand." The name of *Maimonides'* code of law.

Yechida: One of the five levels of the soul; the *essence* of the soul. See fn. 48 to main text.

Yesh Me'ayin: "Something from nothing"; *creatio ex nihilo.*

Yesod: See fn. 98.

Yetzer Hara: Evil Inclination.

Yetzirah: See fn. 45 to main text.

Yiddishkeit: Jewishness, Judaism. A term covering the traditional culture of Jewry.

Yom Kippur: Day of Atonement, tenth day of the Hebrew month of *Tishrei.*

Yud: Hebrew letter; numerical equivalent of ten; one of the four letters of the Tetragrammaton.

Yud Shevat: The tenth day of the Hebrew month of *Shevat.* Anniversary of the passing of the sixth *Lubavitcher Rebbe,* R. Yoseph Yitzchak Schneersohn (1880-1950).

Yud-Tes Kislev: The nineteenth day of the Hebrew month of *Kislev.* The festival of *Yud-Tes Kislev* commemorates the release from Russian prison of R. Schneur Zalman of Liadi, founder of *Chabad.*

Zohar: Classic *Kabbalisitic* work by R. Shimon bar Yochai.

OTHER TITLES IN
THE CHASIDIC HERITAGE SERIES

THE ETERNAL BOND *from Torah Or*

By Rabbi Schneur Zalman of Liadi
Translated by Rabbi Ari Sollish

This discourse explores the spiritual significance of *brit milah*, analyzing two dimensions in which our connection with G-d may be realized. For in truth, there are two forms of spiritual circumcision: Initially, man must "circumcise his heart," freeing himself to the best of his ability from his negative, physical drives; ultimately, though, it is G-d who truly liberates man from his material attachment.

᭟᭟᭟

JOURNEY OF THE SOUL from *Torah Or*

By Rabbi Schneur Zalman of Liadi
Translated by Rabbi Ari Sollish

Drawing upon the parallel between Queen Esther's impassioned plea to King Ahasuerus for salvation and the soul's entreaty to G-d for help in its spiritual struggle, this discourse examines the root of the soul's exile, and the dynamics by which it lifts itself from the grip of materiality and ultimately finds a voice with which to express its G-dly yearnings. Includes a brief biography of the author.

᭟᭟᭟

TRANSFORMING THE INNER SELF from *Likkutei Torah*

By Rabbi Schneur Zalman of Liadi
Translated by Rabbi Ari Sollish

This discourse presents a modern-day perspective on the Biblical command to offer animal sacrifices. Rabbi Schneur Zalman teaches that each of us possesses certain character traits that can be seen as "animalistic," or materialistic, in nature, which can lead a person toward a life of material indulgence. Our charge, then, is to "sacrifice" and transform the animal within, to refine our animal traits and utilize them in our pursuit of spiritual perfection.

᭟᭟᭟

FLAMES from *Gates of Radiance*

By Rabbi DovBer of Lubavitch
Translated by Dr. Naftoli Loewenthal

This discourse focuses on the multiple images of the lamp, the oil, the wick and the different hues of the flame in order to express profound guidance in the divine service of every individual. Although *Flames* is a Chanukah discourse, at the same time, it presents concepts that are of perennial significance. Includes the first English biography of the author ever published.

ଵଵ ଵଵ ଵଵ

THE MITZVAH TO LOVE YOUR
FELLOW AS YOURSELF from *Derech Mitzvotecha*

By Rabbi Menachem Mendel of Lubavitch, the Tzemach Tzedek
Translated by Rabbis Nissan Mangel and Zalman Posner

The discourse discusses the Kabbalistic principle of the "collective soul of the world of *Tikkun*" and explores the essential unity of all souls. The discourse develops the idea that when we connect on a soul level, we can love our fellow as we love ourselves; for in truth, we are all one soul. Includes a brief biography of the author.

ଵଵ ଵଵ ଵଵ

TRUE EXISTENCE *Mi Chamocha 5629*

By Rabbi Shmuel of Lubavitch
Translated by Rabbis Yosef Marcus and Avraham D. Vaisfiche

This discourse revolutionizes the age-old notion of Monotheism, i.e., that there is no other god besides Him. Culling from Talmudic and Midrashic sources, the discourse makes the case that not only is there no other god besides Him, there is nothing besides Him—literally. The only thing that truly exists is G-d. Includes a brief biography of the author.

ଵଵ ଵଵ ଵଵ

TRUE EXISTENCE *The Chasidic View of Reality*
A Video-CD with Rabbi Manis Friedman
Venture beyond science and Kabbalah and discover the world of Chasidism. This Video-CD takes the viewer step-by-step through the basic chasidic and kabbalistic view of creation and existence. In clear, lucid language, Rabbi Manis Friedman deciphers these esoteric concepts and demonstrates their modern-day applications.

ৰ্চ ৰ্চ ৰ্চ

YOM TOV SHEL ROSH HASHANAH 5659
Discourse One
By Rabbi Shalom DovBer of Lubavitch
Translated by Rabbis Yosef Marcus and Moshe Miller
The discourse explores the attribute of *malchut* and the power of speech while introducing some of the basic concepts of Chasidism and Kabbalah in a relatively easy to follow format. Despite its title and date of inception, the discourse is germane throughout the year. Includes a brief biography of the author.

ৰ্চ ৰ্চ ৰ্চ

FORCES IN CREATION
Yom Tov Shel Rosh Hashanah 5659 Discourse Two
By Rabbi Shalom DovBer of Lubavitch
Translated by Rabbis Moshe Miller and Shmuel Marcus
This is a fascinating journey beyond the terrestrial, into the myriad spiritual realms that shape our existence. In this discourse, Rabbi Shalom DovBer systematically traces the origins of earth, Torah and souls, drawing the reader higher and higher into the mystical, cosmic dimensions that lie beyond the here and now, and granting a deeper awareness of who we are at our core.

ৰ্চ ৰ্চ ৰ্চ

THE PRINCIPLES OF
EDUCATION AND GUIDANCE
Klalei Hachinuch Vehahadrachah
By Rabbi Yosef Yitzchak of Lubavitch
Translated by Rabbi Y. Eliezer Danzinger

The Principles of Education and Guidance is a compelling treatise that examines the art of educating. In this thought provoking analysis, Rabbi Yosef Yitzchak teaches how to assess the potential of any pupil, how to objectively evaluate one's own strengths, and how to successfully use reward and punishment—methods that will help one become a more effective educator.

❧ ❧ ❧

THE FOUR WORLDS
By Rabbi Yosef Yitzchak of Lubavitch
Translated by Rabbis Yosef Marcus and Avraham D. Vaisfiche
Overview by Rabbi J. Immanuel Schochet

At the core of our identity is the desire to be one with our source, and to know the spiritual realities that give our physical life the transcendental importance of the Torah's imperatives. In this letter to a yearning Chasid, the Rebbe explains the mystical worlds of Atzilut, Beriah, Yetzira, and Asiya.

❧ ❧ ❧

ONENESS IN CREATION
By Rabbi Yosef Yitzchak of Lubavitch
Translated by Rabbi Y. Eliezer Danzinger

Said by Rabbi Yosef Yitzchak at the close of his 1930 visit to Chicago, this discourse explores the concept of Divine Unity as expressed in the first verse of the Shema. The discourse maintains that it is a G-dly force that perpetually sustains all of creation. As such, G-d is one with creation. And it is our study of Torah and performance of the mitzvot that reveals this essential oneness.

❧ ❧ ❧

GARMENTS OF THE SOUL

Vayishlach Yehoshua 5736

By Rabbi Menachem M. Schneerson, the Lubavitcher Rebbe
Translated by Rabbi Yosef Marcus

Often what is perceived in this world as secondary is in reality most sublime. What appears to be mundane and inconsequential is often most sacred and crucial. Thus at their source, the garments of the human, both physical and spiritual, transcend the individual.

THE UNBREAKABLE SOUL

Mayim Rabbim 5738

By Rabbi Menachem M. Schneerson, the Lubavitcher Rebbe
Translated by Rabbi Ari Sollish

The discourse begins with an unequivocal declaration: No matter how much one may be inundated with materialism, the flame of the soul burns forever. This discourse speaks to one who finds pleasure in the material world, yet struggles to find spirituality in his or her life.

THERE ARE MANY IMPORTANT MANUSCRIPTS THAT ARE READY TO GO TO PRESS, BUT ARE WAITING FOR A SPONSOR LIKE YOU.

PLEASE CONSIDER ONE OF THESE OPPORTUNITIES AND MAKE AN EVERLASTING CONTRIBUTION TO JEWISH SCHOLARSHIP AND CHASIDIC LIFE.

FOR MORE INFORMATION PLEASE CONTACT:

THE CHASIDIC HERITAGE SERIES
770 EASTERN PARKWAY
BROOKLYN, NEW YORK 11213
TEL: **718.774.4000**
E-MAIL: INFO@KEHOTONLINE.COM

COMING SOON!

YOM TOV SHEL ROSH HASHANAH 5659
Discourse Three
By Rabbi Shalom DovBer of Lubavitch
Translated by Rabbi Y. Eliezer Danzinger

HACHODESH 5700
By Rabbi Yosef Yitzchak of Lubavitch
Translated by Rabbi Yosef Marcus

VE'ATAH TETZAVEH 5741
By Rabbi Menachem M. Schneerson, the Lubavitcher Rebbe
Translated by Rabbi Yosef Marcus